D0855901

The Children of Ham

ALSO BY CLAUDE BROWN

MANCHILD IN THE PROMISED LAND

The Children of Ham

CLAUDE BROWN

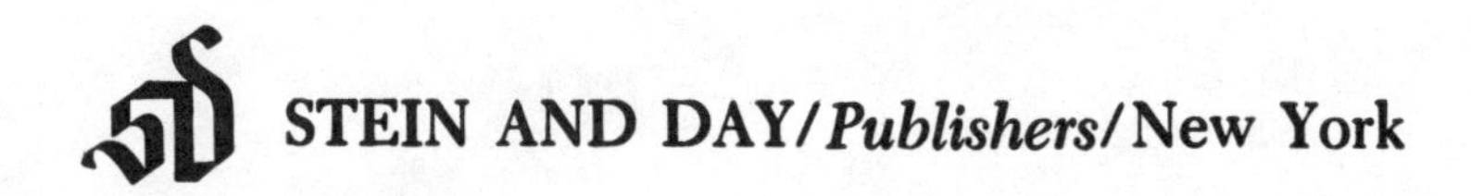

STEIN AND DAY/*Publishers*/New York

First published in the United States of America, 1976

Designed by David Miller
Printed in the United States of America
Stein and Day/*Publishers*/Scarborough House,
Briarcliff Manor, N.Y. 10510

SECOND PRINTING 1976

Library of Congress Cataloging in Publication Data

Brown, Claude, 1937-
The children of Ham.

1. Negro youth—Harlem, New York (City) 2. Slums—Harlem, New York (City) I. Title.
HV1437.H37B75 362.7'3 75-14469
ISBN 0-8128-1837-7

Contents

Foreword

There is a building in upper Harlem on a shabby side street with several other buildings that resemble it in both appearance and condition. This building is in an advanced state of deterioration: only cold water runs through the water pipes; the rats here are as large as cats. The saving grace of this building might very well be the erratic patterns of the varied and brilliant colors of the graffiti that adorn it internally and externally from basement to roof. There is no electricity in the apartments, but the electricity in the hallway lamp fixtures is still on. Some of the apartments have garbage piled up in them five feet high, and that makes opening the door a very difficult task for those whose nasal passages are sufficiently insensitive to permit entry. In some of the apartments and on the rooftop, the garbage and assorted debris are piled only one or two feet high, and the trash has been there so long that plant life has generated.

This building is adjacent to a fully occupied tenement whose inhabitants are families, some of which include several children. A few steps are missing from the staircase above the second floor, and there are no lightbulbs in the hallways; it's a very unsafe place for trespassers, even during the day.

The last family of tenants was emancipated more than two years ago. They hit the numbers and moved to the Bronx, shouting, "Free at last, free at last, thank God for the number man."

Prior to their liberation, the "last family" had lived a most unusual existence. Somebody had to be at home at all times to protect the family's second-hand-hot television from becoming a third-hand-hot television; there were too many junkies in and out who used the vacant apartments to stash their loot until they could "down" it and who also used some of the apartments for sleeping and as "shooting galleries." For protection, the last family had a large, vicious German shepherd. This dog was needed for the rats as well as the junkies. A cat would be no help at all. The sight of the rats in this building would give any cat smaller than a mountain lion instant heart failure. The last family considered itself fortunate, despite the many unpleasant, unhealthy and unsafe aspects of its residence. "We ain't paid no rent in two years. I guess the city just forgot that we was here, or they was just too embarrassed to ask for it," said the head of the last family.

This building has holes in the walls large enough for a man to walk through from one apartment to the adjacent one. There are holes in the ceilings on the fourth and fifth floors, and when it rains, the rain settles on the floor of a fourth-story apartment. This building is not unique. There are many others like it in the ghettos of New York City. And like many others, this building is owned by the City of New York.

Aside from the rats, the lice, and a few privileged junkies, this building is inhabited by an exceptional group of teenagers. The three apartments which are used as residences by the group members contain two or three bedrooms and a living room. Cots and mattresses are scattered throughout. The group members freely admit that they stole one mattress, but most of the cots and mattresses were left behind during the great exodus of two years ago. Some were found on the street and in other abandoned buildings, of which there are many in this block. The inhabited apartments are lighted by running extension cords from the hallway sockets (apparently the City continues to pay Con Ed for the electricity in the hallways). Some of the gas ranges are still operating, and they provide enough heat to render these places habitable in cold weather. The members of the group do very little cooking; they usually eat frankfurters, hamburgers, potato chips, and sandwiches. The gas range is often left burning day and night, for weeks at a time. Nobody is concerned about who pays the gas bill; it hasn't been paid in two years, and the gas is still on.

The group's members, whose ages range from fourteen to twenty-two, have a sense of possession and pride about their apartments, which they call "spots." Somebody stole a chair from in front of a vegetable store and brought it home. So now there is one genuine wooden chair in one of the spots and mattresses and wooden boxes in the others. The members have done some interesting things in their attempt to make the spots resemble homes. Two of them now have curtains, and some of the rooms even have shades. In the third spot, where there are no curtains, one of the members wove a very intricately constructed spider's web, from string, across one of the windows. This strange work of art gives the spot an air of décor and very appropriately symbolizes the building's motif. In several of the rooms, the walls and ceilings have been covered with multicolored tinfoil to conceal the cracks and the peeling paint, which can no longer resist gravity's pleas to abandon the walls and the ceiling. The air of abandonment is so pervasive in this building that every sign and sound of human life conforms to the motif. In one of the spots, I saw an old pair of women's shoes, abandoned by their owner. The water pipes had been abandoned by hot water; electrical wiring had been abandoned by electricity; the City had abandoned the building; humanity had abandoned the members of the group. So why shouldn't the paint abandon the walls and the ceilings?

Generally speaking, the group loathes junkies—"heroin worshipers," "dopeys"—though it does make exceptions. Some members have personal reasons; others don't like what the worshipers represent. But the primary reason is the junkies would steal the formaldehyde out of a corpse and sell it back to the mortician if they could. Even unguarded brooms don't last long around this building because the junkies steal them and sell them to janitors for a quarter to support their "scag jones"—heroin habit. The junkies will also set the building afire when the cold weather comes to town. The fires are started to bring the fire engines and the New York City Fire Department's relocation agent. If someone is burned out of his or her apartment in New York City on a cold night, the Fire Department has the authority and responsibility to provide emergency shelter. So when the relocation agent arrives, every junkie in the neighborhood converges on him swearing that he or she has just been burned out and demanding emergency relocation. It frequently works. The junkies get put up in welfare hotels, sometimes for as long as a couple of months.

Some members don't want worshipers around because this is the reason they left home in the first place, to get away from a parent or two parents who were both junkies.

The junkies have been a big problem, but the group members

have now worked out an uneasy understanding, an entente, that can be simply stated: "If we catch any dopeys in here uninvited, they get carried out or violently assisted out of a first- or second-story window." Most of the neighborhood junkies respect the agreement, and the group proudly compares its victory and final usurpation of the building to the Early American frontier struggle. (The junkies are the Indians. But, of course, there is a paradox here because none of the members could see a Western and support John Wayne.)

What is most surprising about the group is that none of them have succumbed to the lure of scag. Only a few have ever had any experience with it; most of them have never had a desire for even one try. They do get high though, practically every weekend. They drink whiskey and "gage up" (smoke pot), which in this neighborhood (where people walk up and down the street snorting cocaine as though the law didn't exist, and everybody's got a drugstore in a shopping bag or in his back pocket) quickly stigmatizes one as "square." This doesn't seem to bother them; they all appear to be very much together.

Most of the group members like school and have a strong sense of the importance of attending regularly. Ask any member what his goal is, and most likely he will reply that he wants to finish college, if nothing else. So really, a secondary bond for the group is a common goal, the fervent desire to finish school.

The primary common bond of the children of Ham is probably the same one that unites most teenagers, the need for friendship and a sense of belonging.

The Children of Ham

ONE

Salt-Noody

Salt-Noody is a nickname. He doesn't know how he came by that name, or when. However he got the name, he likes to paint it all over the city. Salt-Noody prints his name in larger-than-life-size letters in fancy script with an aerosol spray can. He says, "There's nothin' more wrong with it than for all those white people to put they names and pictures up there in subway trains, on posters, on buses, and all over the place. They don't want nobody else to put they names up in places as though they think they're the only people in the world."

He has just as much right as any of those other people, he says. "I'm here just as much as anybody else, and my name is just as important as theirs is. They like to see they names up, and I like to see mine. So I'm gonna put mine everyplace where I can see it."

Dujo, who is more or less the resident psychologist for the Hamites, says that the reason Salt-Noody puts his name up all over the city, and especially around the block, is that he is behaving like a dog. Dujo says that whenever a dog urinates on a hydrant, he is staking a claim. "It's like that's his mark, he's lettin' all the other dogs know that I have been here and this is my territory." Dujo says that Salt-Noody is doing the same thing. He's letting everybody know, "This is my territory. I belong here, and everybody else had better stay out." Salt-Noody just says, "Well, Dujo's entitled to his opinion, so that ain't soft or solid."

Salt-Noody decorates the Hamites' place as well as the walls of the city. In one of the spots, in a room where there are no curtains, he wove an intricately constructed spider's web from ordinary string across one of the windows. His strange work of art gives the spot an air of decor and appropriately symbolizes the building's motif. I don't think anyone else would have thought of something like that. In several of the rooms, he has covered the walls and ceilings with multicolored tinfoil to hide the cracks and the peeling paint and to conceal some of the air of abandonment that pervades the apartment.

In one of the spots, I saw an old pair of women's shoes. They had been abandoned by the owner. The water pipes had been abandoned by hot water. Electrical wiring had been abandoned by electricity. The city had abandoned the building, and humanity had abandoned the Children of Ham, but in everything Salt-Noody does he tries to counter this sense of abandonment. It seems to have personal significance for him.

Although Salt-Noody is fifteen, he's only in the seventh grade. He doesn't like school, but he usually doesn't mind attending. He tries diligently to understand his courses, but he feels humiliated when the teacher calls on him to recite or answer questions. So he plays hooky occasionally. His speech is very slow, and sometimes it seems as though he's straining to talk, and for several days on end he'll walk around and not say anything to anyone. Sometimes he just smiles all day. He seems to have nothing to say, but he likes to be around the Hamites, just listening.

Salt-Noody is a third child in a family of four children. When asked if he likes his family, he says he likes his little brother, but he has very little feeling for either of his parents. He sees them almost every day, and they don't even bother to ask him how he's doing or anything else. He says his mother sometimes tells him how dirty he looks and how shabbily dressed he is. He has a pronounced limp when he walks. "Once when I was a baby my father got drunk and accidentally stepped on my ankle, and it was never right again," he explains.

When one has any kind of physical deformation, most people tend to look upon him a little bit as an abnormal person. They look at Salt-Noody that way.

When he was four or five years old, one day his father beat him for doing something, and he began to cry and he wouldn't stop crying. His father took him and locked him in the bathroom, which was very dark, and in a corner there was a large rat hole. He had always been afraid of the bathroom because of the rat hole. Because of this fear he always left the door open when he went in there, and the other kids did, too. But on this day, Salt-Noody was locked in the bathroom in the dark, and his father kept telling him that if he didn't stop making all of that noise the rat would get him. Even when he stopped crying, his father did not open the door and pretended that everybody had gone out of the house. Salt-Noody was very much afraid. Eventually his father let him out of the bathroom and from that time on, Salt-Noody stuttered. He stuttered for about the next ten years of his life, all the time that he lived at home with his parents. He stopped stuttering about two months after he moved into one of the spots.

One day Dujo, Salt's running partner on the street, who had moved into one of the spots with the other Children of Ham, brought Salt-Noody up to show him the place. Salt didn't want to go home, and other members of the Hamites didn't want him to stay because they felt that once his parents found out, and they were certain to find out eventually because they lived right around the corner, they would make trouble. They thought Salt-Noody's parents cared about him because he was always clean and neat. Nevertheless, they let him stay at the spot for two days. He said his parents didn't care, but the others didn't believe that, so they urged him to go home, and he did. But a couple of days later he came back, and he brought a flowerpot with a plant in it and said, "This is for the house."

Shortly thereafter, he started collecting other little household ornaments. He found this old picture, one of those dime-store, living-room pictures, and he brought it in and hung it up on the wall. Next he brought in one of those black-history calendars and put it on the wall, and the others could not imagine why they hadn't ever thought of doing that before. After about two weeks Salt-Noody came back and stayed. Nobody had the nerve to tell him that he should go home, and, like the others, nobody came looking for him, and that became his new home.

Salt-Noody says that he'd been waiting for a long time to leave home. In a sense, everybody waits to grow up and leave home, but that wasn't exactly what Salt-Noody had meant. He said that when he was a little boy about six or seven years old, one night he went into his mother's room, and she happened to be praying for his brother, who was seriously ill with pneumonia. And he heard her ask God something like, "O Lord, please, if you've gotta take one of my children from me, please don't take this one, 'cause he's a good boy and he's smart and he's good-lookin' and he's precious. Lord, if you've gotta take one of them, why don't you take my crippled child, 'cause he's just gonna be miserable in life, anyway. Lord, he's just crippled in mind and the body, and life ain't got that much to offer him. So if you gotta take one of my children, please take the other one."

Salt-Noody said he left the room and he never said anything to her, but he never felt the same about his mother or about anyone ever since. And I asked him if he hated his mother as a result of what he had overheard, and all he could say is, "Ain't nobody nothin' anyway."

Dujo has insisted that Salt-Noody be treated like a full-fledged member of the group. Initially, around the spots everybody treated him as an equal, and it was workable though most of the fellows felt that he would be something of an embarrassment to them if he went out in public with the family. Jill didn't care for that attitude at all because she was extremely fond of Salt-Noody. She was like a big sister to everybody, but he was a favorite of hers. He was constantly bringing her flowers and doing things that nobody ever did for her, and it touched her. Not just her but most all the girls in the family loved Salt, and they tend to overrespond to any gesture of kindness. This is especially true of Jill.

They hadn't received too much affection prior to becoming members of this family, the Children of Ham. Now they were making up for it and in some cases trying to make up for all the affection and kindness they were likely to miss throughout their lives. Jill almost babied Salt-Noody and would insist that the other members of the group treat him as they treated each other.

Salt-Noody takes great pride in doing his part in the group projects, whatever it might be, and usually his part isn't too difficult because they wouldn't trust him with any difficult chores. But however simple it might be, he feels very gratified if he does it right, and Dujo will usually compliment him and he'll just sit there and smile all over himself, basking in glory. Even if it's something as simple as washing the walls. One of the Hamites will come in and say, "Salt-Noody, who washed the walls?"

Somebody else answers, "Salt-Noody did it."

"Wow, Salt, you really took care of business with those walls."

And he just beams. When they want to get him to do something, they tell him how great they think he can do it. He is one of the more valuable assets when it comes to decorating the place and also in the area of obtaining furnishings for the spots when there might be dogs guarding whatever the item is that they want to take, because Salt-Noody gets along with dogs, even—or especially—mean ones.

The Hamites keep pigeons up on the roof, but nobody is more concerned about them than Salt-Noody. Salt-Noody can achieve even this outstanding feat: He can get the pigeons to go into their coop at night without any food. Nobody else in the family can do that. He seems to have the same kind of secret language with pigeons that he has with dogs. Somehow they understand each other just through vibrations and nothing more. When it's raining, the pigeons all stay in the coop, and Salt-Noody goes in there and talks to them. And when it's lightning he's been known to go to calm the pigeons down. Or if a rat gets up there, he goes up and he stands guard, throwing bottles at it. He's the guardian of the pigeons, and they seem to appreciate him.

Salt-Noody usually doesn't have much money, and when he gets some it goes very fast, between the pigeon food and the aerosol spray paint cans. When he needs money, he gets his younger brother, Jimmy, who is nine or ten, to hustle for him. He'll ask his brother to go into the bars in the afternoon, usually after the last digit of the "number" has come out, and ask out loud to the men hanging around there and wanting to be big-time spenders, or the number taker, "Mister, do you have any errands that I can run, because I'd like to earn a dollar so I can go to the movies?"

Now, sometimes they might give him an errand, or somebody might say, "Run across the street and get me a cup of coffee." But even if they say no, chances are they will give him a dollar anyway, or a big-time spender down at the other end of the bar may hear it and in trying to impress one of the women in the bar will say, "Here, kid, here's two dollars. Take one and buy yourself some candy." Or something like that. Or somebody else may hear it, or maybe a woman, and say, "Here's fifty cents."

On most of the blocks in Harlem there are about two bars to

every block, so Salt-Noody will have Jimmy go down the avenue from one bar to another. And within about five blocks, and maybe fifteen minutes, it's likely that Jimmy will have collected anywhere from ten to fifteen dollars. Salt-Noody will take the money and buy Jimmy some ice cream or some little reward and then go and buy pigeon food and spray cans. He'll let Jimmy come with him and help him feed the pigeons or help him use the spray cans to put up some graffiti.

There are more than a couple of places along the block one can see, up very high and in huge letters, "Salt-Noody," inscribed with multicolored spray cans, and below that, in smaller letters, "Jimmy." And we know Jimmy had been out hustling for Salt-Noody that day, and Salt-Noody took him on a graffiti-spraying excursion.

Dujo says that maybe Salt-Noody ought to be a farmer. "In Harlem, down around 131st Street, there's a dude who is a barber, he grows corn about ten feet tall in the back of his barbershop. Salt-Noody once went down there and spent the whole day, played hooky from school and spent the whole day just starin' at the tall corn. We got some corn seeds and he planted some in a pot out on the fire escape, and he got what he called dog manure because he thought dog manure would be good for fertilizer, and put it in the pot, and nothin' happened for a long time, but he didn't give up. The corn didn't grow, so he thinks he could be wrong about the dog manure. He sure would like to get some horse manure. He's gonna go down to Central Park now and try to get some horse do-do from one of those hansom cab horses, they always messin' on that drive that goes through Central Park. He says he's gonna go down there with a paper bag and scoop some up one day, bring it back and put it on his corn. He's got it out on the fire escape where it gets rain, and it gets a lot of sunshine, so he can't figure out why it's not growin'. Maybe the guy in the store sold him the wrong seeds. So he's gonna go back down there and talk to that barber and find out what kinda seeds he's got. But sometimes people don't want to tell you their secrets about growin' things.

"That's how he gets his jollies, watchin' things grow. Like one time he was passin' by a old lot where people throw junk and stuff, up on the hill between Amsterdam and Broadway where they still had those private houses and brownstones and some people even have gardens out there behind their brownstones, flower gardens and vegetable gardens."

Ever since then, Salt-Noody's been trying to interest the family in growing a vegetable garden like the people have up on the hill. But nobody gets too excited about it. The other Hamites feel that the farming thing is not too practical in the city unless you have a private house that nobody can come into.

Salt-Noody went up on the hill one day and saw an old toilet bowl in a lot, and he saw a pretty plant growing out of it in the midst of all the debris. He wanted to start a garden in an old commode up on his roof. He kept pestering Hebro until one day Hebro finally broke down and took a commode from an abandoned house. Salt-Noody put some dirt in it and planted some vegetables. But it was the wrong time of the year, and nothing came up. Salt-Noody says that next summer he intends to grow some huge tomatoes just for Jill.

Last year the Hamites had Salt-Noody growing some smoke (pot) up on the roof and on the fire escape, and Salt didn't know what it was. As a matter of fact, there were a few other members of the Hamites who didn't know what it was, either. Dujo says, "Most people don't know what a pot leaf looks like unless they see it rolled up and in a joint, ready to smoke."

Salt-Noody got excited about growing this plant that Chips brought in for him. Chips knew what it was, of course, so did Mumps and Dujo and Shaft and Hebro. Salt-Noody should have been suspicious when all these guys became so concerned about this one plant, but it didn't bother him and it made him feel more important because they depended on Salt-Noody to see that the plant became ready and ripe. He was very proud to be the custodian of the plant.

In the winter Salt-Noody took the plant from the fire escape and put it in the corner near the kitchen stove because it didn't get much sunshine. When the sun was shining he put it out on the windowsill. And it wasn't until the plant was full grown and ready to be smoked that Salt-Noody found out what it was he had nourished for months. Then he really felt great.

The Hamites took the leaves off, stripped the plant on the fire escape, and put the leaves in the oven. They rolled up about twenty joints from the baked leaves, and everybody got high, "a real dynamite high." The following day they were all thanking Salt-Noody and drinking wine. It was a day of celebration honoring Salt-Noody and his plant-growing talent. They made toasts to him, and of course he got the first drink of the wine, and it was his day.

It was some of the best pot they'd ever had, "a monster." It was better than anything they had bought from the streets in a long time, and they all agreed that it had to be better. It was fresh, green, and homegrown. They were raving about their homegrown smoke for months. And every time Salt-Noody would hear them mention the term "homegrown," his ears would perk up and a smug smile would cover his face because he knew that he was the person responsible for the homegrown.

After the homegrown experiment, Chips and Dujo told Salt-Noody that they were going to put him in business. They would grow their own smoke. They wouldn't buy any from anyone else. They'd gotten a long flower box to go on the fire escape, and they were ready to go into business on a big scale. Salt-Noody was going to get a fair cut, an equal share of the money that they made from this pot-growing venture. All they'd have to buy was some bamboo paper, some small envelopes, and they had it made. What they would do is give more smoke in a bag. Their nickel bag would not contain only enough smoke for three joints, or two and a half like the average one does now, but five joints in the nickel bags and eight in the dime bags. Many people were dealing in the block, but nobody else would have anything as great as this. Nobody else would have any homegrown.

But for some strange reason the pot plot never worked out. Nobody knows exactly why. All they know is that it didn't come off. They said they would try again next year. Pot growing would become the Hamites' cooperative business. Everybody'd be in on it, and they would have the proceeds from the pot to fix up the place and even get a color television in there and maybe a small pool table in one of the spots.

Everything depended on Salt-Noody's talent for growing marijuana. But for some unknown reason he was unable to get the plants growing. He didn't stop trying. He was certain that they were going to come up eventually.

It might have been, as Jill was telling him, that he watched them too much and babied them to excess. "It's not like a flower or other houseplants, domestic plants, where they say in the books that you gotta talk to 'em." According to Jill, "Pot is a wild, undomesticated plant. Pot is a weed, and you don't have to be talkin' to pot all the time and babyin' it. You know, it's probably one of those plants that's a nonpeople plant, and they don't care for people talkin' to 'em. Unlike other plants, they probably thrive on not havin' people around and not bein' talked to. Maybe silence would be good for plants like pot."

Jill thinks that weeds don't like people talking to them. Salt-Noody listened to Jill because he has a great deal of respect for her. So he took her advice, and he was not going to bother the plant too much. He was going to treat it like what it was, a weed.

In the meantime, Salt-Noody was having fun growing a variety of other plants, thinking that next year he would probably be rich. And it would be wonderful. Just imagine, he could make his farming pay off in New York City. He didn't have to go down South and become a farmer. He was going to become a pot farmer right up here, and he'd bet that nobody ever did that before. He was "gonna be the biggest pot farmer New York City ever had." Just think of all the spraying he could do with a year's supply of aerosol spray paint cans. He would have his name all over New York City by the end of the year. And next year he'd have to go someplace else, to another city, to find some more wall space for his name. So now Salt-Noody is content with his dream.

Salt-Noody is very good at learning to do repairs fast on just about any machine. One day he watched Stretch fix a refrigerator, and then he tinkered with one that had been in one of the spots for who knows how long, but had never worked, and he fixed that refrigerator and everybody praised him to the sky. Very often other Hamites will bring an electrical appliance that breaks down to Salt-Noody. If the Hamites' television breaks down, he's the first person they want to look at it, and only if the problem is too difficult for him will they go down and get "Mr. Stretch." If he hears about something broken or something not working, Salt-Noody can't just leave it alone. He has a conviction that everything is supposed to be working in life. He's either going to make it work or he's going to replace it because he feels that the spot is his and he has that obligation. He has defined his position there in the group. His position is to keep things working. Perhaps you would call him the maintenance man among the Hamites as well as other things. He's also the farmer and the dog keeper, and to an extent he's the resident interior decorator. The more he does, the more valuable he feels. Not only that, the Hamites also let him know that he is very valuable to them.

Frequently somebody, maybe a storekeeper, will say about something that's obviously beyond repair, "I was meaning to throw that thing out. You know, you can throw it out for me if you want to."

Now what Salt-Noody will do is take it and repair it. As a matter of fact, they get many pieces of furniture in this manner. He'll take it, fix it, and put it in one of the spots, and it usually turns out to be a very functional piece of furniture. He's even gotten a record player like that, and a cot that was supposed to be a folding cot that wouldn't fold anymore. Well, he made it fold, with the help of Stretch, who is the neighborhood carpenter.

Salt-Noody can fix things, he can make things, he's got a green thumb, he can handle dogs, and he can handle pigeons. He does so many things well, and still he has a deep inferiority complex about being unable to express himself adequately verbally.

It's strange that some adults seem to feel that this very likable and well-behaved kid who is always doing something, and usually something constructive, is retarded simply because he doesn't do much talking. Not only that but he's also very polite and gets along well with the old people on the block. They all like him because he's always nodding to Mrs. So-and-so and Mr. So-and-so, to the older folks that most people don't even say anything to or walk by and don't even notice. He will stop and ask them if they want him to do something for them. Maybe they want him to go and find out what the number was today, or something like that, or maybe they want him to go the store for them the way people generally do with much younger children, but he doesn't feel that he's too old for it. He does it, and he won't accept any tips for his services, and he's very mannerly.

But most of the adults don't have enough patience to be "bothered" with him. It seems that only the older people who possess patience acquired with age can appreciate somebody being polite to them and giving them some attention and some genuine respect, really like him, so he gets along well with them and the Hamites and a few others, a very few others.

Some others he gets along with are kids. He makes scooters out of two-by-fours and one roller skate, and he sells these scooters for two dollars apiece. And when spring comes around and kids are really coming out onto the streets in droves, they are looking for scooters. There are many kids who don't have older brothers to make scooters for them, so Salt-Noody will make them. Scores of children will come to him and beg him to make them scooters, and they'll stand in line. So it's a business for him in the spring when the scooter season comes in. In the summer his business is still thriving, and he's fixing bicycles as well as making scooters, and he's also fixing radios, and sometimes he puts the simple little cassette tape recorders back together again. He's very enterprising.

Salt-Noody says he wants to finish school, but he doesn't think it's important. He'll probably stop school and open a shop one day in the not-too-distant future, a kind of general fixit shop. But Jill tells him that he should try to learn something in school. She tells him that he's got to learn how to read "because you can't go into business if you don't know how to read. People send you bills, and notes, and they'll complain and send you letters, and so you gotta know how to read. But not only that, you can get a lotta fun outta readin'."

He reads, but far below his age level, and he reads very slowly, too. Jill's working on that problem, and it seems as though she's making some headway.

Salt-Noody likes to pretend sometimes he's a preacher. There are three mirrors in one of the spots. He'll get in front of a mirror when he thinks nobody's around, and preach. There's a storefront church around the corner, and he likes to go and peek in the door and watch the minister preaching. He can sit there in the doorway of that little storefront church for hours upon hours and listen to the preacher just ranting and raving and going on and on. Salt-Noody sits there in utter fascination.

Salt-Noody also likes to listen to Jill's version of Bible stories, so maybe one day he'll combine the two pleasures and become a preacher. Then he'll have it made. In the meantime, if he's not up at the pigeon coop with the pigeons and not caring for the plants in the spots or not in the street with the dogs someplace, everybody knows that he's probably around at that storefront church. He forgets about eating, forgets about everything else, watching this preacher go through his act.

The Hamites say, "It isn't that Salt-Noody is so strange, it's just that strange things happen to him, like things that don't happen to anybody else. He had a pair of shoes that had worn out on him, and he left 'em in a closet in one of the rooms in the spot. There was some dirt in it at the bottom, and before anybody knew anything a plant started sproutin' up in his shoes. It seemed weird. People don't grow plants in their shoes.

"And, you know, those mean dogs that don't like nobody, they like him. He can go places where people got a dog watchin' the spot, and the dog wants to follow him home. He has to stop and just about pet every dog he sees. Mumps trained a dog for Stretch to watch his shop and tools. But Salt-Noody likes to talk to dogs, and that dog seems to be able to talk to him, and other people seem to find this kinda behavior strange."

Salt-Noody had a reputation on the street of doing some other strange things, like the time when Salt went into the carpenter's shop down the block. Stretch gets along well with most of the kids in the block, not just the Hamites. All of them like him, and he's fond of them. Stretch was talking to a customer in his fixit shop, and Salt-Noody waited patiently for ten minutes and then said very politely, "Mr. Stretch, I'm makin' some shelves for one of the spots, and I wonder if I could borrow your hammer for a little while."

Stretch knew that Salt-Noody was a junior handyman so he gave it to him without any hesitation, just telling him to be sure to bring the hammer back when he finished with it. About three minutes later, Salt-Noody came back and returned the hammer and said, "Thank you very much, Mr. Stretch, for your hammer."

"Okay, Salt-Noody, anytime. Did you get the shelves fixed?"

"Yeah, I got 'em fixed all right."

Nearly fifteen minutes later, Stretch heard sirens in the block. He went outside to see what was going on and saw an ambulance and a police patrol car, and it seemed that some boy had been hit on the head with a hammer. When Stretch heard this, he thought about it and said, "Oh my Lord, I hope it wasn't my hammer." But he couldn't imagine Salt-Noody doing anything like that because he didn't bother anybody and nobody bothered him.

It turned out that Salt-Noody had been spraying one of his aerosol cans on one of the walls across the street where the community center is located, and some kid who lives around the corner came up and said to him, "Why don't ya stop puttin' that stupid name all over everything?"

The boy took the can from him and sprayed it down his back. Salt didn't even try to resist. The bully returned the can to Salt and told him he'd better stop with spray cans because if he saw him doing it again he was going to repeat what he did to him. Salt-Noody sat down on the curb for a while, looking at the can, feeling his back, and looking at his artwork on the wall. After a few minutes, he just got up and went to Stretch's carpentry shop and borrowed a hammer. He walked back up to the corner, hit the boy in the head, turned around, and walked casually back down the street to Stretch's shop and returned the hammer. After that, he went over to the wall, finished painting his name, and then went to a movie. Everybody said that the boy had it coming because he shouldn't have interfered with Salt-Noody, especially at a time when Salt was engaged in his art-work. Most people would know better than to do that.

The ambulance took the boy to the hospital, but the police don't get too concerned about what Harlemites do to each other. They couldn't find Salt-Noody that day, and fortunately the boy didn't die, so it became a minor incident in the community. It was just one of those everyday occurrences. But because of things like that, the fellows were reluctant to let Salt-Noody get high.

Once Salt-Noody had gotten high and a couple of junkies asked him—this was before the hammer incident—if he would go into Stretch's shop and borrow a crowbar and a sledge hammer. They had promised Salt-Noody a five-dollar bag of smoke. The junkies took the crowbar and the sledgehammer, which had Stretch's name carved on the handle, and they broke into an apartment and burglarized the television, stereo, tape records, suits, and a whole variety of pawn-able items, plus some money and whiskey. They left the crowbar and the sledgehammer with Stretch's name on it in the apartment, and the man who lived there found the tools, got his gun, and went down to Stretch's apartment looking for Stretch and threatening to kill him. The burglary victim knew Stretch and therefore had no diffi-culty believing his explanation. They found Salt-Noody on the stoop, still waiting for the junkies to return and bring him the five-dollar bag of smoke. There was nothing to do but for Salt-Noody and Stretch to help the victim look for the junkies. A couple of days later, they found one of them, and he told the man where some of the loot was, and he was able to retrieve some of his things from the pawnshop.

Salt-Noody gets angry with the group from time to time, and he'll go away and stay with an aunt, his crazy aunt who lives in Queens. Salt-Noody's parents used to send him to stay with her when he got into trouble for playing hooky from school. But Salt-Noody said he couldn't stay with his aunt and her husband for long because they are crazy. According to Salt-Noody they eat health food that's not real food. They eat seeds and wheat germs. "They even got to a point where they thought the toilet paper was bad for you. She had read someplace that the colorin' in toilet paper was harmful for you, so she said we had to stop usin' any kinda toilet paper. She didn't believe that the white toilet paper had a natural color, so we stopped usin' that, too, but napkins was all right."

When Dujo asked him what he thought people did before they used toilet paper and napkins, he said he didn't know. "Yeah, what did Christ use?"

Dujo began telling him that Christ and the disciples didn't wash their hands before they ate, "and back in those days there wasn't any toilet paper. So what's so bad about not usin' toilet paper now?"

Of course this was a put-on. Salt-Noody said he didn't know what Christ and his disciples did, but he suspected that they used leaves.

Sometimes he would go and stay with his folks, but they gave him such a hard time that he had to stop going there, too. And so what he would do when he got peeved in recent times is go upstairs on the roof and sleep with the pigeons, or he would go into the basement of the building across the street, in the building where Hebro lives. The janitor has two mean German shepherd dogs, and they wouldn't permit anybody to come down there, but Salt-Noody could go down and sleep with them and they never bothered him.

Before Salt-Noody became a Hamite, nobody ever gave him any encouragement or any praise for the things that he accomplished. Therefore, coming into the family was an important positive move for him. He doesn't trust very many people because he's never met many adults who liked him. Before becoming a member of the Hamites, he really didn't have a social place. The kids in the neighborhood would take him someplace to use him for their entertainment, to help them break into a store and then make fun of him, that kind of sport, and so he was very distrustful until Dujo came along.

Dujo liked him and took him under his wing. This was the beginning of a profound experience for him. Probably for the first time in his life he knew some people who treated him as an equal and like a full-fledged human being, like somebody that had some value.

One of the reasons Salt-Noody left home was that he had more value to the Hamites than he had to his family. His parents viewed him as an embarrassment—like the family idiot you want to hide in the cellar or attic, if you have a cellar or attic. But here he has a lot of things that he can show off, like the lamp he made from the wine bottle and the spiderweb instead of a curtain over the window that he made from ordinary string, and the beer-can-top-rings curtain that he made from beer-can rings. Since he's been here he started becoming a person. If he had been living with the Hamites for all the years of his instead of just one year, he might be much more advanced along the road to finding himself than he is now, and he'd probably have fewer and less serious emotional problems. He's profited from the relationship, and they've profited from it.

His parents, when they see him, don't bother him, not only because they're embarrassed and ashamed of him, but I think they realize that his living situation now is healthier for him and so it wouldn't make sense for them to ask him to come home, even if they wanted him to.

TWO

Jill

Jill is like a big sister and mother to the Children of Ham. She is almost eighteen years old, but she has forty-five years of mileage to her credit, and every mile straight uphill. Since the age of twelve, Jill has been seriously overdeveloped, physically. This condition can present an unending series of difficult problems for any young girl, especially on the streets of Harlem. Coupled with the fact that she is not at all unattractive, it's quite clear that Jill's early destiny was trouble.

Jill has been more or less on her own since her mother died seven years ago. She has been a junkie, she's been to reform school and to jail. She's been a prostitute and she's sold drugs, though she's sort of straight now. She would like to try marriage to somebody—if only for a short while.

Jill is the eighth child in a family of ten children from five different fathers. She never found out who her father is or was. She asked her mother only once. The Hamites are the closest thing she's ever had to a real family. Everything she knows, Jill says she learned on the streets. She told me she was hustling, doing a little bit of everything, even when she was very young. She sold dope. She knew hustlers. "I know a lot of dudes who couldn't wait till I got older. They been tellin' me they been waitin' for me and waitin' for me."

She got busted for dope, got caught with a half an ounce and about twenty sets of works, and since it was her first bust they let her go. "They called my foster mother, you know, and paroled me in her custody. She tried to put me away a lot of times, but what could she do 'cause I don't stay with her."

Jill just stopped going to school, but she would really like to go back, she says. She claims she got good grades when she was there. She went on the Harlem Hospital program for detoxification, and she was in group therapy every day. She says, "They was tryin' to help me."

I asked her how she avoided the methadone syndrome, with everybody out here walking around with a wine bottle hooked under his arm, on methadone, sniffing a little coke. How did she escape the methadone/wine, cocaine bag?

" 'Cause, you know, I like to get high, but I know when enough is enough, and I know when too much is too much, and all that's just too much. I was takin' meth and drinkin' wine. I used to find myself too high. Superhigh. And I didn't like the feelin', like I was gonna fall out. Now I don't even shoot coke no more. All I do is smoke dope and cigarettes. I don't even drink. All that's too much.

"I had a experience with one dude, a fellow that I 'sposed to be goin' off with to make some money. He had took me to this buildin', and I noticed that it seemed like he was the only one in the crib. So I say, 'Do anybody else live in the buildin'?'

"It was a condemned buildin', and I knew somethin' was wrong. So when we got in this room it was dusty and dirty. So the dude locked the door and pulled out a pistol, and he hit me on the head with the end of the pistol. He was goin' to pistol-whip me, you know. So like I pretended I was faintin' and begged him to get me some water, and when he went to get the water I jumped out the third-floor window. And I broke my leg. The way I landed I was lucky.

"I never saw the dude again, but if I see him, I know him. I could never forget him. I told 'em at the hospital that I twisted my ankle runnin', you know, runnin' down the street. I was scared to tell 'em what really happened. I told 'em this dude was chasin' me and I was runnin'.

"Then one night I was at the bus stop waitin' to go home. You know Thelma's bar on 148th Street? Well, while I was waitin' for a bus to go home, some dudes had took off [stuck up] this bar. All of a sudden I seen police cars pullin' up and cops jumpin' out and startin' shootin', and I panicked, and so this fellow Preston who was with me ran to the gas station.

"I was standin' in front of the newsstand, and the getaway cab ran into the newsstand and knocked me down. Then the police thought I ran outta the cab, so when I got up and ran, they came runnin' behind me, shootin'. So I ran into the closest apartment building and was knockin' on doors and beggin' people, you know, 'Let me in, help me.' They'd say, 'Get away from that fuckin' door, get away from my fuckin' door. Whatever you did, face up to it,' and all that shit.

"And I was sayin', 'Let me in, the police is shootin' at me.'

"I could still hear the police downstairs, bustin' in the door, comin' up behind me. So I ran all the way to the roof. Then I said, 'Well, I can't jump off this motha, so I'm gonna just go back down, but I'm gonna start yellin' so they won't think I'm sneakin' up on 'em'. So when I went back downstairs I started yellin', 'Wait, don't shoot, don't shoot.'

"One cop grabbed me and start harassin' me, you know, throwin' me all against the wall, smackin' me and goin' in my collar. Then he put my hands behind my back and handcuffed me. When he got me outside, it just so happened the sergeant or somebody said, 'This is not the woman. We lookin' for a white girl.'

"When we got outside, the police started apologizin' and cleanin' up fast. He started sayin' to me, 'Oh, I'm sorry, I didn't mean to hurt you,' and askin' if I was all right.

"I said, 'Yeah. I coulda been shot for nothin'.'

"And then they woulda seen that I wasn't the girl, and it woulda just have been a innocent bystander who got killed. No big thing. It wouldn'ta meant nothin' to 'em, you know. That woulda just been my life gone.

"I remember one dude I went off with, I was gonna trick with him, and when we got to this house the guy was artificial. He had a false eye, false teeth, and a false leg. He was real drunk, so I beat him for his money. I got somethin' like two hundred and eighty dollars. I had to snatch his leg off so he wouldn't come after me. I threw it right over that fence in 145th Street, right there by the pool. I was runnin' down the street with it under my arm. I said, 'Damn, I can't run down the street with this leg,' so I threw it away right there."

Jill takes pride in claiming that when she went out on the street tricking for Georgie, in a period of less than two years she made forty thousand dollars for the dude. Now, that's a lot of money for any woman to make out there turning a trick. She was dealing dope and doing a few other things as well, but if it's anywhere near true, I guess it is something of an achievement.

She was on stuff at the time, and she claims that scag helped her maintain her ambition and drive. She said when she was using drugs she would go into a nod and "As soon as I got the needle in my arm and was takin' off, I would be thinkin' about where I was gonna get my next shot from, and already I would be thinkin' about what I could steal or who I could turn a trick with for some money. And if I saw somethin', especially when my jones was down on me, like I'd see a truck with the door open and it would hit me right away, Hey, there's no man around, like that. And I would get some fellows and take them where it was, and we'd take it off. Like if I saw somebody with some money in his hand, and he put it in his pocket, I would go over to him and try and make him notice me and try and get some of that money as quick as I could.

"But it's like sometimes when I wasn't jonesin' I would sleep these things. I wouldn't even think about doin' anything all day. You know, like a week would go by or maybe two weeks would go by before I got a idea how I could come up with some money. But as long as I was jonesin' I never had time to stop thinkin' about makin' some money and makin' some money quick, because that jones kept me goin' and would never let me stop to even rest. So in a way it was good because it kept my ambition up."

I asked Jill where she lived after her mother died. She said she doesn't think her mother had a funeral because her mother was on welfare. But even people on welfare have at least a pauper's funeral. All she remembers is going out of the apartment one day and coming back to find the door locked. There was nobody inside, her mother had died, and she didn't know where to go. When asked why one of her older brothers or sisters who were married and had places of their own didn't want to take her in, she says they didn't have space for her.

She ended up living with different people until something happened that messed up the arrangement. She said, "I lived with Jimmy's family down the street for about a month or a couple of months. I was just hangin' out with him one day, and I went home with him and I stayed there. I was tight with his sister, and his mother thought I was just stayin' over for the night. And she didn' ask me anything till she saw me there a couple of days later and she said, 'Don't you have to go home? Don't you have some folks worried about you?'

"I told her no, because my folks had died.

"In the summertime I was walkin' the streets, or I would hang out with somebody who I could go home with and change clothes. I didn't have too many clothes, so I had to start stealin', and one or two friends would lend me a dress just once in a while, and I could go someplace and get a bath or at least wash my face and wash up and be halfway clean. I would stay in all kinds of places, people's cars, and men would take me home with them and would let me sleep someplace. Or I'd give one of the supers somethin' and they'd let me sleep down in the cellar as long as I didn' bother anybody and as long as I gave 'em what they wanted."

She said her older sister asked her once just casually where she was living, and she told her that she was staying with a friend of hers. She was afraid to tell her sister she didn't have anyplace to stay because her sister might have sent her down South to her aunt or some other relative, and Jill was determined to stay in New York City.

She lived like that for two years, on the street, knocking about here and there. When the weather got cold, she could usually find a fellow, or some janitor, who would let her stay for a night or two. Or if she met a new girl friend and got tight with her, she would tell the girl's mother that her mother was sick and in the hospital and she didn't have anyplace to stay. And as time went by and she'd been there for, let's say, a month, or even longer, they would start questioning Jill about her mother's illness and when she was expected to come home. She would make up the visiting days and get dressed on Sunday and say she was going to the TB hospital to visit her mother. She would return late in the day and tell them how her mother was doing. But eventually there would come a time when Jill had to get her walking papers.

When she was about thirteen, and had been out on the street for a little more than two years, she got busted for stealing and was sent to the New York State Training School for Girls. She stayed there for about a year. She was paroled in the custody of a foster parent who didn't care very much about her. When she came out, she started using drugs and hanging out with the junkies and learning new and more daring ways to survive on the streets. The first guy she tumbled for put her on the corner and had her turning tricks and making money for him. And he was okay for her because she hadn't known any great life previously, and she liked it. She was in love. Then she got strung out, and she got busted again. She went to jail and got on withdrawal, came out, got into a program, and stopped using stuff.

A little more than a year ago, when she was about sixteen, she started hanging out in this block. She found one of the spots and met the group of kids and moved in and sort of started keeping house for them. And gradually they all developed into something of a loose-knit family with Jill as mother of the other children.

I asked Shaft one day, "What about Jill as a woman, not a swift street broad? How do you rate her?"

"Man, it ain't ten dudes in all o' big ol' New York City who knows what to do for Jill. If she ever finds out what she is really all about, every dude in sight is gonna be in big trouble."

Jill is the Hamites' biblical authority. Many times when Jill wants to relay something to the Hamites she will tell them that they can always go to the Bible and verify it. She has boundless faith in the Bible as an authority on life.

One day Jill was telling the Hamites how precious a man is and what he's really worth. She told them that they didn't have to believe her. "Anybody who can read can go to the Bible and check it out. But things in the Bible are usually sort of disguised and you have to kinda dig 'em out." Jill says that in Proverbs, Chapter 31, "Lemuel's mother almost let the cat outta the bag in tellin' him and lettin' everybody else know what a precious creature a man really is. Some men don't know it, so they suffer for not fulfillin' their natural destiny. They become addicts, alcoholics, tricks, snakes, all kindsa sufferers as punishment for not fulfillin' their destiny of bein' precious men."

As Jill sees it, all men are kings and they have only to realize it to ascend a throne. According to Jill, when King Lemuel's mother was telling him what not to do if he wants to be a king, "She was really tellin' him how to be a man instead of a clown. She told him not to waste his strength on women, like he shouldn't go around chasin' pussy all the time or even wastin' his strength on women with screwin' and all that because it was just a nut [silly]. He could use that strength to do things that would be more beneficial to him. And she told him not to drink because this is what fools and weak men do. She was tellin' him all these things a man should not do if he wants to be a man and rule like a king, you know, and be his majestic self throughout life."

According to Jill, all this is right there in the book, all the prophecies, but most people can't see. Most people won't even take the trouble to look. She says, "If black men were to ever realize, you know, what precious beings they are, there wouldn't be any junkies out on the street or in places like Harlem. There wouldn't be any winos, there wouldn't be any alcoholics, there wouldn't be any perverts, any beggars, panhandlers, nothing but kings. You know, like all the Harlems in the country would be lands of Judah.

"It's like we've been into the white-book bag for so long that we've forgotten the religion of the black land in Africa, the secrets in the Bible that were never secrets to the Africans. They knew that man was a very precious thing. But when we got to this country and whitey spooked our parents, at least our mothers, through Christianity, God and the Devil and all that, they did a wicked number on us. But our generation didn't go for the spookism. We learned to read, and then we saw things on television, and we gettin' out into the world and seein' all the hypocrisy instead of just layin' back and listenin' to a whole lotta garbage, like our parents' generation, who bought it and got spooked right outta their minds, started runnin' around believin' in Jesus and callin' on the Lord."

Jill says the Bible is a fairy tale, and most of it wasn't written to be taken as anything serious, but a lot of it is just common sense. "Ain't nothin' heavy about it or deep or secretive."

She says it messed up a whole generation because black men wouldn't buy it. When she was staying with one friend, after her mother died, she said her friend's mother was always in the kitchen calling on the Lord, calling on Jesus to help her, and her friend's father was always in the bathroom cursing out God. She was certain that all of this was a result of Christianity and the "spookism that's messin' up people's minds. Like the man couldn't buy it because there was too much game involved, goin' and shoutin' for somebody to come down and do somethin' for you."

She says she liked her friend's mother and felt sorry for her because this was something that sort of tore their marriage apart. The father was dead set against all this God nonsense in his house because the mother was in love with Jesus, and she thought that at times maybe the father was jealous of Jesus for being so tight with his wife. "The mother was always hollerin' about Jesus, and the father would just come out and say, you know, like, 'F——Jesus,' and, 'It ain't no Jesus, you gotta talk to me.'

"Every time she called on the Lord, the father would say, 'I'm your lord, I do all the providin'. Jesus ain't paid the bills or the rent in this house, electric bills, or the telephone bill, or nothin'. So if you wanna call on somebody to help or provide, you gotta call on me. I bring home the paycheck and pay the rent. Yeah, I'm the one that goes out and works every day.'

"And I think that's why, you know, the husband hated it so much, because instead of his wife appreciatin' what he was doin' for her and bein' a good provider, here she was lookin' up at Jesus and talkin' about Jesus when this dude was goin' out every day breakin' his back and all. He mighta dug it if he was able to see that there was a Jesus someplace, but as far as this dude was concerned, Jesus wasn't doin' nothin'. He had to get up early every mornin' and go out there and meet the man. What did Jesus have to do with it?

"This crazy old broad is wrapped up in Jesus instead of appreciatin' his efforts. Yeah, I guess that woulda weighed hard on anybody's mind, because it looked like when he wasn't there, Jesus was on the set takin' care of business. That Jesus thing just mighta been carried to the bed, too. The dude mighta thought that Jesus was there sort of cuttin' in on his stuff, you know, sorta gettin' the rewards."

Well, anyway, all of this came out of the spookism of Christianity as Jill would run it down to us. Jill is a pretty swift girl, as they say, but anybody who has been through as much as that girl has been through would have to be very swift to survive it in any kind of condition.

Jill once had this dude that she dug a whole lot. They'd been tight for a long time. According to Jill, Sly was one of the mellowest people you could ever meet. She says that Sly taught her some deep game stuff about out there on the street, and if it hadn't been for him there were times when she would have been dead. She talks about him from time to time. She'll come out of a long silence and say, "You know, I was thinkin' of somethin' that Sly told me one time." And you can see the gleam in her eyes, like a little light that comes from deep down inside, like he really lit her up at one time lastingly. The Hamites know how much she cherishes his memory, and when she talks about him everybody listens in respectful silence.

Jill says once she OD'd in a hallway, and Sly came and found her and started smacking her to bring her around. Being a junkie, he knew he needed something cold. So he asked the people in the restaurant for some ice, but they were going through changes and didn't want to give it to him. Everybody gives junkies a hard time because they don't trust them and they suspect that they are up to no good all the time, and they usually are.

He got a quarter and bought a little bit of ice for her and put the ice between her legs and told his brother to smack her, and she began to regain consciousness. They got her up and walked her around for a little while, up and down the block a couple of times. She said they were really very tight after that, and she would give him money even after she had stopped using stuff. Even after she hooked up with the pimp and was making all that money for him, she would still give Sly "somethin' to keep him goin'."

"Sly was a special junkie among junkies. He wasn't just an average dopey out there who didn't care about himself and nobody else. He cared, even though he was a dope fiend. He never wanted to hurt anybody. He cared about people, he cared about himself, you know, and he made other people care. If you can care, you never get so lost."

Jill says they never had a sex thing going, but you get the impression that she wanted something sexual with him but somehow it just never came off.

Jill tells Hebro that if he'd known Sly he would have a completely different attitude about junkies. "Straight people go around sayin' they are a fouler form of life than they actually are. Junkies are individual people just like anybody else, you know. Most people who have never had a jones don't know that, you know, that junkies vary in degrees of being foul. All junkies won't steal from their mothers. All junkies won't cut their granddaddy's throat to cool out their jones."

Jill would say that Sly was like a prince among junkies, "The kinda dude that the Bible would talk about in bein' a king and keepin' yourself together, but he slipped one time, and that's all it takes. A person slips and becomes a wino, and it's like then he sorta lost out in the game of kings and bein' the precious man fulfillin' his destiny. Carin' for other people was his trace of class and kingly dignity that he never lost and that always distinguished him from the average junkie out there, and perhaps he was aware of it. If somebody had gone into a coma or had passed out or maybe it was a risk of messin' up his high, as long as he could show some kinda concern for somebody else, he would save them."

Jill makes Sly sound like the junkies' guardian angel on the street. About a year and a half ago, Sly passed out after getting high in a hallway. He went into a coma first and then he passed out. The sad thing, the sad and ironic thing, is that there was nobody around to walk Sly. When Jill tells it she says, "It's funny that there was nobody even around to give him one slap to help him come out of it."

Jill used to frequent after-hours joints a lot and different dope dens and houses of ill repute to visit her friends, not necessarily to take care of any business. It was her way of getting away from the group and taking a look at some of the other side of life occasionally. She decided not to go to these places anymore after being present at a crazy stickup of one joint, "Because of all those dangerous maniacs out there. All the madmen."

Jill figures she's had too many close calls already. She's fortunate to be aboveground and she shouldn't go around pushing her luck anymore. She thinks she has already spent eight of her nine lives. She said she also wanted to get out of the life.

Some people still call her "VD." When asked why, Jill says that when she was out there turning tricks and somebody would come up to her and offer her some money and she didn't want to, she would tell them that she had VD. Often the person knew that she was running the game, but somebody else would come up and say it out loud, "Don't touch that broad, she's got VD."

Now she's in the process of living down the nickname, and she hates to be out on the streets with any of the Hamites when somebody comes up to her and calls her VD, especially with any of the other girls like Connie or Dee Dee or Nita.

She's trying to stay away from all those places where she might have trouble and might get busted or be around when the wrong thing goes down or when the place gets busted and she goes along in the wagon on a humble just because she was in the wrong place at the wrong time. When she starts talking about these things, she sounds like an old woman who's been through the mill three or four times or the mill was just a revolving door. You hope that she'll get married one day and that it'll work; she's such a sincere person.

Jill claims that she's tried every high in the world, methadone, peyote, LSD. She's smoked opium and smoke, and she's had morphine, and scag was her thing, and of course she's had cocaine and hashish and amphetamines and mescaline. She says she's had just about everything high available, but she thinks that the best high in this life that anybody can get is sex. She believes it could be the final solution to the drug problem. "You know what the older folks should do is, you know, just tell the younger ones that the best high in the world is sex, this is like the truth because a high is supposed to take you up or pick you up when you're feeling lowdown."

I asked Jill what it is she's looking forward to most in life. Her answer was Memorial Day. Puzzled, I said, Why? I thought maybe she wanted to go to her mother's grave, and I asked her if she puts flowers on it every Memorial Day. She shook her head, no. Instead of doing that, she says, she's waiting for Memorial Day so she can walk somebody for Sly.

Jill, who's simply loaded with compassion, has more compassion for Sheryl than anyone else. "Sheryl never had a chance because she grew up in a sort of drug shop."

Sheryl's mother Mae was, for many years, the major dope dealer in this community. She didn't try to hide it from her children, and they just grew up into it. At early ages, even by Harlem standards, they began using drugs, and they all eventually became addicted. She was also a fence, she started off in numbers, but there wasn't enough money in it, so she went into something more lucrative like dealing drugs. Sheryl sometimes stays at the spot when she doesn't have a place to stay, but she's not really a fully accepted member of the group. After Jill's mother died, she stayed with Sheryl for about three months until Mae got "an attitude" one day and put her out.

Jill, being the motherly type, likes to worry over the brood. The worry thing is reciprocal because the Hamites worry about Jill also. If she decides to vanish—she has a habit of doing this, nobody will see her for two or three days—they become apprehensive. They wonder where she is and what she's doing, and they'll ask each other, in what they believe to be a casual manner, has anybody seen her. They're wondering if the mother hen has left the coop for good or if she's coming back. So far, she's always returned.

Apparently they like the idea of having someone around who knows a little bit more, maybe much more, about life in the raw than they do, and somebody to play mother to them. If she's gone too long, they will sneak down the street, look around the block, and try to find out what's happening with her. I think she likes it, the feeling or the knowledge that somebody really cares about what will happen to her.

It's highly probable that this is the first time in Jill's life that she ever felt that if she were to walk away or not come back, somebody would be concerned. She would be genuinely missed. She once said, "It's a real sad feelin' to feel like a stranger in a house where you grew up at."

This has probably more meaning to Jill, or at least as much meaning to Jill, as it has to all the other Hamites who have never had even a poor imitation of the American concept of a home.

From time to time, Jill will say something about getting married, just to get a reaction out of the others. It's interesting to observe the way they respond. The girls will start talking about what they don't like about the intended groom. The fellows will start lecturing about how such a guy isn't good enough or swift enough for her and that she'd be wasting herself on him.

Once she said she was going to marry this guy around the corner. There was a long silence, and Mumps said, "You know, I saw this color television in this joint that was easy to cop from and I think I'm gonna get it and bring it here and put it in the crib tomorrow."

Somebody else said, "Yeah, that'd be outta sight, then we'll have a real spot. This'll be like home. All we need is a refrigerator now that works and we'll sho'nuff be doin' it to death. You know, like this will be a sho'nuff crib for everybody."

After a while she broke down and said, "Yeah, that would be really some dynamite stuff to put in here."

I think she realized that they all loved her, but at that particular moment she had a powerful need to have it verbalized. "If there's anything we can do for you, we'll do it. If there's anything we can get to persuade you to stay, we'll go and get it."

For a long time after that, she wouldn't mention getting married or deserting the Hamites, even teasingly.

Jill has long fingers and is a very skillful pot roller, so various members of the group are always giving her the bag to roll up from. And she's as neat as a cigarette machine, so it seems.

Jill also has a talent for massaging. She has taught the Hamites how to massage each other, but she's still the best. Jill can give massages to stimulate, and she can give massages that will put one to sleep, and she claims that she knows a great sexual massage. Well, nobody around the spots needs any sexual stimulation, not at their ages. Jill might give Dujo a massage, and if you see him five minutes later, he's either asleep or looking as though he's at peace with the world and never had a worry or a care in his life. Perhaps that's another reason that Jill is so valuable to the group.

Jill is more or less the manager of the spots and the mother figure, the one who does most of the worrying and tells the others what's needed and what has to be done before they can go off on any of their kicks.

Jill doesn't like most women, and she readily takes to all men, I mean any man. Shrinks say that sort of thing happens as a reaction to not having a father.

She often sings around the spot. The Hamites have a record player, and people are always bringing her recordings. Almost every week Mumps will give Jill a couple of albums that he "picked up" someplace. Jill says that maybe she was destined to be a singer like Billie Holiday because she has had a life that's very similar. She saw the movie *Lady Sings the Blues* four times.

This girl has been out on the streets longer than any of the rest of the Hamites, and knows more about it and has knocked around hustling in every conceivable way that a woman can. When she was on scag she supported her own jones as well as that of a few other guys she was going with at the same time, and she has made a pile of money for a couple of pimps in her spare time. In spite of all this, Jill says it's unnatural for women to sell their bodies. "You don't see animals goin' around sellin' themselves to other animals. They were put here to keep on producin' their kinda creatures, and it's the same thing with man and woman. But since there's so many stupid men around who wanna buy it, well, why not sell it? It's just somethin' that's gonna make 'em happy."

Jill, who should know, says that pimps do very little screwing, much less than the average man. She claims that women who give their money to pimps are not necessarily screwing them or doing anything sexual. They give it to them for knowing how to handle them, "Knowin' what to say when the woman is feelin' bad, and just knowin' how to make her happy when she's feelin' low, and sayin' the right thing at the right time. And also the flash has got a lot to do with it. Most women like to be seen with guys who are flashy and eye-catching and everybody's gonna look up to them."

She says that's the main thing, not fantastic sexual feats. She calls the sex fable "pimp pipe dreams and pimp propaganda."

According to Jill, Solomon was the biggest pimp in the history of the world. Not because of his four hundred wives and seven hundred concubines, but because of all the priceless gifts that the Queen of Sheba gave to him before he ever touched her. She reasons that "Solomon must have been a dynamite lover because Sheba said that his wives was happy, and that's a whole lotta happiness for one dude, even a king, to be handin' out." And "He gave to her everything her heart desired," so the Good Book says.

But the reason that Jill says Solomon was the greatest pimp in the history of the world is that "The Queen of Sheba gave him one hundred and twenty talents of gold, not to mention the spices and precious stones that she gave him. She also gave him a whole lotta other things like myrrh and wood that couldn't be found anyplace else but in Africa. The one hundred and twenty talents of gold would now amount to about three million nine hundred and sixteen thousand dollars, which is almost four million dollars that she gave to the dude before anything ever came off between them."

Jill says, as far as she knows, nobody in the world ever got that kind of money from a woman without even touching her. "So Solomon would've had to be not king of kings but pimp of pimps."

And that's the way Jill interprets the Bible.

The Hamites' housemother's repertoire consists of several dozen of these uniquely interpreted Bible tales, and some of them are very entertaining. It's like Jill is certain that the forbidden fruit in the Bible was smoke, not a "apple they ate." It was the hip weed in the Garden of Eden that Adam and Eve smoked and got high, "started havin' a ball and just diggin' some sex and didn't wanna do anythin' else, and that's why God got mad at 'em and threw them outta the garden."

One of her more interesting tales is the tale about Christ being the first junkie. She says, "Christ and his disciples were all just some dudes strollin' around in the wilderness or on the countryside gettin' high all the time, and Christ would be stoned, like really out of it all, you know, spaced, and he'd stop different places and tell people to listen to a sermon he was about to give. You know, every time he got high he wanted to rap. It's like a lotta people are into that. They get high and wanna rap. Well, Christ was deep into it, too, just him and his disciples. You know, they were junkies who went walkin' around gettin' high all the time on some o' that bad scag they had back there, and one day Christ was rappin', you know, everybody dug his thing, his rap game.

"Well, one day he was out in the countryside with his fellows, and they gettin' high and takin' off and he said to Peter, 'Look here, Peter, you know, I got a idea for somethin' that we can run on the gators [hicks] out here, and they'll never forget us. They'll be talkin' about us for two thousand years or more.' Peter's ears perked up, and he said, 'Yeah, J.C., what is that? Like run it to me, tell me what it's all about.'

"J.C. said to Peter, 'Well, look heah, what it comes down to is like I'm gonna get some real brown [good] scag, and get high, and let the Romans catch me and crucify me. But 'cause of this scag, I'll be so spaced on, so dynamite, I won't be dead. I'll go into a deep, deep nod, and before I have a chance to bleed to death from the nails, I'll be in this nod and lookin' limp. I'll look like I'm iced.

" 'That's not long enough to bleed to death. So then what you can do, you and the fellows, y'all come cut me down; and then take me over to our crib and cool me out. You know, tend to the nail holes. You dig it. And a couple of days afterward, I'll show on the scene again, like we'll do it 'round Eastertime, and I'll look like I was resurrected on Easter mornin'. Now, can you dig this? People will be talkin' about it. That would really give Christianity a big push, and people will be talkin' about it for the next two thousand years at least, and maybe the next three thousand years, if these folks here can last that long, you know.'

"So Peter said, 'Yeah, J.C., that's a pretty swift scheme, but it's kinda gamblin', too. You know, like anything can go wrong, or a lotta things can go wrong, and it may not come off right, and if it don't go down right, you know, it's like we done blew you, baby, and what's the rest of us goin' do? We won't even know how to get high anymore. We won't have anybody with us to support our jones, so you don't wanna risk that, do you?'

"And J.C. said to Peter, 'Now, look here, fisherman, you ain't scared that you ain't goin' be able to support your own jones if I'm not here, are you? One day you goin' have to get out there and shift for yourself anyhow. So like that's no sweat right now because I'm not goin' anyplace. You got some faith in me, haven't you? I'm not goin' go up there and let those dudes just off me like that, like nothin' happened. I know what I'm doin'. Haven't I always pulled it off real brown? Remember that dead man's stunt we pulled off?'

"And Peter said, 'Yeah, man, but that was different. That wasn't you. And you wasn't playin' dead yourself.'

"He said, 'Yeah, but remember the bit about walkin' on water? Don't my games always get over?'

" 'Yeah, J.C., but I don't know about this shot, baby.'

" 'Peter, you dig how it is, how the people get excited and treat us, you know, like royalty when we hit a town now? They treat us better than the Roman generals. Now, after this shot, when we put this over, they goin' treat us like the Kingdom has come already.'

"So Christ convinced Peter that he would be able to pull this scheme off, and Peter went along with it sorta half-ass like. Christ went on, let the Romans bust him, and then he had some stuff with him to get high on just before they nailed him on the cross. When he fell and stumbled, and the cat who came in there to help him put his cross on, that was the dope man who slipped him the dope, and it was a monster, so he'd be able to go out there and take care of business. He wasn't goin' be bleedin' as fast as he normally would.

"Everything went off according to schedule, just about. They nailed J.C. up on the cross, and he was just hangin' up there, and then, you know, there was these two Roman soldiers who were down there on the ground shootin' craps for his robe. Well, you see, Christ didn't count on a mishap like this. What had happened, the Roman soldier who lost the crap game got mad. He wasn't goin' do nothin' to the other soldier there, but he was mad, you know, because he lost his money after shootin' for the robe, and then started shootin' for money. So he lost his money to the other soldier, and in his attitude he snatched up that old rusty spear of his and stuck J.C. in his side.

"When his disciples, J.C.'s fellows, came and took him down and took him to their crib, Christ died from lockjaw from bein' stuck in the side with that ol' rusty spear by the Roman soldier. But they couldn't go and tell everybody that the great J.C. died from lockjaw. Now all that risin', well, you know, only two people saw him."

When Jill was in jail she used to read the Bible often. At first, because she had nothing else to read, so she read the Bible, and then she got interested in reading about all the incest and the countless other goodies "that was goin' on, about how everybody was screwin' their daughters and their sisters and all kindsa depravity stuff," and she was fascinated. "They was doin' stuff in the Bible that's almost as mean as the shots that people do out in the streets of the Apple [New York City]. They were just offin' people, messin' over people, rapin' people, turnin' everybody into stone and doin' it to death, and it's like, you know, it was interestin'. It made it a little hard to believe that you had this God back there who was doin' all o' these wicked numbers on people, and the people that he was supposed to be doin' it to didn't wanna do anything that cold-blooded to him.

"Sometimes they make God seem like a silly old man who was just spiteful and vicious to people. Then other times they made the people who dug God seem like fools, like Job. Now he played so much stuff on Job, and the chump said, 'Well, it's cool, you know, if you come back and tighten it up.'

"But it seems impossible for anybody to go around like takin' somebody's squeeze [wife] and money and children and everything, fuckin' up a man's whole life, and then comin' back later and sayin', 'That's okay, I'm give you another one.'

"It just made Job seem like a first-class ass that the man could come and play with him like that, take anything he wanted to and blow his whole life, then come back and give him another one. Now what reason did Job have to believe that this silly-ass prankster called God wouldn't come and do the same thing all over again, 'cause it was clear that he was capable of it. Looked like Job was the main dude that he wanted to run some of those silly games on."

Some of Jill's reasoning makes a lot of sense, and some of the things in the Bible that she points out as not making too much sense, she has a pretty good argument for. She can actually make some bona fide Christians stop and wonder if the Bible isn't just a collection of nonsense or fairy tales told to some children. And Jill says like she doesn't think that the Bible was written for adults.

"At one time, when people and the world went through the Dark Ages and people wasn't that hip, it's like they started runnin' it down that this was the for-real truth and spookin' people into bein' afraid of a Holy Spirit and God and all that kinda scene, and they told 'em like here was The Book. Black men had never seen white men, white men had never seen black men, and red men had never seen white men or black men, and yellow men had never seen white, red, black, and red had never seen black, yellow, and white. You know, it's like the whole world was strangers from each other, and because there was so much mystery surroundin' everything, people was more naive and gullible and they believed just about anything they heard.

"Now people are outgrowin' Bible tales. They know more about the world, they get educated and learning about geography and customs and different groups and different strokes. Some preachers still goin' 'round and tryin' to sell the Bible and the sweet Jesus rap game as some real serious stuff, but it's just a hustle, everybody's hip to that. The preachers are the biggest players [hustlers] around."

To Jill's way of thinking, "preachers" is merely a synonym for politicians.

"First it was the preachers and the church, and then came the politicians, and to show you that there ain't much difference between the two games, preachin' and politics, well, most of the politicians in the black community came outta the church. I mean years ago this was true, and everybody knows it. They do a whole lotta playin'. It's like the black preachers was always playin'. Right after slavery, they was the first black players. As soon as they learned to read, they got the callin' from the Lord and went 'round and started preachin'. But then, you know, when black folks started goin' into politics and they found out there was a lotta money to be taken off in politics, well, they started gamin' on that.

"Five or ten years ago it was true, especially in New York City, where we had Adam Clayton Powell, but not only in New York City. A lotta throwback preachers who were politicians came out and started hustlin' politics because they saw that there was some money in it and they could lead the flock any way they wanted to. And just like the politicians would be runnin' games on top o' games and trippin' up on all the lies they tell, the preachers had a lyin' textbook so they could always point to the Bible and say, 'You see here,' and tricks would go peep on it, and they would buy it for the truth. Anything they wanted to say, they could find somethin' in the Bible to prove it.

"It's pretty much the same scene when people go and they listen to politicians who be lyin' and schemin' and stealin' and swearin' up and down that this is like the gospel. It's the same thing, and it's like people never seem to get tired of, or to get hip to, the lies or the politicians. It could be that the politicians just don't put all that godliness in it no more. It's like they wouldn't dare—the politicians wouldn't dare come out and tell people now in this day and time that God's goin' solve the problem of unemployment and light pockets and inflation, because if they was to do that, they'd be run right off the set.

"Years ago when everybody was doin' bad, preachers would be comin' 'round their houses to eat on Sunday, durin' the Depression, sayin', 'Everything is goin' be all right, you just gotta trust in the Lord. The Lord is sure goin' make a way for you. Let's have a prayer meetin'.'

"But today if some dude was to come 'round, if some preacher was to come 'round or a politician was to come 'round and say, 'Well, I don't know what we goin' do about this inflation and the recession, but what we should do is sit down and have this great prayer meetin' and the Lord is goin' come out and make a way for us,' they would run him outta town or think the man wasn't wrapped too tight. It's like the people have grown a little wiser over the years, and they could still be fooled, most of them with light stuff, but not the same way that they used to be flammed by those Bible fairy tales.

"So now, you know, instead of runnin' those Bible fairy tales, the politicians have to tell the people that they're goin' solve all these problems, you know, by next year or sometime in the future. It's the same flam, the preachers kept the tricks lookin' up in the sky while they ripped 'em off, and the politicians keep them lookin' in the future. You just give 'em somethin' to look for. I mean somethin' real. You can't tell 'em about God and about be patient because God is just tryin' you like he did Job or somethin', or God's got all this wisdom and he ain't goin' let nobody down because he always found a way in the Bible.

"In about another twenty years or so, people goin' get too hip for this kinda stuff, too. They ain't goin' be listenin' to politicians no more and them sayin' that they goin' solve problems that they know they can't solve. And people goin' be runnin' them out of offices and turnin' away from politics and turnin' away from the polls, and nobody's goin' be payin' no attention to 'em, just like they don't pay no attention to preachers no more.

"The whole world just keeps on gettin' swifter and swifter every day. The games keep on goin' down, but they ain't the same kinda games. They may be basically the same kinda games, but they not played in the same way. You always gotta change it, or change up on the people, or they'll get ahead of you. You know, you just can't keep on comin' back with the same tricks. It's like the world grows up, you know.

"I mean not just that kids get older. You know, when kids are young they believe in Santa Claus, and then they get to be about eight, they don't believe in Santa Claus no more. Well, the world grows up in the same way. The whole world's grown up out of the Santa Claus fairy tale hang-up. The people who runnin' down the games, the lawmakers, you know, and the politicians and the police, the government, they just start runnin' down more grown-up games on 'em, that's all. But it's like the thing never really changes, it really don't get that much different."

We keep hoping that one day somebody will devise a solution to this affliction in Harlem. The common tragedy among these youngsters is that by the time they reach the age of nineteen or twenty they are thoroughly and irreversibly demoralized. All the ambition and the drive that they once had is permanently crushed out of them. I'm hoping that this doesn't happen to Jill. She appears to be one of the fortunate ones who just might be able to escape that usual fate of forsaking her dreams.

THREE

Lee

This block has been one of Harlem's most notoriously violent and has had one of the highest drug-addiction rates in the enitre city for the past twenty years. The dope fiends are practically all between twenty-five and forty. This might be a positive social phenomenon in the community. But it is too early to draw any conclusions. The Hamites have now worked out an uneasy truce with the junkies in the block. If they catch any dope fiends in the spots uninvited, they get carried out or violently assisted out of a first- or second-story window. Most of the neighborhood junkies respect the agreement, and the group proudly compares its victory and final use of the building to the early American struggle.

Among the junkies there are three or four whom the Hamites do not actually despise. But only one of the younger ones is allowed to come up to the spots. As a matter of fact, he's allowed to live in one of the spots. This is Lee, who is twenty-three and has a bachelor's degree in sociology. He deeps himself clean and about as neat as a junkie can be. He says he'd like to get a job. I think he views this as a solution to all his problems, and it might be, if this solution comes soon enough.

"I first came up here from Florida in the fall of 1971. I knew nothing about dope. I knew what wine and winos were, but that was it. And I'd see the junkies on the corner noddin' and lookin' greasy and sick, but I really didn't know what they was doin'. I'd go upstairs and I'd ask my cousin, 'Hey, Ann, you know why those people sleepin' on the corner?

"And, you know, like she would tell me that they was sick, but then her husband would tell me that it was dope that made them nod like that, but I didn't know what dope really was."

Lee has been a bona fide, vein-puncturing member of the heroin-worshiping cult for only a year, which means that he might still be salvageable. He is a quiet guy whom everybody likes, of an obvious intelligence made questionable by his scag jones. The Hamites like him because he can be trusted far beyond the limits of any other worshipers they know. Lee runs the errands for them that they cannot run for themselves: to the liquor store to "cop a jug" or something. If Lee's habit is down on him, or getting to him, he will inform the Hamites without hesitation, "Man, please don't put any money in my hands today." And they won't.

The Hamites allow Lee to stay in one of the spots because he's clean, quiet, doesn't bother anyone, and he's a nice guy who can be trusted. But he knows not to come around the spots when he's high, and he never brings any of his junkie friends there. Lee is the kind of junkie that none of the Hamites has ever seen in a nod. They see him high sometimes and his eyes may bat just a little bit, but he's not a nodding junkie and this is important.

Lee has been in New York City for fifteen months. He says if he gets a job eveything will be all right because he feels his problem is just that he never got started in New York. Sometimes he feels that he got involved with the dope fiends because he was a gator, he wasn't from one of the big cities. He had relatives on the block. That was how he got onto the block. If he had been from the city and didn't have to prove anything, he would never have started using any stuff. But he wanted to prove that he wasn't a gator, a creep, or very square, a farmer, somebody who just got off the bus. He didn't want to be that.

When Lee was in school at the University of Miami, he heard about drugs and stuff like that. He said he smoked, but he never tried anything else. And so when he came here and he got the challenge, junkies seemed to be really mellow people, with a whole lot of cool, and sophisticated. He was working with one of those summer programs for a while, and when that ran out of funds he was unable to get another job. He kept on hanging around the block, and before he knew it that's all he was doing, hanging out and using dope. And because he needed a place, the Hamites let him come in, and he stayed there. He didn't bother anybody. Sometimes he feels that all he wants when the pressure comes down on him is to get carfare back to Florida. It might be the best thing for him, too. If he really wanted to get back home, all he'd have to do is deprive his arm for a day or so and he'd have carfare. Or if he were to come out and tell the Hamites that he's in trouble and really wants to get back home, they would probably help him out.

There's a crazy group around the corner that goes around shooting people. They shot one boy in the head who was dealing smoke. They have been trying to lure Lee to come in with them. Eventually Lee is going to have to go someplace. He's going to have to belong someplace.

There are all kinds of cliques on the block. There are the straight-up people who work, and they're very few. And there are the junkies and the winos and the potheads. There are some people who just snort coke. There are people who deal in digits, and they don't do anything else—all they do is take care of business. The digit fellows had tried at one time to pull Lee into the group, but he was too involved in his own thing to get into it with anybody. His own thing was just getting into his jones good. But everybody likes him because he's cool, he's calm, he doesn't cause any static. He knows how to approach everybody, and he doesn't make any wrong moves. Everybody who has seen him in the block since he's been in there has known that the cat is right.

There are a lot of choices, and I guess that's what made it so difficult for him to make up his mind. Everybody wanted him, and most of them still do to a point, although I think the junior gangsters are cooling toward him.

Lee doesn't stink, and he bathes from time to time and keeps himself looking halfway respectable, and that may be one of the reasons everybody is trying to pull him into their thing. If he's on the street he's usually talking to the junkies, and people probably figure it's not going to be long before he'll be a full-fledged junkie out there chasing the bag all day and all night long just like the other junkies. And they're trying to save him while there's still time. Some of the people that want to save him, however, want to save him from a fate that may not be worse than the one they want to bring him into.

A couple of the Hamites stay with him, like Mumps stays, and some of the times Chips stays. He likes to cook tea, and he comes up with his jailhouse cooker, one of those little pieces of wire that you put into a cup and it heats up. He brings his tea bag, and in the morning he'll have a cup of tea. He goes to restaurants and puts some sugar in a napkin and brings it out, asks for a glass of water, or maybe he'll buy a doughnut or something. If they have sugar cubes, he'll take out a handful. That's the extent of his housekeeping.

He's always available and willing to do what he can for the various members of the group, which makes him a valuable asset, too. When somebody gets into trouble in school, like Snooky or Salt-Noody, he'll go to school with them and say, not that he's the parent, but that he's their older brother and the mother is dead or in the hospital and he's in charge of them now. He'll act like the guardian. He's usually pretty good at the game.

He's also one of the preachers around, always sermonizing on the ills of using stuff. People don't pay too much attention to him because they know he hasn't stopped using it. It's more effective if you get it from an ex-addict than an addict—the sermon, that is.

One of the reasons that he is still so trustworthy is that he hasn't really gotten a full-fledged jones yet. If he had been on stuff for two years, it's very, very difficult to imagine that he would still be as righteous as he is. It is impossible to believe that anybody can get a genuine jones and not turn foul on everybody. I guess everybody else in the block watches Lee closely to see if he'll get foul.

The Hamites' acceptance of Lee is a symbol of their tolerance because they all, especially Dujo and Hebro, despise junkies. Hebro shows the most obvious contempt for them, and next is Dujo. Dujo says the reason that he doesn't like them is that they're so untrustworthy. But even Hebro and Dujo have accepted Lee at this point. It may be because there is something a bit tragic about Lee. He seems to have an air about him of impending doom. And maybe that's one of the things that attract people to him or make people want to take him in and do something for him. He doesn't know where he's going or what he's doing. He isn't certain what he wants, and it's pretty easy to drop off the face of the earth or drop out of life in a community like this one. It's just like walking in the jungle and having no idea where the dangerous paths and pitfalls are. I think that many people in the community, the Hamites included, wish that they could show him the way. Even though he's older than the Hamites, to them he's something of a babe in the woods. Even Snooky tends to look on Lee as a little brother. And Lee is at least nine years older than Snooky. The fact of the matter is everybody knows that Lee is a nice guy but that he has no business in the community, especially in that block. Lee becomes a little more uncertain with each passing day, and a little more lost. I have seen him come out of the spot and turn around two or three times, starting to go, beginning to walk in one direction, and immediately changing and starting to go another way, and then come back as if he doesn't know what to do with himself. And this sort of summarizes just where his mind is. A lot of people, especially young people, in the Harlem community start using scag just because they don't know what to do with themselves or don't have any specific purpose or goal. Scag was something that would definitely occupy their time, even if it did it in the worst way. And that's probably what happened to Lee.

Lee walks around telling people, "I'm goin' back home. I'm goin' to get me carfare, and as soon as I get it up I'm goin' home to Florida."

And people will wish him good luck, or they used to. For the first three months he was doing that, everybody was saying, "Yeah, okay," and different people would give him a few dollars. But then the people who wanted to be helpful began to suspect that that was his way of getting money to buy scag. And so after a while people wouldn't respond. But I don't think he was ever really trying to hustle up dope money by telling people he's going home. I've listened to him closely, and I appreciate his sincerity. It's just possible he doesn't want to go back as a failure or have people suspect that he couldn't make it in New York, and there's also the thing of running. New York City, especially Harlem, can be downright frightening to someone who really is a gator.

Lee said he really became excited about New York when he saw the film *Superfly* and in 1971 he made his mind up right then that he was going to go and see it. He wanted to see all those people who went around snorting that cocaine and driving those fancy cars. And he wanted to see some of those spots where everybody went and danced all night long and dudes smoke marijuana right out there in the open and snorted all kinds of coke like it was legal, almost. He had heard a lot about Harlem, which is to most blacks in the South really New York. But if you've never seen Harlem, if you've never seen one of the major urban ghettos in the country, it's rather formidable when you do. There are a lot a blacks all over, very unrepressed blacks, who are just walking around letting it all hang out. They seem to have no inhibitions whatsoever. To a person from the country who isn't a naturally extroverted type, this can be a very intimidating experience. Lee has never gotten over the shock of it.

That's why he listens like a younger brother to the Hamites. He's learning a lot from them, too, practically all he's learning, about survival in New York City. But he didn't learn about shooting scag from them. That's something he picked up on his own.

Almost every time you ask Lee why or how did he start using scag, you get a completely different story, and you begin to suspect that he doesn't know or can't face the real reason. One of the most memorable answers I received was, "I was a gator and wanted to be swift. They used to call reefers in school dope, but that wasn't any real dope. People used to talk about usin' LSD and the pep pills and stuff like that. You know, nobody went into any noddin' things. You knew that cocaine in the movies didn't make people nod or look all sleepin' and carryin' on like that.

"And I used to stand there on the stoop and look at the junkies noddin', and they be peepin' me, too, and one might come over and say, 'Hey, man, can you spare a quarter or something? I ain't had nothin' to eat in some days.'

"And yeah, I'd give them a quarter. They really looked like they needed it. It seemed like if somebody had a quarter that he could spare, that's the least he could do for a guy like this because he was in sad shape. If a quarter could help him, I was ready to give it up in a hurry. I had heard about heroin, but everybody was talkin' about scag, and I didn't know for a long time that scag was the same thing as heroin. When you hear about or you read about dope, it's really far removed from you and your way of life and the people that you live around. It doesn't come home as something real. But then you get here and you start seeing this and when you find out that that's heroin, you say, 'Wow, yeah, so that's what it does to you.' Suddenly heroin became alive. Heroin was all those dudes out on the corner. Like somethin' had a hold on 'em from the inside, turnin' them up, turnin' them around that way and puttin' them like on the wall, or layin' up against the wall. It's like havin' a whole lot of sadness deep down in their eyes. If you look deep enough, you could see it. You know, it was somethin' that you really couldn't talk about on the outside.

"Heroin seemed to be somethin' that was inside of these people, like demons possessin' them, and I was always like sort of peepin' at it to get an idea of what the demon looked like on the inside. Of course, it's like I was sure it was a demon that had a hold on a whole lotta people at the same time, but nobody could see him. All they could see is what he was doin' to the people on the outside, and I knew that that demon was mean and foul. I mean I didn't know what dope was, but I knew what it did to people.

"I became afraid of dope fiends because they looked like somethin' had a hold on 'em. And then you always hear people say that they broke into somebody's house or stole somethin' from somebody or from somewhere. Maybe that's why I started usin' drugs, so I wouldn't be as scared of the junkies no more. It's like a kid openin' a closet that he'd heard there was somethin' bad in it for a long time. He keeps peepin' at it. He keeps peepin' at it, like tryin' to see what's it really like without openin' it up because it might jump out and grab him or eat him up. Some sort of weird, childish fear like that. Well, that's how I was about the scag thing, but I was really curious, too, because I wanted to know what it was. It seemed that the more frightened of it I was, the more curious I became. Maybe that's why I started using stuff, so I wouldn't be afraid of it or the junkies anymore.

"Maybe people would even be scared of me. So I thought, Well, let me go on and see if I could become a part of that frightenin' crowd. I was more afraid of the dope than dope fiends, but I wasn't scared of gettin' an overdose or anything like that because I saw too many of the dope fiends out there on the corner, like livin' a long time. It was just, you know, people lost respect for you, and you lost respect for yourself, too. It made you not care about your parents, made your arms and hands swell up, stay that way all the time. It not only made you act like a fiend, it made you look like one, too. Another thing I was scared of was stickin' a needle in my arm. It seemed like just stickin' a needle in your arm all the time would make you sick even without dope. Like real normal people didn't go around stickin' needles in their arms. There was somethin' science fictional about it. You know, the junkies came off like creatures from another planet who in order to stay alive on earth had to be constantly takin' injections.

"But still I had to find out about this thing. And I thought maybe, like the kid at the closet again, I could crack it open and peep just a little way in, and I could see it without really goin' in. It's like exposin' myself, or being snatched in by this fiend and held captive or killed or something like that. I suppose that's really how I got into it. When I started dabblin', that's what it amounted to. I was peekin' in the closet. When the monster jumped out at me it's like I wasn't quick enough because he sho'nuff caught me. But I'm not cryin' about my life because I know there's a lot of dudes out there much worse off than I am. I don't have a real heavy jones, but I got a jones and it's a thing that I can give up anytime. So I'm not worried about it, and I got a pretty cool thing going. I don't cause nobody no kind of friction. I ain't got nothin' to do. I know if I get a job everything will be straight in a minute. Just let me get a job and you'll see. This thing'll be something of the past. My jones will leave so fast it'll be like it never even happened. And I think everybody around here knows it."

Well, there are some people who suspect it, and they want to know it, but they're not so certain about Lee right now, and foremost among these people are the Hamites. But they have faith in Lee, and they believe in him, and, more than that, they like him and accept him as a kind of human misfortune. Not as a junkie or a dope fiend out there. No, just a guy who is lost, somebody who has yet to find his way.

FOUR

Dujo

The Hamites don't have a leader. They don't believe in leadership. But Dujo is the member of the group who is most often listened to. He's something of a politician and diplomat who's continually settling conflicts and calling meetings to discuss any problems that may arise for the Hamites or even for their neighbors outside, and especially friends in the block. When somebody is having a problem at school and he thinks that it affects the group or that the group should be concerned about the individual's problem, he immediately calls for a meeting. He does this despite his awareness that the others don't relish meetings and discussions, but they are certain that Dujo is going to clarify some issues and provide some food for thought at these meetings, so they all attend. Therefore, it's reasonable to assume that Dujo would be the leader if they had one.

Dujo is a bright, sixteen-year-old kid. He has been on the streets for a long time. When asked how he came to be shacking at one of the spots and why he left home, Dujo replied, "I didn't leave home, home left me. I left home when my mama became a worshiper, a heroin worshiper, you know, a dopey.

"I hung around for four years, waitin' for somethin' to happen and takin' care of my brothers and sisters. One day a lady 'cross the hall came to take us in with her. She told us that Mama had taken ill and had to go to the hospital for a while. I was scared because I thought maybe Mama had OD'd or shot some bad stuff or somethin'. But in a few hours the wire was on the street that Mama got busted shopliftin'. She was in the Women's House of Detention, not in the hospital. She showed back in about a week, but she didn't bother to go across the hall and scoop up the kids. She just asked how they were doin' and slipped [went into a nod]. It seems like she's been into that same nod ever since.

"At this point I just faced up to it. Home was long gone, and it wasn't comin' back, so I tipped. But I still drop around my aunt's to see the kids, and when I finish school I'm gonna get a job so they can come live with me. They shouldn't have to suffer on account of scag. They never messed with it."

Dujo's ambition is to finish college, earn a goodly sum of money, and take his younger brothers and sisters in to live with him.

Dujo has a special hate on for scag because of what it did to his family. But he says that it's impossible for anyone to grow up in Harlem and not try heroin at least once. Even he checked it out. He explained how it happened. He had tried to persuade Mumps and Snooky to "take off" a blind woman, and Mumps told him that it was nut city, but if the others were down, so was he. He tried to get Salt-Noody into it, too, "But he said, you know, like he didn't think he could deal with it, so I didn't force him."

Dugo was planning to rob a blind lady who frequently came around the block to get some wine. "I wouldn've thought about doin' it ordinarily, but I needed some money real bad to get my pants out of the cleaners, and I didn't like her anyway.

"After a while, Snooky said he was down with me, and Mumps came on in and said he'd go along with it. So we took her off. We didn't get that much money, we split about three dollars apiece. It came off kinda brown. I mean it went down the way we set it up. We set it up like we were goin' in there to see somebody. Once we saw there was nobody else in there, we went into our act. We closed the door when we got down there in the basement and told the blind broad that this was a sho'nuff stickup. I put this piece of wood up to the broad's head like it was a piece and told her to give it up. I guess it felt like it was a piece. It was wood, and the broad was blind.

"Snooky grabbed her wig off because he figured she had somethin' in it, and it turned out to be scag. Mumps said, 'Come on, let's down it,' and I said, 'Let's try it.'

"And so we decided to try it. Everybody got curious and said, 'Let's all try snortin' some.' We snorted the scag, and we went to a movie and just laid in the movie and grooved behind the high. I think I was too messed up to tell whether I liked it or not. And everybody else was sorta messed up, too. We were into some heavy slippin', and

I don't think anybody remembers what the flick was all about. Then we bought some sangria, and we decided to go up to the spot and drink the wine."

Crazy Mary was the last legitimate tenant in the building. But she hadn't been paying rent for a long time, Dujo told me. "When she started to tip she told us, and we thought it would be brown not to have to pay rent. Everybody wanted a spot anyway. So when she moved out, we moved in.

"Crazy Mary left a dresser behind, that was all. But we got old furniture from people movin' away who didn't want to take it with 'em. We bought a few sheets and bed things, some of it from junkies, some a girl friend would drop on us, or we would steal a blanket. And bit by bit, piece by piece, we sort of slowly put it together, anything that we could find or steal without too much sweat.

"The joint didn't really get off the ground until Mumps showed because Mumps had been out there boostin' since he was four or five years old. His brother was in Greenhaven Prison for dealin', but he was a second-story man until he got shot in the leg, and then he dealt scag, and he got busted for that. Mumps learned the boostin' game from his brother. His brother hipped him to just how to do it, do it with class. Mumps had been livin' at a foster home and stealin' just for himself. He's the cleanest one like of our whole crowd, but then when he decided to move into the crib, one of the spots, he started stealin' stuff for the spot, and then we really started shapin' the place up. It was just like a little bit here and a little bit there until Mumps showed on the scene."

When asked how they got their order established, how they developed the impressive measure of respect that they have for one another, Dujo said, "From the jump, everybody was doin' a little hustlin', and everybody thought they was gettin' over, and when they started doin' good they didn't want to speak to each other and they didn't want to know anybody. One night I dug where they were comin' from. I dug how they was messin' one another around, so I told 'em we was gonna have a meetin' with everybody in the spot at about eight o'clock. Everybody showed at the spot, and we weren't all livin' there then, you know, it was just a few of us was stayin' there, like me and Shaft and Lee, you know, junkie Lee. But the others would hang out there. We all grew up together, but we was sort of pullin' away from each other without meanin' to. Everybody was sort of gettin' into his own thing and gettin' kind of sassy and gettin' to feel that he was better than somebody else. And I decided to talk about it.

"I wanted to get the dudes back together the way we always was. So I told them about the meetin' at the spot. To my surprise everybody showed, and I brought it right down front. I told 'em, 'No matter if somebody is gettin' over better than somebody else, we all still down together. We was always tight. I don't know what this funny scene is now. A lot of times a dude might be dealin' some smoke, and somebody else is dealin' against him, which is like puttin' everybody in jeopardy.'

"Most of the dudes sat around mumblin', but they listened. We had the shoutin' thing goin' on, like for a short time, I guess. Finally we started givin' one person the floor, and other people started listenin', and we started seein' each other's points. We always been stickin' together. If somebody was to get in some static, we all rolled on the set. But it wasn't hooked up quite as tight until, you know, until I ran the rap to everybody. And a couple of other dudes in the group just moved into the spot, too, and we really got down and tight, or even tighter, for that matter, because then the real family thing started."

The Hamites had a violent conflict a few weeks ago that tested Dujo's talent for diplomatic negotiations in a very practical way. "Me and my brother-in-law Mumps, we was in the spot gettin' high off a fifth of vodka. And we was feelin' kinda mellow, so we went downstairs, and the fellows was on the stoop and we started rappin'. Then I sat down in a chair on the street by the numbers joint that turned out to belong to the joint. I guess the dude in the spot didn't like me, so while we rappin', the dude comes and snatches the chair from under me, you know, instead of sayin', like somebody with some sense, to get up, he just snatched the chair from under me. And me bein' high, I asked him why he snatched it, and he came outta his mouth on me, so I called him a pussy. I punched at him and missed him and hit the store window and broke it. And then, you know, Mr. Paul, who owns the cleaners about two doors away from the numbers spot, he comes grabbin' me. Then this other dude from the numbers spot comes grabbin' me, and he swung on me and hit me in my eye while Mr. Paul was holdin' me. Then Mr. Paul let me go, and he went back into his cleaners where he should've stayed in the first place.

You know, because he came like he was helpin' the enemy or somethin', or wanted to help them do a real number on me.

"Well, when he let me go I fell on the ground. Then another dude comes out of the numbers spot. They started stompin' on me, and one of them cut me. That's when Mumps swung on the dude with a golf club. Then along came Big Junior, and he was holdin' him, and told him to give me a fair one."

Big Junior is Hebro. He serves as kind of a shotgun (henchman) for the family, a kind of big brother. Only the Hamites call Hebro by this name. Everybody else calls him Big Junior.

"Nobody was gonna mess with Big Junior. When Hebro hits a dude he don't get up, so they got kinda cool until Big Junior walked away, but then as soon as he got into a distance, then came the stuff on me. I swung. I thought maybe Hebro was behind me, or maybe I wouldn've got so bad. Then I realized there wasn't nobody there but me, and I was sort of like in the trick. But me and Mumps, we had to go on and play the hand all the way to the bust, which is what we did.

"The dude's brother, Funny Head Oscar, ran out of the numbers joint and ran up and tried to stab me. He pulled out his knife and swung at me, but I had got up off the ground, and Mumps was pullin' me back, and I'd already been cut, so he took me to the hospital.

"I was in the hospital a week and three days. It was sorta nice, you know. Everybody came by to see me, and it's like I just laid back and took it easy. A hospital can be a groove, especially if you ain't hurt too bad."

But Hebro, meanwhile, was out for revenge.

"From jump street, Big Junior, he broke bad. He said, 'Let's get them mothers right now.' And I said, 'No, don't mess with them now because if we roll on them now half of us is gonna wind up gettin' shot up. We don't have any pieces or even blades. We don't have one piece between us all, and everybody in the numbers spot got a pistol.' I said, 'I think we ought to just lay in the cut until we get a pistol or a couple o' pieces together because we ought to have somethin' to hurt 'em with when we roll on 'em next time.'

"When I heard the story about what really came off, I thought about it and said we should leave 'em alone and just rap to the dudes and find out what really went down. The dude said that I cracked the glass, and that's what really started it. Now, because I was all messed with vodka, I didn't really know myself like when it started because, you know, like the first thing I remember was like Mr. Paul was holdin' me, and the dude was hittin' me, and then I saw the knife and the feet, and I knew I was hurt, and I wasn't sure how bad. So I figured they had come down on me and did a job on me for no reason at all.

"Big Junior was all messed around because he was feelin' real bad about it. He felt that they wouldn't have moved on us if he had laid on the set, and they was takin' advantage with him not bein' there, and he felt bad about walkin' away behind what they did to me. So he said, 'Come on, let's go and get them now.'

"He had already laid out the plan, you know, how we could come down on them. He wanted to come up the block from Eighth Avenue and from Seventh and catch 'em in between. And I said, 'No, don't come that way, because when we get outta the cabs they might be there and start firin' us up. And they could fire us up before we even knew where they was.'

"So I said, 'Let's get out on the avenue and just walk on up the avenue, and this way we can peep everythin'.' So we did it.

"They was comin' down the avenue behind us, sneakin' up behind cars like they gonna fire us up, and so we met, and I said, 'Come on, man, wait a minute, let's rap.'

"And so this dude Gregg, the dude from the numbers spot, seemed to be about the coolest one in the whole group, and he said, 'Okay, like, yeah man, 'cause we don't need this. All it's gonna do is bring a whole lotta unnecessary heat on the spot.'

"And it turned out that they was really just as scared of us as we was o' them. Like they figured we was some silly kids who was gonna mess up their thing.

"I think Gregg is about seventeen or eighteen, and his brother Oscar may be about nineteen, and sometimes they run the spot for their father. What really started it is he was scared that his father was gonna show back at the spot and complain that he's got those kids sittin' there, hangin' 'round the joint when he's supposed to be in there takin' care of some serious business. If he had sounded me from jump street, I woulda gone 'long with it and said, 'That's cool. I'm not gonna mess with yo' thing,' but I didn't even know that I was sittin' in their chair.

"I told Gregg, I said, 'Look, man, you know too many people

likely to get hurt in this unnecessary hassle, and whatever business me and you got to handle we can do that all by ourselves. But, you know, it may be a good idea for you to come around and talk about it. Like let's rap and see what this thing is all about.' But I said, 'Ain't nobody punkin' out or nothin', you know, I just want to know what happened, you know, before we take it on to the point o' no return. So if you and yo' people want to take it like a gangster act, well, we can take it like that, too.'

"He said, 'I don't even know what happened, man.'

"I said, 'Well, you ran out there swingin' at me, and your brother came out like first with his knife cuttin' and then came out with his pistol like he was gonna fire somebody up.'

"Well, the dude said, 'Well, I came out with my pistol because I didn't know what was goin' down, and all I knew is that you was gettin' to it with my brother, and your man was swingin' on him with the golf club.'

"So then he said, 'Okay, well, tomorrow I'll bring some of my people 'round here, and we'll rap about it.'

"So next day the dude showed. We was sittin' on a car that day, and I noticed when Gregg came up the block. Nobody knew what was comin' off, but everybody was ready for anything. First, it was gonna be Hebro and Victor. They was gonna rap about it—they was the biggest in the group—and find out if we was gonna have to go to war. If they would've come off sour or if any kinda stuff would've come outta their mouths, like we was gonna roll on them. We was gonna finish our beef right there. So I guess he knew what was happenin' because he didn't come outta his mouth with nothin'. He said, 'Forget it, we'll buy the window ourselves. We'll put the window back in.'

"I said, 'The next time yo' man throws me outta a chair, ain't gonna be no scene like this no more. It ain't gonna be nothin' to talk about because you know that was foul. You ask somebody to move or give you your chair or anything. You know that was really, really like some wrong action.'

"So he said, 'Yeah, well, man, you should have got up from jump street.' He told me that Victor had been yellin' at me to get up outta the seat, and I said I ain't goin' nowhere, and that's when he came and grabbed me and pulled me out of the seat and said I swung on him, and then he said Oscar grabbed me and started hittin' me, and that's when Gregg started hittin' me, and that's when Hebro came up and grabbed Oscar. And it's like Mumps ran and got the golf club while Big Junior was holdin' Oscar. When I punched at whatcha-callum, when I punched at Gregg, that's when I hit the window. That's what I couldn't understand. I thought sure the dude was there. You know, I wasn't in any kind of shape to be doin' things that made sense anyway. So we all apologized, and, you know, the dude said yeah, I was right, he had no business like snatchin' the chair."

Not even Dujo, who is as much of a leader as the Hamites have, has any respect for leadership. I asked him once about black leaders, what he thought about black leaders in the community, and he answered, "Leadership is somethin' that exists in the minds of white folks." He says, "For blacks folks it had a meaning once. That was a long time ago."

Most of the group members don't remember Malcolm X or Martin Luther King because they were too young when these men died. But Dujo believes "Those dudes must have been dynamite because everybody talks about them and writes about them, and Martin Luther King's the only black dude who ever had his birthday made into a real holiday, sort of."

He wishes he could have met Malcolm X because he knows "Malcolm was a swift dude and was hip to a whole lotta games. Malcolm was a dude who knew what he was talkin' about and laid down a heavy rap and opened up a whole lotta brothers' eyes to stuff that was goin' on. I could believe in a leader today who would really be hippin' people to what was goin' on and could really peep all the games. That's why they had to off Malcolm X, because Malcolm was too hip. Wasn't that much gettin' by him. He was so swift that whitey couldn't put too much over on other brothers out there as long as Malcolm was on the scene peepin' all the plays that whitey made. So that's why they had to off him, because he peeped too much. But now if another Malcolm was around, I think that maybe somethin' could come off today."

I asked him about the other figures whom the black folks call leaders in the black community.

"You mean that the white folks call leaders in the black community."

"Yeah, you know, like your borough president, you've heard of him, haven't you?"

"Yeah, man, I heard of him."

"What about your congressman and leaders such as Jesse Jackson?"

"Well, you see, I really don't know that much about those dudes. I mean I heard about 'em, I know they out there doin' their thing and all that, but it's like they sorta hang out with the other people in Harlem, you know, the people who are into the church on Sunday thing, the people who hang out around Seventh Avenue in Harlem, and 125th Street, and who're mouthin' a lot. They ain't interested in none of the real people and what's really goin' on up here. I bet they ain't never been uptown, any of those dudes.

"The black day is comin'. A good day is comin' for black folks. It ain't far off. You remember how before he died Elijah Muhammad was always rappin' about we livin' in the last days o' the decline o' the white world? Well, man, you can see it all around you, and in seein' this you can see how the black man is comin' into power. It's like the Arabs—who woulda ever thought that the Arabs would be sittin' in the catbird seat? But look at where they are now. You know, it's just a matter of time before blacks are sittin' on top o' the heap, too. I mean the day's gotta come. We been on the bottom too long and been strugglin', and we peeped a whole lotta game.

"Who can be a better expert, or more than expert, on game than black folks? Man, you know, it's like blacks have had every game in the books played on us. I mean any game anybody can think of. It's like blacks in America and blacks throughout the world have had some game played on 'em. It's not just the slavery game but all the games we had to play in slavery. This worldwide flam [flimflam] goin' on to keep us in the dark and inferior to whitey, at least economically, and mentally, too, if they can keep on brainwashin' us to believe in it. But it ain't as easy as it used to be 'cause everybody's got a television and blacks ain't down in the woods no more down South. We up here peepin' everything that the white folks're peepin', and they know where it's at. We don't have to buy any o' that goin' to church and listenin' to all that spookism no more, man. We peepin' what's happenin' out there with whitey and the bucks.

"So it's hard to keep black folks still feelin' that we inferior. It's almost impossible. Even those who're feelin' that way, they gettin' outta it faster, outta that feelin' o' inferiority faster than they use to, let's say, about ten years, even five years ago. It's like we gettin' there. The black day is comin', you know. The messenger was right."

"Yeah, okay. Look, Dujo, you know that everybody has a pet peeve, right? You know, like a pet gripe about something he doesn't approve of in the community. You know, it's like something he's really down on. It's like with Hebro and the junkies, for example. You know Hebro has a mean hate on for junkies. What's your pet peeve or your mean hate?"

"Well, I'll tell you, Hebro ain't too cool. I don't think the dopies ever did anything to him personally, but he just goes around like hatin' people for the way they look or the way they live. I don't care for the dopies either, behind some of the things they do, but I think they do the worst harm to themselves, so I don't hate 'em. I can't go around hatin' nobody just because he don't care about himself. But I guess I got a pet peeve now, that's probably with the raise. I've seen the police do some foul numbers in Harlem, man. There ain't nobody, nobody lower than them, I mean behind the things they do. I've seen the police do some stuff here, I don't see how anybody can respect those dudes. If they just come up in Harlem for a little while and peep the action that's goin' down, nobody would ever dig 'em again or ever want 'em 'round 'em. The raise have a club, and it's their club that really controls things, especially in Harlem or probably all black neighborhoods. They seem to think that they special. They get real upset when one of 'em gets killed, I mean more than when an ordinary untrained, unarmed, unpaid citizen gets killed. Now that should show you where they comin' from.

"Cops are some of the foulest forms of life out there. You see them askin' to be killed all the time with those stupid acts, all the silly changes they take people through. The go around beggin' to be killed. That ol' racist white police department down there, they send those stupid young white cowboys full of racism to black neighborhoods, you know, and let 'em raise hell. Then they act surprised when somebody ices one of 'em. That's because whitey thinks blacks supposed to keep on goin' for it.

"I mean like look, we been goin' for all that flam they been playin' on us for nearly four hundred years now, so I guess they figure, Well, why should it stop? And then when black folks get mad and scream a little bit, it's like the police department gets upset because ain't nobody supposed to get mad at 'em for messin' over 'em. And that's crazy. You know, but the raise, man, they are some sick dudes, I mean really foul. You know, Malcolm was right—it's a racist system, but especially the police system.

"That's the one thing, I think, Malcolm overlooked. He shoulda given special attention, you know, like in his rap, to the police system all over this country. They have a few blacks in there, here and there, doin' a little bit of flunkyin', because that's all it amounts to. It's always run by whitey. I really don't see how anybody, how a black dude can live with bein' a cop.

"You know, they probably have to dance [Uncle Tom], you know, like go and do their steps when the white dudes tell 'em to. They probably have to dance for the white raise I mean, it's a dancin' gig. If you're black, how can it not be when you know the other raises, the white raises, openly treat black police like less than equal, even when they not shootin' 'em by accident. I mean they don't really respect 'em. You ever hear of any black cops shootin' any white cops by accident? Or where some black raise went into some white neighborhood and accidentally shot a white eleven-year-old kid, some white fourteen- or fifteen-year-old kid, in the back, accidentally, and then they let him walk behind for it? You know they would hang him on the set. He'd never even get to jail if that was to come off with some black raise in a white community, and they gonna talk about bein' equal.

"I don't see how a black dude can live with bein' a part o' that action. He knows what police are all about, and he knows that a raise is the lowest animal out there, and a black raise has gotten be the sub-lowest thing out there. I mean he's even lower than the white raise because o' the way they treat him and he goes for it. They're dancin' when they even work with those dudes and be actin' halfway friendly with 'em when they know the white raise hates you. To real black folks it's just so plain. How do you tell yourself that you not bein' a Tom when you workin' every day with a dude that hates you so much he gonna go around and shoot your children the first chance he gets and call it a accident? I mean when he hates you that much, and you know it, and still you go 'round smilin' and actin' friendly with him every day, that ain't nothin' but dancin', man. Ain't nothin' else you can call it.

"And they like brainwash the black cops before they get into it to accept it. Like that's your role and it's all right. When he's around whites he'd better go into his act or he might be thrown off the force or might get lynched in a white neighborhood. You know, it's a dancin' gig for blacks, and any fool can see that. So they go out there and they roll on the brother in the street, and he ain't no dancer. But it's like the only blacks those white raises know about are the black raises, they see the dancers and then they think the other brothers, all brothers, are dancers, so they come out here and they get hurt because they mistake another brother out on the streets for that dancer that they got on the force with 'em.

"A white racist walkin' 'round in the black community with a gun on his hip, how you not gonna have trouble? But the whites who run the system know this, and they want it that way. They want trouble so that they can keep blacks under their gun control. They try to tell us like we'll sic that cowboy with the gun on his hip on you if you don't be cool, know your place, and get up every mornin' and go downtown and make me some bucks. Yeah, work hard for whitey, you know. That's the way they play their games with the raise, and they need some tricks to play the game on. Joinin' the police force in New York City, that's almost like joinin' the Ku Klux Klan. You might as well say you gonna be a black honorary member of the Ku Klux Klan.

"Now I've peeped some things go down with the police that's really unholy. To really show you how unrighteous it is and how little they care about a black raise, they got the club thing goin'. The police department runs New York City. They do what they want to, take advantage of anybody they want to, and every once in a while they get one o' them nuts out there like Nadjari, a honest dude! Like they consider him a nut. You remember when he started investigatin' everybody and talkin' about graft? But they live on through that, and they lay dead until he gets what he wants. If he wants to become district attorney, governor, or lieutenant governor or somethin' like that, they just bide their time for a while. They gotta be a little cooler while they got this madman runnin' 'round there investigatin' everybody, and they know that the action's gonna be slow. Or when somebody's comin' up for election, they wanta make a whole lotta busts and the heat is on, so the judge just says, 'Well, we gotta be cool and lay dead.' Well, the raises do the same thing. When somebody like Nadjari starts runnin' his investigations, they can't make as much money, they gotta be cool on the graft for a while and let the thing pass by. Once this dude gets what he wants, it'll be business as usual.

"I guess the raises down 'round Madison Avenue and Park Avenue and Central Park West, they don't go shake nobody down. But uptown in Harlem, the raise come knockin' at the door, and the folks come to the door with their wallets in their hands, 'cause they know what they're lookin' for. It's like black folks really know what it's all about. We didn't need a Knapp Commission to tell us. Everybody black knew that. Little kids in Harlem know that when they six and seven years old. Maybe white folks might be a little shocked or act surprised when they read somethin' like the Knapp Commission rap. Black folks don't pay any attention to that. You grow up in neighborhoods where you know the raise is on the take. Kids on the street can tell. They see 'em always goin' into candy stores where they sell whiskey on a Sunday, or they see 'em goin' into the fence joint, and they don't never come out with nobody handcuffed or makin' any arrest, so they got to be on the take, right? That ain't too swift to figure out.

"Let me tell you somethin', show you what racists the police are. Let me tell you about a number when me and my uncle saw a raise get killed one day in the Bronx up on Tremont Avenue, It was pourin' down rain, and we saw a raise get killed and told the PBA who did it. They put out a reward of five thousand dollars, and they busted the dude who we told 'em did it. It was a white dude, and they never gave us the reward. He was sentenced and all that, you know how those rewards read, 'for the information, reward for information leadin' to the arrest and conviction of So-and-so.' Well, that's what we did. We gave 'em the information that led to the arrest and conviction, and they put the dude in jail, but they only gave him four years.

"Well, it was only a black raise, so what? I just figure, Well, maybe they don't give out rewards for black police or maybe they don't give out rewards to blacks. But anyway, let me tell you how it came off because it was in the newpaper a long time.

"It was on a Saturday, we was helpin' my aunt move, and me and my uncle was in the car comin' down the hill on Tremont Avenue near Jerome, and it was pourin' down rain. It was rainin' real hard. You could hardly see anything. Just as we was comin' down the hill, you know, like one man ran across the street in all that rain, between cars, and he wasn't lookin' or anything, and so my uncle said, 'Wow, did you see that, I almost hit him. Man, that dude's gonna get killed out there or somethin'.'

"And then he stopped and went slow, and then another dude was followin' the first dude, and he ran across the street, and this blue taxicab was comin' down from the other direction and boom, hit him, and he went flying way up in the air. The taxi kept gittin' up, man, I mean it knocked him on the other side of the street, and a car that was comin' the other way hit him, hit the dude who was already hit, and he got caught under the bumper. It drug him. There was a big pool o' water in the street, and you couldn't tell whether the body was down under the water or was on the other car. So my uncle said, 'Man, did you see that? I'm follow him and see where he's goin'.' He had New Jersey license plates, and he was in a old Ford, sort of beige-colored, and we followed him, runnin' down that dude. He had to know that he hit somebody.

"Now, the other dude, who was in front, turned out to be the brother of the raise who got killed. Nobody knew he was a cop yet, just a black dude in plain clothes. Now, the dude who ran out there first was his brother, and he don't see none o' this. But when he gets on the other side of the street he turns around, and he's lookin' for his brother. He don't know that this dude's been hit and is bein' dragged or pushed by the front of the car on down the street.

"Now, the first car that hit him, the cab that hit the raise, he's goin' on across Tremont Avenue. My uncle is followin' the second car over to Grand Concourse. He knows somebody is behind him, so he starts gittin' up. Now he goes all the way down to about 153rd Street, and he stops. Like he's runnin' red lights and dodgin' in and out traffic. So about 163rd Street he's tryin' to hide, and you know how there's sorta side roads on the Grand Concourse up there in the Bronx, well, he goes in there. So my uncle pulls up in front o' his car to block him off, and he stops him, but he hits another car.

"It turns out to be a raise car, and there're police in there. So the police get out, and they get mad about my uncle for hittin' their car. So my uncle says to the dude in the car, 'Hey, man, get outta that car, like get outta that car because you hit a man. There's a man under the front of your car dead.' And, sho'nuff, he looked under the car and there was this dude. His head was busted all open, you know, like the scalp was off, you could see meat hangin' outta it. His chest had this big hole in it, but he was twitchin' like he was still alive, or it might've just been the nerves. And so this dude gets out, and he looks at the car. It's a big fat white peckerwood-lookin' dude, you know, with a big belly hangin' over his belt and big fat red neck with big pimples on it, and he gets out and looks at the car and says, 'Yeah, how did that happen?'

"He gets in his car to back up, to supposedly let the body fall loose from the car. Instead of gettin' outta his car again, he just backed on up, got in the clear, and got in the wind, you know, and started gittin' up. So it's like he's goin' about ninety MPH through traffic and everything, and my uncle is stayin' on him, followin' him all the way until 'round the South Bronx someplace, and then a cop got behind my uncle, another cop, not the one the guy hit, 'cause that one stayed with the body, and flagged him down for speedin', and sayin' like they wanna give him a ticket, and he's tellin' 'em, 'Hey, a man's just been killed back there, and I'm followin' the guy who hit the man and killed him.'

"They acted like they thought it was just a flam he had goin', runnin' a story, and they said, 'Okay, well, come on, let's go back to where the guy was hit.'

"My uncle kept tryin' to explain to 'em that the guy who did it is gettin' away. They wouldn't listen to that.

"Now, on the way back to the spot, they hearin' somethin' on the radio that a policeman was killed by a hit-and-run driver up in the Bronx somewhere. Then when they get to the set, they find out that this is the raise. They're not too concerned about it because they see that he's black. It seemed that once they peeped that the raise who had been hit was black they became more concerned about bringin' some charges against my uncle for hittin' that police car when he was tryin' to cut the dude off and keep him from gittin' up.

"The next day the PBA put out an announcement that there was a five-thousand-dollar reward for any information leadin' to the arrest and conviction of whoever was responsible for killin' this black raise. About three days later, they came and got me and my uncle and had us goin' down to the DA's office every day like they was serious. About two weeks later, they caught this dude for somethin' else. We identified him and said yeah, it was him. Well, somehow we never gave testimony, we only identified him. And it seems that the grand jury indicted him without our testimony.

"A detective with the DA's office was tellin' us that they had this guy and they wanted to get him bad. Now, they got a whole lota charges against him, but they wanta get him for murderin' this cop, and they did. I don't know if they got him for that or not. But somehow he just got about three or four years, so they probably let him cop a plea to a lesser charge. It was just a black cop, it was no big thing like killin' a white cop.

"You see, I got a idea for how they can make the police department really work. The way to do this would be to only put black dudes on the police force. If they would only put black dudes on the force in the black community, it's like they would be halfway cool, especially if they didn't have any white cops 'round that they have to dance for. The mayor and all the people who are over the police, the city council and all, wouldn't have to worry about the cops hasslin' the nice people in white neighborhoods because they know that the black raise gonna be dancin' when they go 'round white folks in the nicer neighborhoods. You wouldn't have white raise goin' 'round shootin' black babies anymore. Everybody knows that black raise never have those careless gun accidents. White folks would go for it because they figure blacks are supposed to be servants anyhow. And then the police would be what they was really meant to be, like public servants.

"They're public servants in white communities, but it's when they get in black communities the police're not servants. As a matter of fact, they act like the citizens in black communities are their servants, and they come in like they gangsters or big and bad and superior to everybody else. It's like they're the storm troopers or the conquerors who come in here and, you know, gonna run over people, gonna tell 'em what to do. It's like they're not servants, they the rulers.

"I think that's the coolest way, you know, to get this thing off. Only that or scrap the whole police department and give everybody a gun and let 'em go for themselves. Yeah, they say it would be chaos, but as I see it, you know, we got pretty near chaos now. I don't see how this thing is so great. It didn't work for Clifford Glover and it didn't work for Claude Reese, * you know. I don't know who it's workin' for other than the raise. I see the police as bein' on the level of junkies. Snakes, police, and junkies. That's how I feel about it. Maybe it'll change, but I don't see how."

* Clifford Glover was an eleven-year-old black boy who was shot and killed by a white policeman who claimed the boy had a gun, which was never found. Claude Reese, fifteen years old, suffered the same fate the following year. The slayings occurred in New York City in 1973 and 1974.

FIVE

Dee Dee

Dee Dee is fifteen, I think, and she's tight with Shaft. She's been in the spot for about a year. Generally speaking, the girls in the family are not committed to any one person in particular, with one exception, Shaft and Dee Dee. They have a "serious" thing going now. Dee Dee used to go with Dujo but says she outgrew him.

At various times the girls in the group have all been committed to one guy or another, but they like to say, "I outgrew him, so we're just friends." These young ladies certainly do a considerable amount of growing. Actually, the kids have known each other for so long that they've all become used to each other, the girls and the fellows. I guess it was very natural for Dee Dee to hook up with Shaft. She has a soft spot in her heart for junkies.

Dee Dee says the reason she came to one of the spots, and became a member of the family, is that her mother was on stuff almost as long as she can remember and their crib was a shooting gallery. Her mother deals scag, so the apartment had a stream of junkie traffic through it all the time.

One morning Dee Dee got up and was on her way to school, and her mother and her mother's old man were taking a guy's shoes off of him, somebody who appeared to be sleeping. So she paid it no attention and went on to school because something like that was always going down at her crib. but that afternoon when she returned home from school, she saw the man her mother and her mother's old man, Charlie, had beaten for his shoes earlier the same day. He was in the bed with her two younger brothers and sisters, and she was wondering why he was in the bed with them, and she asked the kids, "What is this?"

Her mother had told her not to worry about it and not to go into the back room. But, of course, she was concerned about "who this dude was." Her attitude was, "If he was sleepy or somethin', let him go outside." She went back into the room, and her siblings simply said, "Mamma told us not to move and to stay in here."

And so she took it upon herself to "try and wake this dude up" who was in bed with her younger brothers and sisters. He wouldn't wake up. She touched him, and "he was kinda cold." She kept on shaking him and felt his heart. She realized he was a corpse.

Dee Dee asked the four-year-old how long the man was there, and he told her he'd been there since this morning and Mama told them not to get out of bed. So she began "puttin' it together."

When she was going out of the apartment that morning, on her way to school, there were junkies around, "takin' off," and copping, nodding, etc., which was a regular scene in her home because it was a shooting gallery, so she didn't pay much attention to it, but apparently the guy who was being relieved of his shoes had no further need of them. He was dead. And her mother and Charlie didn't want her or anybody else to know because if the junkies knew that the guy was dead, that somebody OD'd, it would panic the place. Nobody would come around for a few days except the police, who would "show and squat," and the heat would be on the spot. So what Dee Dee's mother and Charlie were attempting to do was conceal the death from the outsiders, from everybody else who came around, and pretend that he was all right, that "everything was cool," that he was just sleeping. In the meantime, of course, they were going to beat him for whatever money and valuables he had.

The word was that this guy had just gotten out of the joint after a couple of years and hadn't used any scag in a long while. So he sat there and fired up. The stuff was a "monster," it was much too strong for him, and he nodded into eternity.

When Dee Dee showed from school and discovered what had gone down, she was shocked. The idea that her mother had put this dead body in bed with her little brothers and sisters just blew her mind. Her mother was using the story that the kids were in the back room sleeping as a part of the ruse to keep other junkies from straying back there and having somebody discover that this guy had OD'd. What they were waiting for was a time when the traffic slowed down or when there was nobody there and they could sneak him out into the hall, upstairs on a floor above, or downstairs, a flight below them, and make it appear as though he had died outside in the hall someplace. Better yet, if they could get him out of the building or up on the roof. But they hadn't gotten a chance to do this before Dee Dee returned home from school.

When Dee Dee got there and found out what had taken place, she became enraged and she started screaming at her mother and carrying on. Her mother smacked her, and then they got into a physical struggle, and Dee Dee ran out of the house and "dropped a dime" on her mother. She called the Children's Aid Society or the welfare or somebody. Anyhow, it was the Children's Aid Society that came to the house with the policemen and arrested her mother and her mother's old man and took the kids from them. And of course her mother was angry with her and threatened to kill her for dropping the dime.

When the neighbors heard about it, they didn't know what had really occurred. They were actually protecting Dee Dee's mother and Charlie. They thought it was just the Children's Aid Society coming around to "take somebody else's kids from them." They kept telling the man and woman from the Children's Aid Society, "Nobody lives there, and we don't know where she lives."

People in Harlem tend to band together against the authorities. But if they had known what had really happened, or what her mother had done, I think they would have been much more cooperative. As it was, they gave the officials a hard time.

So the police came and demanded that they open the door, and the junkies started cleaning up and throwing drugs and syringes out the window, and everybody got scared and started to panic. The policemen got in and said they wanted to see the kids because they heard some kids were being abused there. Linda, Dee Dee's mother, got the kids and brought them out into the living room so the policemen could see that they were all right. But they had been informed, and so had the social worker from the Children's Aid Society, that there was a corpse in the bed with the children. Therefore they insisted on going into the bedroom, and they found the corpse. They announced that "Everybody in here is under arrest."

But the junkies had already thrown their stuff out of the window or flushed it down the toilet or hid it in their shoes, and all of them had sneaked out the door while the policemen were going in to check out the bedroom. By the time the police had determined that the corpse was actually a corpse and returned to the living room, practically everybody was gone. Charlie tried to "get in the wind," too, but the policemen caught him at the door and said, "Hey, nobody leaves." Of course, they called for assistance and wanted to know "who was in here when he died," and what time he died, and other details. And that was the end of the gallery.

Dee Dee wasn't there at bust time, and when she got back a policeman was at the door and her mother and Charlie had been arrested. They got some time, but it wasn't much, I think. Because the apartment was in Dee Dee's mother's name, she got most of the time. But they had determined that Charlie was living there, so he got something like one year.

By the time Charlie got out of jail Dee Dee had been living at the spot for a long time and she had a new family. She hasn't yet found out what became of her younger brothers and sisters. The Children's Aid Society social worker told her that they were living with a foster family in Queens and she could see them after they had really gotten settled. She and the other people at the Children's Aid Society were telling her this story for about six months before she finally realized that they weren't going to let her see them. Linda, her mother, had told them that Dee Dee was on scag and that she didn't want Dee Dee to be around the younger children.

Dee Dee keeps saying that when her mother gets out she's going to have to leave town because her mother is going to try to kill her. I don't think that will happen, but she seems to feel that there's a good chance of it, and she knows her mother much better than anybody else. Linda has to do about another two years in jail before she gets out and can carry out her threat to get Dee Dee if she still has a desire to do so. In the meantime, Dee Dee's making the most of it. She's going to school and living at one of the spots with the Hamites. She's well entrenched and truly enjoys being in the family.

Dee Dee's father was a junkie, too. He was called Karate Carl. He was a seriously strung-out junkie. He was on stuff for about eight or nine years before he got killed, which was six or seven years ago. Karate Carl was a neighborhood character, one of the first persons in the neighborhood to know about karate—long before the martial arts films became popular. He mastered karate back in 1958, when he was a teenager and hardly anybody in New York, or at least in Harlem, knew what karate was. When he began using stuff, Karate Carl also began going around gorillaing drug dealers. He would shake them down. He'd approach a person who he knew was dealing—and he knew all the dope dealers, everybody knew them, especially the dope fiends—Karate Carl would go up to one of them and say, "I need a bag, I don't wanta hurt you, but I need some scag, so you better give it up."

And very often the dope dealers would give him stuff when they saw him coming or if they saw him someplace to keep him off their backs because he was a threat to them. They knew he was bad news with his hands. Nobody was going to try to fight him. That would be suicide—he'd break them up.

But one day he ran up on a dope dealer everybody used to call Dirty Bob. Karate Carl had shaken down Dirty Bob before and he got away with it, and he'd been shaking down everybody else, so I suspect he figured this would be okay. He'd get away with it this time, too. Nobody had seriously objected to what he was doing, and the dope peddlers couldn't complain to the police. Some dealers had made threats behind his back and talked to other people about doing a job on him, but nothing had actually happened to him, and, besides, he had a good thing going. He didn't have to go out there and gamble, pulling stickups and robbing places and stealing. His thing was a solid groove. It was like being the ward of all the dope dealers in the block.

Until one day he ran up on Dirty Bob for maybe the third time. He told him he was sick and needed some stuff real bad, so Bob told him, "Okay, why don't you have a seat in the living room?" He'd go fix him up a shot. He went in the kitchen and cooked it up. When Karate Carl shot up he died almost instantly because Dirty Bob had given him a hot shot. The dope was mixed with lye. and so he shot some lye up in his veins and he croaked.

Of course, nobody saw when Dirty Bob got Karate Carl out of his apartment and into the hallway, but they knew he was dead in the hallway. The other junkies who had been in the crib and saw him there had figured it out after they got the word that somebody had given Karate Carl a hot shot. They put two and two together and knew that it had to be Dirty Bob. They didn't call Dirty Bob Dirty

Bob for nothing. Other dope dealers in the neighborhood wanted to congratulate him because he did something that they all wanted to do but didn't have the nerve.

Anyhow, that's the way it went down. Dee Dee has been around stuff all of her life with her father and mother both junkies.

Shaft is the only male member of the group that's ever had a "sho'nuff" scag jones. It's logical that when Dee Dee finally decided to commit herself to one of the Hamites, Shaft was the most likely prospect. He says that he'd like to marry Dee Dee one day, and she says, "Well, maybe that would be all right," too, she might like to try it, but as it is they're semimarried already. Most of the other Hamites respect their relationship like it's a "marriage thing." She'll cook or sew something for other members of the group sometimes, or she'll iron. She likes doing these domestic things, but she doesn't do them for everybody. She doesn't do half as much for others now as she'll do for Shaft. Before, she used to do things for everybody. As a matter of fact, she used to do just about everything for all the fellows, but knowing the relationship she and Shaft have going, the other guys don't ask her to do anything often now. They'll go to Connie, Anita, or Jill first.

The fellows say Dee Dee once gave Shaft the clap, and Dujo said he was walking around with his peter burning off and saying he didn't have money and was too busy to go to a doctor. He was in terrible pain. So the other fellows had Hebro, who is the strong arm of the group, "snatch him quietly." And they took him to the doctor whom they all go to see when they have minor problems. Dee Dee felt very bad about it and said that she didn't do it because, she said, she's very clean. Shaft "wouldn't speak on it," and he couldn't say that somebody else did it because he was supposed to be too tight with Dee Dee for that.

Anyway, they sent her to the doctor also, because they all agreed that if she was not responsible for Shaft's condition she must at least have gotten it from him. So she went away angry and stayed out of the spot for several days. She said she stayed with a friend. After a while everybody stopped teasing her and told her, "Don't let it get you down. Why don't you come on back? Nobody said you had to leave."

She came back, and all was well. They forgave her, and she forgave him, or somebody forgave somebody, and they tightened their thing up again. Of course, she had to be cleaner afterward. Everybody felt that experience had taught her a lesson if nothing else, just in case she needed a lesson.

Dee Dee says the fate she fears most in life is becoming a junkie like her mother. She says that's why she doesn't "use" anything. That's why she doesn't think she'd ever do anything more than smoke some herb or drink some wine. "They make me feel good. Why should I try anything else?"

She doesn't like any kind of whiskey. It's too strong. She "can't handle it," and she knows what "the other stuff will do to people." Dee Dee claims she's never tried cocaine either, and this, more so than the other available drugs, is very accessible in the block, but she says she's never been tempted to try it. From what she's heard she can't understand why people would bother with it. Growing up in a gallery, she would see addicts mixing it, speeding some scag and "fixin' up," and she thought that was all people did with it until she was thirteen years old. She's never been tempted to try anything stronger than smoke. She says Shaft has told her a lot about the evils of being addicted to scag, and that frightened her more than what she glimpsed.

She said there've been times when Shaft's told her about some of the things that he's done to people close to him, and she said they are more "foul" than the numbers she had seen her mother and Charlie do on other people. And she said she'd be afraid to mess with it because it takes away all of anybody's concern for other people, even for your children. "I know that it's something that's too mean to mess with."

Dee Dee had another younger brother who would be about eleven years old now had he still been alive, but he got killed by an automobile in the block a few years back. This is something that happens on the average of once a year to one of the kids in this godforsaken block. She says he might have been the lucky one in the family.

She feels that there is something cursed about the block. "Everybody in it is sort of doomed to suffer some kinda misery."

Dee Dee says she intends to graduate from high school, go to college, and become an actress, but she says that there's very little chance her dream will come true because she lives in that block and the odds are so "heavy" against her and everyone else who comes up there. But she's determined to give it her best shot, as she puts it.

Dee Dee is at worst a very, very nice girl, and perhaps if she lived in another block she would be the kind of "nice girl who just goes to school and the other changes that nice girls do." She isn't certain what that is. In the spot she is treated very much like one of the fellows. She sits and raps with the fellows, and they treat her just like anybody else. They get high with her. Every time somebody pulls out a joint they pass it to her, the same as they do with one another.

"Last year when they had that monster on the street, when everybody was paying seventy dollars an ounce for that smoke that was really messing people up, sending them out of their skulls," she says, "can you imagine four dudes"—she's including herself as a dude, too—"so high that after walkin' seven blocks they stop and not one of them can remember where they're goin' or why? Well, that happened to us a couple of weekends last year. That's when that monster was still on the streets, and everybody was smokin' it, and it was takin' folks through some mean changes. It really turned us dudes around."

Dee Dee's a very feminine type of girl. She's similar to a girl growing up in a house with only many brothers for companions. But she and the other girls are rather tight, too. As a matter of fact, she brought Connie into the Hamites. She and Connie were tight, and Connie needed a place to stay, so, when the time came, Dee Dee showed Connie the spot and invited her in, introduced her to the Hamites, and she was instantly accepted because she was a friend of Dee Dee's and Chip's former squeeze.

If Dee Dee gets mad at Shaft, she sometimes spends the night at her friend Aggie's house. Aggie's her main friend outside of the group. Aggie's always lending her money, and sometimes she even lets her wear her clothes, like teenage girls do. They play sisters and that sort of thing. Aggie is a valuable friend because she has a home and a place where Dee Dee can get away from the Hamites when she wants to or needs to, and the girls tend to have that need from time to time, because living at the spot is similar to inhabiting a huge house with a big family and sometimes there's just no room for privacy. Dee Dee can go to Aggie's house, and she can take a bath there, and when she and Shaft don't get along she spends the night there.

The fellows don't like Aggie. They call her Superman, and Dujo says it's because she thinks she's a man. The way he puts it, "How can anybody dig a chick who thinks she's a superman, you know, it's like, man, the broad thinks she's just a man who happened to have a hole in the middle."

I thought that he meant that Aggie was a "creep," "snake," a homosexual, but he didn't. He was merely saying that she just wasn't their kind of people. She was on her own trip.

Dee Dee, like the other girls, is so love-starved. They tend to overract to kindness, and one has to be careful that they don't misinterpret kind gestures simply because they aren't used to them.

Aside from being "hooked up" with Shaft—very much in love, as she terms it—Dee Dee is seriously into astrology, horoscopes, and palm reading. She's always "running down" stars and somebody's astrological sign. She likes to amuse herself by guessing people's sign: So-and-so's got to be Sagittarius, or Capricorn, or Taurus, or something or other. She "reads people." When she's got nothing better to do, she runs down horoscopes for the Hamites. She can read palms also, and she does from time to time when she tires of the stars. The palm reading is only a one-shot deal. The palm doesn't change, but she can tell people their horoscopes for a whole week. Dee Dee, being Gemini, says she stays away from Libras and Piscean men, and she shies away from Gemini men, too, which is okay, because Shaft is Scorpio.

The first thing Dee Dee does in the morning is to check out her horoscope to see what kind of day it's going to be. She looks up at the sky, maybe she reads the clouds, too. She wants to be a tea reader in Harlem.

Quite a lot of tea reading goes on in Harlem. Harlemites have tea-reading parties on the weekend. Women will come to have their tea leaves read in a cup of tea, and they sell food. It's almost like an old-fashioned rent party or house party where everybody pays to get in, and they sell food because people have to wait around. It takes the readers about twenty minutes to read each person's tea leaves, and the people will pay something like five dollars for a reading and then buy some food while they're sitting there waiting, and the sponsors make a modest sum of money. The readers often sell good-luck charms, figurines, and candles, too.

Various people in the neighborhood will have a tea reading, and they'll cook big pots of pig feet, fried chicken, potato salad, collard greens, etc. They'll be up all night cooking, so that when the tea reader comes and she starts taking care of business, they can start selling. The reader will be there for close to eight hours. Maybe she'll arrive around one o'clock in the afternoon, on a Saturday, and stay until nine o'clock that night. She's cleaning up. She's making about fifteen dollars an hour, and she's going to give something to the houselady, just like a gambling party or something like that where you give a cut to the houseman. And the houselady is making money of her own by selling dinners. It's a kind of going business in Harlem.

You can read in the black newspapers about Madam So-and-so who tells the future and can give you valuable advice. They advertise as "advisers," or something like that, but they are usually tea readers or some other type of soothsayer. They're listed in the telephone directory in New York City, and I suppose in other cities, too. Anyway, it's a thriving industry.

Dee Dee said she had thought about going into this lucrative profession and setting up shop as Sister Mystique. "You know, you gotta have an exotic name like Sister Pocahontas or, you know, Madam Zee Bee, and settin' up a shop like the gypsies do around here for tellin' people their fortunes." But she says that she found out she's too young and that the women who patronize these operators "don't trust a young person for readin' their tea leaves and for tellin' their fortunes and helpin' to solve their problems."

Their problems consist of things like getting their man back from another woman, or getting a daughter or son "away from that dope," or getting out of the neighborhood, or getting out of an extramarital affair, and similar situations, And they can't imagine telling such things to someone who's so young.

Dee Dee claims that she's "as good as anybody out there and probably a whole lot better than most of 'em" because, she said, she's read all the books by the leading soothsayers and clairvoyants and she knows the whole game about reading tea leaves and palms and then some. And right now she's into, or she's just gotten into, the tarot cards. And she says she's pretty good at it. She thinks she's "as good as any of those women out there tellin' people what they wanta hear, like first gettin' all the information from 'em and runnin' it back to 'em another way and guessin' about it mostly."

She said the reason she thinks they hesitate to confide in a young woman is that they're ashamed. "Like they come on out, they tell their deep secrets. A lotta these women'll tell one of these advisers, as they call 'em, things that they wouldn't tell their doctors or preachers. And it's like they be just too ashamed to tell it to somebody young. Maybe they figure, Well, if it's an older woman, you know, she's done a lotta foolish things, too, so it's all right then. I mean it's all right to tell it to her, but when it's a young girl it's just gonna make 'em feel all the more silly. And then, you know, they worry about it being a rip-off, that the young people would be phony. 'They haven't been around long enough to know what it's really all about.' Well, the same thing could be true about these other people, and it probably is, like they've been around and it's only so much to learn. It doesn't mean just because they're old they know what they doin'. I mean you got some old fools out there, too."

Dee Dee believes the stars have a lot to do with people and their behavior. She says, "I've seen a lotta things about people, a lotta common traits that people with the same sign have in common." And she says that predicting what a person would do on the basis of his astrological sign usually comes true because people tend to behave in accordance with astrological patterns.

Dee Dee said that she wished she could do "my thing" for money. And one day, she says, she is going to try it. She said she thought about "puttin' on a wig and dyeing' my hair, you know, like a old lady." She wants to be an actress anyway, and she says, "You know, if I could get over with this, it would be like my crownin' performance"—if she could pass for a fifty-year-old lady and call herself Madam Zooloo or Sister Buzzard or something like that and set up shop.

But she knows she couldn't do it in the neighborhood because everybody knows her and knows how young she is. She thinks she could go downtown, perhaps in the area of 125th Street, and really pull this thing off, and she thinks one day, maybe in about a year, when she's tried her acting some more, has it down pat, when she and Shaft have some money, they are going to go downtown and rent a place, or maybe let somebody hire her or put her in the back of a beauty parlor in the afternoons when she gets out of school. She could tell fortunes and read signs.

"You know, you'd be surprised to see how many black women have gotten away from all that root business and tea reading, and a lot of 'em have gotten sophisticated enough to be goin' and buyin' astrological sign books and readin' their horoscopes every day in the newspapers and really livin' by it. That's a whole big field out there now, and I could combine that with the tea readin', you know, successfully. I could get two generations. And after school, if you're really good you could charge ten dollars a shot, or fifteen dollars sometimes. Like bein' in a beauty parloer, you always got customers comin' in there, especially on the weekends. You could get rich just on the weekends. The women will walk out, and they'll go around singin' your praises, tellin' everybody what Sister Who's-it told her or Madam Such-and-such told her. They been used to the gypsies now for a long time for tellin' fortunes. But now they gettin' used to havin' a sister get out there and tell the fortune and read the tea leaves."

Dee Dee says that she's going to get this wig, the whole costume, and learn to walk, because she believes the main hurdle when it comes to acting the part of an older woman is learning how to move, not to have too much pep in your movements. "Not just the way you walk, but even turnin' too fast, movin' your hand too fast. As people get older they just sort of naturally slow down." She's going to practice sounding like an old woman, and she thinks that she'll get away with it.

Dee Dee really wants to be an actress, so she says. She's always acting. She's always "putting on airs." She's kind of funny, comical, when she does this. She said that one day she'd like to join the Negro Ensemble Company. She thinks she'll be ready for it by the time she goes to college, or after she has been a tea-leaves reader and a fortune-teller for about a year.

I've asked Dee Dee, tried to provoke her into telling me, what she really feels about the stars and all that, and she says, and I think she was serious, that she does believe in the stars. She doesn't believe that they control all things. But she believes that most people and their personalities are controlled by the stars. If you've got the time to listen, Dee Dee will analyze each member of the Hamites according to the stars. She says, "There is no way in the world for Hebro to be anything but big and rash, and I mean not too thoughtful and quick-tempered and not about to think things out, because he's Taurus, and Taurus is a bull. They go charging into everything. And he is kinda clumsy, especially when it comes to people's feelings and such things, you know, social relationships." She can analyze each member of the Hamites in just this manner, and she's often very convincing.

Anyway, that's her "thing." She has this other thing, too, about people dying and life and death and the stars. Dee Dee says that when people die their spirits go shooting out into space and become stars, and every spirit of everybody who has ever lived, good or bad, is one of those stars that we see twinkling out there in the heavens at night. Well, other people believe things that sound stranger. So she views death as taking one's place among the stars. She says of course she's in no hurry to get there and nobody should want to rush becoming a heavenly star. "You know," she says, "it's an inevitable thing and we'll all get there sooner or later, and just how bright we shine at night depends on how good a life we lived, I mean in terms of what we contributed to the earthly brilliance of the world."

She can point out stars and identify the historical personality to whom the spirit originally belonged—all this solely on the basis of the star's brilliance and the way it twinkles. She says she thinks the world will end when every spirit on earth is a part of the stars. That's what the world is waiting for. "When all the spirits have become heavenly stars and the heavens have been filled with all the stars that they were destined to have, then life and the world is finished. It's all over, and all the stars are doin' now is waitin' for the other stars to join them, and then, you know, the universe and all will be no more." It sounds as good as most of the fables one hears about what's coming afterward.

Dee Dee claims she read somewhere once that there are three kinds of people in the world and they can be spotted when they're very young, four or five years old. She said, "People are things people, ideas people, and people people. The idea person is always thinkin', you know, likes to think, every chance he gets he'll be thinkin'. He'll do more thinkin' than anything else. That's his natural bent, his God-given jones, death is the only cure on ideas.

"The second type of person is the things person, the person who likes to putter and collect and be botherin' with things, who can't see anything pretty and leave it alone. You know, people who like to gather antiques and cars and clothes and all kinds of luxury things, cameras, gadgets, or stereos. It'd be different from bein' like a record collector, who is really somebody who likes music and just collects the records not for the sake of having the records but, you know, for the music, really. It's not just the thing and doing somethin' with the thing, you know, like they're music lovers. But the things people like the idea of havin' a thing to play with like a toy. But a person who likes to play with an erector set, he is really an ideas person who wants to build somethin'. He's not a things person. A person who becomes a book collector, but he doesn't read, is really a things person. He likes havin' books, not readin' them.

"The third type of person is the people person. It's like he *is* the person. The people person likes people and has to have people around him all the time. This sort of person can be a politician, a lawyer, or an actress or somethin' where he can work with people. He can never be a scientist who spends his time alone in a laboratory doin' experiments, or a writer who spends his time at a typewriter all by himself, or a concert pianist who spends maybe a third of his life at a piano with no people around. He just isn't made that way.

"You can recognize these kinds of people by the signs they were born under. Most Pisceans are people people, they can't become concert pianists. But there have been some deviant people under every sign.

"As a rule, the theory holds true for most people, and the people person and the things person and the ideas person can all be identified in very early childhood. The kid who likes to sit around and think, even though he's not withdrawn or retarded or anything like that, you know, but he just likes to sit around and think about things and ask questions, and when he's given answers he comes back and thinks about 'em or asks his mother or his father or his sister or his brother about an answer that they gave to him last week because he's been thinkin' about it since that time—this is usually an ideas person, and in all probability this person will be a Sagittarian.

"Another kid on the same block likes to putter with things and collect things and be botherin' with things, you know, he likes to break up things or just take things apart. Everything new that he sees and doesn't know what it is, he wants to fumble with it, not necessarily see how it works, just to do somethin' with it. He wants to hold it and fondle it and see what it feels like, shake it to see what it sounds like, that sort of thing, just have it for a while. This, of course, will be the things person, you know, and in all probability the things person will be a Gemini or Scorpio, Leo, or a Taurus.

"And for the third type of person, the people person, every time he goes out of the house he'll bring all the rest of the kids in the block back home with him. This is the people person. He couldn't be the concert pianist. He would have to be a Cancer or Virgo, or a Pisces, and maybe an Aries or Aquarian. It's like he's just made that way, to spend his life with a lot of people."

Dee Dee said she can point them out in the group, she knows who's who among the Hamites, but that's a waste of time. She knew what their astrological signs were before anybody told her. She knew by watching them and seeing what kind of persons they were. She said they all fell into categories, with the one exception of Jill. But she says Jill is so complicated that she's very hard to classify because "Jill's been out there."

"Jill could probably be an actress since she's played so many parts," Dee Dee says. "Jill is so difficult to pin down to a sign because she has been so many things and she is so many people. She just squeezed so much of life into a short period of time that it's kind of impossible to tell who she is."

As a matter of fact, Dee Dee doesn't think that Jill is certain as to who she is just yet because she had problems defining herself or discovering who she was in her family. Nobody really was any particular person. Dee Dee says, "Family members and everybody will help to define who you are and help you to discover yourself because of the way they react to your different moods. You're born with nothin', but whatever your sign is, you have to be able to develop into it, and most people will, regardless of whatever comes at 'em in life."

She says that Jill never got an opportunity. "Her family thing was so confused, and there was always so much other stuff interferin' with what was comin' off that her sign just sort of got lost in the confusion. But with most people you can tell what they're about by just observin' them for a while and seein' what kind of people they are, it's all right out front for everybody to see."

Dee Dee says she's got a kind of extrasensory-perception type of feeling, especially when she gets high. When she has some good smoke and some wine, she senses things she doesn't ordinarily sense, and she knows it's got nothing to do with what's actually going on around her in the immediate physical environment or what's happening at the present time. She says that's how she and Shaft really got tight. They got high one night, and she could feel vibrations when he touched her, she could feel some spiritual power passing through from him to her. And it made her feel extremely strong, stronger than she'd ever felt in her life as a person. She says that her ESP is not like what they commonly mean by ESP. She doesn't have any visions, and she doesn't have clairvoyance, and she hasn't seen anything that was going to happen before it happened. She can't tell what somebody's got in his pockets like they do on television, and she doesn't think that people can really do that.

But it's just possible that somebody does have some perceptive powers that are so highly developed that he can tell, by merely looking at a person, or touching a person, where he comes from or what his home looks like or what he was doing that morning. She says she might have that, and maybe that's what the power is that she sensed flowing from Shaft to her when they touched that time. But it's probably underdeveloped now.

Dee Dee says maybe one day when she gets thirty-five, or maybe even twenty-five, the powers will get stronger, because she says she's read in some of the books about ESP that one of these guys said he always could see things and he thought something was mentally wrong with him when he was a child. It started happening when he was about ten years old, and as he grew older it got stronger and stronger. When he got about twenty-three years of age he began seeing entire pictures of various things, and he knew what it was all about. He realized that he had ESP, and it was as though he had a television in his mind and he was seeing things that were happening to other people and happening in other cities and places just as they were taking place. Then he would read about them in the newspapers, and he would know what he had seen.

Of course, there are books that say you can develop ESP if you possess it, but Dee Dee says she's not sure that she wants to develop it. She's not certain she wants to know the future or see too much in life anyway. "You might be doin' somethin' that's gonna be kinda hard to live with." But she said if it's there, if she's got it, and if she's slated to become a clairvoyant one day, well, she's not going to fight it. She's just going to let it happen to her, and when it happens, it just happens. She'll be ready to live with it, and she'll know that was her destiny in life. But she's not "gonna go around and tell anybody about anything bad that's comin' at 'em." She believes if she really got to a point where she knew she had ESP and could foretell things about life and people, good and bad, she just might keep it to herself and never tell anyone.

"That would probably be the only way I could get any real peace. We got a whole lotta people around who can't wait to find out what's gonna happen tomorrow or next week, and they'd probably bother me to death. Of course, they'd pay a whole lotta money for it if you could be certain that this is what's gonna happen.

"After Kennedy was assassinated you had like these phonies comin' up from everywhere sayin' that they had predicted it. But nobody heard anybody predict it before it happened. And it makes them all seem so jive because every year in magazines and certain newspapers they have the predictions for the year, especially the political predictions and the predictions on the lives of celebrities, and by the leading clairvoyants in the country or the world or somethin'. Nobody has said anything yet about any of it comin' true. And those that do come true, well, they seem to be just smart guesses. Yeah, it's like things were goin' that way anyhow. Last year it didn't take any kinda clairvoyance to say that America's economy is gonna be in bad shape in 1975. I mean everybody knew that by August of 1974 if not before.

"Those people who make all the predictions at the beginnin' of the year that never come true for some strange reason, they're never put down, people go right on believin' them. Americans have a whole lotta televisions and radios, and they are probably more sophisticated and knowledgeable than other people in other parts of the world where they haven't seen as much and don't know as much about the gimmicks and games mankind has come up with in the past few years. But they haven't peeped behind the scenes of life enough to know that all this stuff can be worked like a magician's trick. I mean, you know, if they were swift enough they'd know that there's no such thing as a sleeveless magician. Or maybe it's just that the clairvoyants and the fortune-tellers and tea readers and dudes like that can just get over better in America because there's more money in America.

"It's just somethin' people really don't need. There's no necessity for knowin' the future or anything like that. It's like if you're sellin' somethin', you gotta go to a place where people got a whole lotta money to spend. In other countries, people who ain't got enough food to eat ain't gonna be messin' 'round with no fortunes. They starvin' and they're not gonna spend today's supper to be hearin' about what might happen tomorrow, when nobody knows. No, they gonna save that, buy some rice or beans.

"If I should find out that I really have ESP—if I start seein' a whole lotta bad things, I'd keep it to myself—but if I should discover that I have powers and see a lotta good, I'd go out there and start sellin' it, too, not sellin' advice but my glimpses into the future. You know, take advantage of the money that's to be made out there just like anybody else would. Who knows, that might be my thing, you know, what I was meant to do. I would just be doin' that to get my actin' thing off, but I wouldn't be doin' anything like that for serious business."

Dee Dee says she's not ready to be an actress yet. She goes to numerous plays throughout the city, the inexpensive ones, to a few plays at that little place down there on Seventh Avenue, "the National Theatre Society or somethin' or other," a few Off-Broadway, a couple on Broadway. She saw *Ain't Supposed to Die a Natural Death*, and she went to see *Raisin* and *The Wiz*, but she says she's not especially interested in musicals. She'd like to do serious drama. But she says she's not ready for that now. She admits to having many dramatic deficiencies, and she's very undeveloped in acting. She was moved by the mother in *Raisin*. It just "shocked" her "to see how powerfully this woman came across to me." And when she goes to see the things at NEC, she knows she's got a long way to go, but she also knows that she's got time to get there.

Dee Dee doesn't want to try acting in school plays because acting is too important to her to fail at. Shaft told her, "Well, you've got a lotta time to go and tighten it up even if you should fail the first time, so I don't see what you worried about."

She says, "No, it's so important I can't even have one slight failure. When I jump out there, I want to be ready."

I guess that's all right—it makes sense. But there are a lot of people who do everything, do everything but the thing that they really want to do, because they're afraid of failing at that one thing. And if they never do it, well, you know, if they never try it, they never fail. Dee Dee's one of those people who'll practice and practice and practice until she knows that she won't look too bad when she goes out there.

Dee Dee's a serious person, and she has mastered quite a few trades for her age already. She's got the household routine down pat, and she's interested in school. Of course, she would probably—I guess this can be said of most of the Hamites—be much better off if she were at home with parents in a real family situation where she could get some adult support and parental guidance. Even though she is sophisticated compared to the kids in the neighborhood, she has her problems, too. They slow her down and distract her from her goal of becoming an actress.

Dee Dee says that if she were religious she would pray that her younger sisters and brothers don't go out there and get strung out, although it's almost a natural thing to do in Harlem. She knows she just barely missed the needle herself. She thinks that if she had known Shaft or had met him when he was "jonesin'," she probably would have tried it because she digs him that much. She likes doing things with him. And he goes along with her program. He participates in skits with her and lets her play off of his scag thing. She is always telling his fortune when they've got nothing better to do, and he's always checking her out now when she tries to get the tarot card technique together. Yes, Dee Dee's going to be a success, I think, at whatever she finally gets into. And acting just might be there waiting for her because she's got a lot going for her now.

SIX

Mumps

Mumps is probably the most serious member of the Hamites. He usually doesn't have time to fool around. He's the businessman of the group, and he's always got his mind on how he's going to make some money, or how to sell something that he's going to steal. He's also the best-dressed member of the Hamites, a flashy dresser. He wants to finish high school and go to college, and he says he'd like to become a haberdasher with a chain of fancy haberdasheries in Harlem.

All of the Hamites have stolen a little something at some time. They steal just enough to get by, but Mumps is the best thief of them all. He's professional. When a Hamite sees something that might add a touch of home to one of the spots, he tells Mumps about it. Mumps will either expropriate the item, supervise the theft, tell the members how to go about acquiring it with a minimum risk of being caught, or explain why it isn't worth it. He never gets any arguments because he always knows what he's talking about and the other Hamites know that he knows. When it comes to stealing things, he's the undisputed expert. Mumps doesn't steal for the fun of it. He's sixteen now, and he's been on his own for a long time. To him, stealing is a serious business.

Most of the members earn money by shooting craps or dealing pot—only to people whom they know—and some work at part-time jobs occasionally, but Mumps earns money by selling the various items he steals in the evenings and on weekends. He wants to be "a salesman," until he goes to college. Probably because men's clothing is easiest to come by, he sells this mainly, but sometimes he sells small electrical appliances in the neighborhood bars. He sells his hot wares to members of the group on credit, but he keeps very good records.

Everybody else pays cash. Sometimes Mumps will permit a member of the group to barter a sport jacket for three ten-dollar bags of smoke, or, in the case of one of the girls, a watch, a ring, etc., for a favor. He says he doesn't have time for a steady girl friend, so he prefers to pay for sex on the spot, walk away from it, and forget it.

How Mumps became a member of the group is still something of a mystery. He's known them for a long time because he grew up a couple of blocks away. He and Dujo were upstate together, in the New York State Training School for Boys, and that's where they "pulled tight." Following his release from the Training School, Mumps lived a few blocks away in a foster home. His mother is a junkie, and he knows her but seldom sees her. He doesn't like his mother too much. He says he doesn't like drug addicts, and he doesn't like hard drugs. He says he's never used scag "except that once when we took off the blind broad." He's never even been curious about it like most youngsters who grow up in Harlem. Mumps claims he's never been afflicted by such curiosity, and he doesn't think that he will be. It's a deeply ingrained hate, which he isn't too willing to talk about. It has a lot to do with the fact that his mother was an addict and abandoned the family, or the children anyway, when Mumps was very young—about nine or ten.

Since that time, until the time he'd gone to the New York State Training School for Boys, Mumps lived around with his grandmother here and an aunt there. After he came out of the New York State Training School for Boys and lived in a foster home, he used to hang out in this block with the Hamites, especially Dujo, who was his running partner upstate. He's come to accept a life of being on his own.

There were eight children in Mumps's family. His older brother was a thief, and is now in jail "doing a dime." Mumps admired him, and I think that's how he learned to steal himself.

He claims that it's a natural gift. In explaining it to me, what his thieving was all about, Mumps says, "A thief is different from other people. Being a thief is somethin' that's within a person—maybe from birth. I don't know—he really can't control it. It's like the controllin' force of a person. Like if a person is a thief, he has somethin' within him that drives him to steal and to get a charge out of that more than, say, playin' basketball or takin' drugs, and he feels his best thing within him, this need, equal to the addiction urge that makes a person go and get some drugs and sort of live for it. With a sho'nuff, sho'nuff thief, stealin' is his natural jones."

Stealing is one of the greatest joys of his life. He says, "It's like Salt-Noody freakin' out when he sees a big brick wall and beginnin' to imagine his name on it in gigantic letters." He thinks "a dude like Salt-Noody would probably be happy in prison if they gave him four hundred spray paint cans and just turned him loose on all the walls. You know how most dudes will see a broad and she's foxy, well, they stop and they start lookin' at her legs and breasts and her shape and all that. They see how pretty she is, and they look at her from that angle because that's what they're drivin by, the sexual attraction thing, and that's the first thing that hits them.

"A thief is a different kinda bird. When a thief sees a woman, he don't look at the legs, not first, anyway. He don't look at her face and how pretty she is. He's lookin' at somethin' else. And anybody who sees him and watches his eyes is gonna know that this is a different kinda duck. This is how the police can spot a thief very easy, from the jump, on a train or in a subway. That's why a thief is always takin' somethin' to look at, like a newspaper, 'cause if a policeman is around checkin' you out and sees you peepin' on this broad who happens to be a fox and you're not lookin' at her legs and the things that dudes look at, he's got you peeped. A thief is gonna be lookin' at a pocketbook. You're thinkin' what kind it is, how does she carry it, does she leave it open, what kinda rings or jewelry she's got on. You're lookin' at the coat and clothes that she's got on to see if it's some good stuff that you can down quick.

"And this is a giveaway to all the police. That's why he always takes somethin' with him—a newspaper or book or magazine—so that he can be readin' it in case the police are on the set and they gonna be pinnin' him if they see him hawkin' somebody, like a woman.

"The thief knows the police by the way he walks, by the way he's lookin' at somethin'. It's like I know who the police are in plain clothes, lookin' shabby and dirty when they get out there in that undercover costume. You know, those dudes don't game on nobody but the people who don't know and don't care anyhow. They don't fool the sho'nuff thieves and the full-time criminals. Just like they know who the criminals are, the criminals know who they are without anybody wearin' any signs on their backs. So you have to sort of have a cool. You have to have somethin' to sort of disguise that difference in your nature that won't allow you to act like other people or what they call normal or average, because you're not. You're a dude who is driven by this urge to steal, especially if it's somethin' that you have always wanted and wanted kinda bad and knew that you never could cop it in a honest fashion.

"Maybe that's what really happened to me. As a little kid I always wanted things, and there was nobody around to buy 'em. Moms didn't have any money. She was always out there dabblin' in stuff until she got strung out, and then all the money she got went into her arms and thighs, so we never could get anything, me and my brothers and sisters. It was always just wantin'. And maybe what happened is that I wanted too many things for too long, and then, like I don't remember when it was, one day I was out there, you know, like coppin' for myself.

"Well I upped and copped a whole lotta stuff for me. Yeah, maybe all that desire like a long-built-up desire went so deep into my soul or inner self or whatever they call it that it just became the drivin' force in me, you know, the want, and it just came out stealin'. I became like a dude who's driven by wantin'. That's okay if you're rich. You just run out and you buy up everything. But if you ain't rich and the want thing is still there, you gotta find some way to get it. I guess that's how I started stealin'."

When asked if he wasn't afraid of getting busted and going to jail for a long period of time and having it interfere with his plans, he said he wasn't really concerned about that possibility because he wasn't one of those average "ham snatchers." A "ham snatcher," he says, is "one of those people, like a junkie, who will run into a store and snatch a coat or somethin' and run with it. It don't necessarily have to be a ham, but they run in other places, and meat stores, too, and snatch the meat out of frozen-food cases and put in under their coats."

He says the supermarket snatch-'n'-run thieves are all ham snatchers. Mumps claims he doesn't do things like that. For one thing, he always knows what he's going to steal before he steals it. He just doesn't go around and take something because it looks easy or it looks like there's nobody around. He says everything that he steals is carefully planned and "pinned." By "pinned" he means watched or observed for a while. He says when he "cops goods" it's almost impossible for him to get caught.

I asked him why he went to the New York State Training School for Boys. He said he got busted for holding some drugs for his older brother, who was dealing at the time. "The police ran up on him." They were chasing his brother out of his apartment. Mumps was coming up the stairs, and his brother was hollering that the police were going to shoot him. Suddenly his brother passed the drugs off to him and told him to run back down the stairs and out the back door of the building, and his brother ran out the front door. It seems theolice thought he was his brother. So they both ran after Mumps and they caught him, searched him, and found the dope on him. He couldn't tell them that his brother had given it to him. That wouldn't have been cool at all. That would have been dropping a dime on his brother. So he took the fall.

I asked what it was like being upstate. Was he afraid of being there? No, Mumps replied, he wasn't. "It was a kinda freaky life bein' away from the streets for a long time, not especially from home because that was no paradise anyway." He said he had some adjustments to make, "gettin' used to callin' people by their last names, as, you know, dudes do up there."

When he was in reception he made up his mind that he was going to survive, "get over up there," despite what it was all about. He saw "a whole lotta crazy things goin' down, dudes goin' around bogartin' others, and everybody runnin' a gorilla game."

He said, "If you were gonna be meek or timid, you were gonna have trouble. It would almost be impossible to have any peace up there. Instead of being cool and just makin' your time, you're gonna be goin' through changes as long as you don't fight and keep a lotta dudes scared of you.

"So I made my mind up before I got out of reception that I was gonna be a gangster dude. You know, 'cause you can't take no stuff from nobody. So I began goin' into the bogart thing just out of fear. It was more like common sense because that was the way to get over.

"The real weird scene about it was the sex thing, though. It's like dudes was goin' crazy and doin' all kinda creepy things, especially to the meek ones up there and the white boys. Yeah, they had a sad life, you know, most of them came out snakes and creeps [homosexuals and misfits].

"There were a few dudes I used to hang out with. One of them was from Manhattan, downtown around 115th Street, a real swift dude, strong game, had a whole lot of heart. He could sho'nuff handle himself. And most of the dudes that I hung out with, they were real bogart dudes. Most of them were from Brooklyn. They were like some pretty down dudes. These dudes went for a whole lot of bogartin'. Like I had only two fights in the whole nine months I was up there, and I didn't have any kind of sweat like after that. I used to gangster people, too.

"Nobody come to see me most of the time. One of my sisters showed like twice, but usually nobody came. Moms showed one day, like she came with my sister, and she was so spaced, I mean she was bent, I asked her not to come back. It was a real bring-down. Your moms show on the set, and she's all messed up off scag. That's some stuff that's hard to live down. Everybody gonna be talkin' about it and laughin'. I just asked her not to come back no more, and she didn't. Since I wasn't gettin' visits too tough, the only way I was gonna have anything or any money to buy stuff with or get any home-cooked food or stuff from outside, books, or whatever I might want, was to play the gorilla game. I sort of became the main gorilla in the cottage. If I said like we do a job on somebody, we fired him up. And I usually didn't have to mess with people too tough because if I'd gotten up and hit a dude in his mouth, usually he knew what the scene was and didn't need no more explainin' than that.

"My main man was Al, the dude from 115th Street. Al is mellow people, a swift dude. He has a lot of personality, fight in a minute. But he wasn't really evil. He had this sex thing. As a matter of fact, he had come up there because him and some of his partners downtown had raped this teacher around his old neighborhood, Lenox Avenue and 117th Street.

"He's been going away since he was ten years old, some places they done tore down by now. In fact, he was the dude who hipped me to everything that was goin' on and how not to be borrowin' cigarettes from anybody and gettin' in debt for cigarettes. He was like hippin' me and settin' me straight to everything that was goin' down. Really, we ran the cottage after we got tight. I remember one day I had gone out on my assignment, and when I got back Al was tellin' me all kinds of skull-bendin' stuff, how they had caught this white boy on the staircase in the administration buildin' and they had done it to him in his behind. I wasn't interested in that scene, it just wasn't my thing.

"Al said, 'We told this white boy to suck our meats after we did it to him, and he said no, he couldn't do that because if he went and did somethin' like that he could never kiss his mother again. So we kept on tryin' to make him do it, but we didn't want to start beatin' on him and have him hollerin', and everybody woulda gotten flagged, and I told 'em,' he said. 'You shoulda been here 'cause you woulda made him do it.'

"Man, when I heard that, I said, 'Yeah, yeah, I woulda made him suck our meats,' and, man, I wasn't even interested in nothin' like that, but I probably woulda done it if I had been there because I knew it was expected o' me. Like here I was, the main gorilla.

"They used to give us lectures on what they called sex perversion up there. Dudes who were head of the cottage, they'd get into it, especially if there was a sex incident and they thought somebody beat up one of the snakes, the girls, the faggots. Or raped somebody or somethin' like that, they be givin' us all these lectures. The dude would have everybody get up in the dorm and pile around on the sides, and he'd say you can get all kinds of disease from sexual perversion. The dudes who were into that sort of thing, he said, it's like if he was to take a pile of feces and throw it down there in the middle of the floor and somebody was to come along or you came and stuck your thing in it, you know, it would be the same thing, just like what you doin' when you stick your peter in somebody's behind. Anyway, that was such a common practice up there, and when I thought about it, it's like my sex thing would come down on me, and I'd be thinkin' about it and I'd be lookin' at one of them sissies and they be lookin' good. I started to do it twice.

"We were supposed to meet the sissy at night, you know, behind the gym, and the sissy didn't show, so like it didn't come off. I just wanted to try it out of curiosity, like people want to try things, not to mention the fact that I'd been there for a while and hadn't been close to a broad in a long time, and Al just sold me on how delicious this sissy was gonna be. I said, damn, I must be crazy. Here I am, you know, like gettin' hots over some boy's behind. We'd been talkin' about it like it was pussy. And I know this ain't no pussy. I said to myself, Damn dude, you better get a hold of yourself. You know what you're doin'? You're out here talkin' about a boy's behind like it's a girl's pussy. In my mind I was thinkin', I gotta get outta here before I go outta my skull. I was just lucky because if I'd been in someplace else and been goin' to places since I was ten like Al, and if I'd been in someplace since I was thirteen, I probably woulda gotten into a rut like that, too, where the first time I came, it coulda been in some boy's behind, and it woulda been a natural thing to just go on screwin' boys in their behinds, makin' it with sissies all the time. As a matter of fact, it was just a whole weird number.

"You know, when I got outta the joint, it's like when Al came out, about two months later, and I took him around to meet some of the different broads. Nita gave him some, and we partied with some of the broads uptown. But when the dude was first comin' out, he was tellin' me, 'Come on, let's go and see some snake out in Queens.' He wanted to go out there and screw a sissy, and I'm tryin' to make this dude understand, 'You ain't upstate no more, and they got girls out here. You don't have to be doin' that. Out here, man, they got real girls with real pussy. You be out on the street and stickin' it in snakes' behinds, that's kinda messed up in the mind. That means you a little bit outta your skull.'

"I got him to come on and get down with some broads and party, we copped reefers and gaged up, and we partied with Lena and that broad Candy she used to hang out with, and, you know, we had some fun. But I really believe that the dude didn't enjoy it as much as he enjoyed screwin' one of those sissies. If that's his hang-up, let him go on and do his thing in the way that he's gonna enjoy it.

"I was thinkin' I was damn lucky. When I started actin' about it, I said, I gotta get out of this place before I start thinkin' like Al. It's like bein' in there just does a thing to you, it warps your mind. You do a while lot of cold numbers that you wouldn't ordinarily do. That's one of the reasons why I go for everybody here in the spot and like havin' the broads here. It's a pretty cool scene because when they're no girls around, dudes start to be more vicious and cold with each other, but havin' broads around, they sort of cool you down a little bit and make you kinda soft in your role. They make you act a little more human. You don't do all the crazy things like always wantin' to jump up and punch somebody in the mouth. They help to keep everything cool, and it's a mellow atmosphere, like it's healthy and it's peaceful.

"I really hope that I never have to go to jail or go away no more to noplace. I don't think I will, but you never can tell. Anything can happen, but I'm gonna try and stay out here on these streets. I really don't think that's too hard to do. You might think that I'm gamblin', 'cause I steal, but like I ain't gamblin' no more than Dujo or Shaft, when they be dealin' their smoke. It's like I guess I'm gamblin' less 'cause there's so many people out there dealin' smoke in this block, everybody's hot. The police may just swoop down here one day and just grab everybody in a net, and they be in it, too. When I go out to boost somethin', I don't do it in no crowd with a whole lotta people. It's just me. And besides, like I gotta have some kinda money to eat with, buy clothes, keep my clothes clean, to keep on goin' to school and lookin' halfway decent. Everybody gotta have some money. I don't go out there stealin' for the kick of it. I'm just doin' my thing to survive. I could be shortstopped on the way to my goal, but I don't think I will. Of course, I can't say I won't, but even if it should happen, well, I tried, didn't I? Like that's the most anybody can do, right?

"Harlem, Harlem is a real mellow place. I think the main thing wrong with Harlem is the junkie scene. If it wasn't for the junkies, Harlem would be like one of the most outta sight places to live. And in spite of it, it's still pretty cool. I haven't been that many places, but I don't know anyplace else in the city that's as mellow as Harlem, where you feel as much at home. I wouldn't want a business in a white neighborhood. One thing is that they couldn't appreciate the styles. Like the stuff that I'd want to wear, it'd have to be some black dudes to dig it. I wanta sell some swift stuff. I couldn't sell the threads that those white dudes wear. They wear all that funny kinda stuff, and those cheap suits with white stitches. I just wanta get into a swift business."

Mumps shows quite a lot of respect for all the other Hamites, and they for him, but he seems to be the one who is most dissatisfied with his condition, with being there and not being someplace else and able to do something else or something more for himself. He gives the impression that he'll probably be the first one to leave, because his ambition seems to be more immediate.

This is a very together youngster. He is the only person there who has a bank account. All the Hamites know that he has a bank account, "money in the bank," but nobody knows how much, and nobody asks him about it. He deposits money each week.

Mumps acquires money sometimes by financing Dujo or Shaft in their smoke enterprises. He'll buy it and let them sell it, and he'll get half of the profit that's made from it. He steals a lot, but when he sees something in a store that he likes and can't steal, he goes in and he buys it. And he buys many things for the spots, too.

Most of the Hamites feel that they'll do something one day, maybe in a few years from now. Most of their plans are long-distance plans. Mumps, on the other hand, has a "right-now" schedule. He wants to get his "thing off" right now. If he weren't so averse to street life he'd probably be out there dealing drugs or fencing hot goods because he's got a business mind on him already and he's in love with money. Also, he's aware of just how much money there is to be made in illegal street ventures. But he doesn't rush to claim his share because he figures street life "ain't where it's at." To Mumps's way of thinking, that's a practice of the past. "If you get out there and you're doin' the street thing, all you doin' is takin' a risk, and everybody is shakin' you down, like the policemen and all the other bandits who have you. This is no big thing. It happens in straight-up businesses, too, but it happens to you in a worse way if you involved in some street activity. Everybody knows you don't have to be bothered with health inspectors, buildin' inspectors, and other different kinds of inspectors, but the police can clean you out all by themselves, and once they latch on to you or once they hook up with you, they don't ever let you go.

"They could be raisin' their graft fee, whatever it might be, and eventually they gonna be makin' more money than you are, and you know if anybody gets busted it's you. They come off with all the dough, and you the dude who has to make some time or take the fall, and, man, that ain't nothin'. You ain't got no kinda hole card if you gonna be out there throwin' rocks."

Mumps just wants to get enough money to "get this thing off right." He thinks that by the time he gets out of college he'll have accumulated enough money to start a chain of haberdasheries in Harlem and have his "thing gettin' off in a sorta mellow fashion." It's a real ambition, and it's something that he can bring off.

Some folks in the neighborhood think that he's into much more than he actually is because they always see him clean and neat. Of course, he's always selling hot goods in the bars and in the barbershops and he's always taking orders for commodities people want and that he will steal. He sometimes brings some very valuable items to his better customers. He'll get expensive leather goods, such as suitcases, coats, and attaché cases. Customers come to him for just these things because he's so reliable and efficient in filling the orders. And people like to give Mumps things, but he's always hesitant about accepting. Maybe that's the businessman in him. He says he wants to pay for whatever he gets because he thinks the giver will be expecting free goods from him and he likes to keep things on a business level.

Mumps often goes in to the bars, though he isn't old enough to drink, but in Harlem many people aren't old enough to drink and nobody pays any attention to it, but he doesn't drink in bars. He's very serious in the bars because he's taking care of his business and he wants to keep a clear head. He knows that a lot of people are "layin' " and trying to beat him for one thing or another. So he makes it his business to keep alert at all times. When he goes into a bar or into a beauty parlor he's friendly enough, but he goes in there not to make friends. He goes in to sell and take future orders. When the lady around the corner who owns the beauty salon wants to see Mumps, she'll always ask one of the Hamites, "Where is that serious boy? Tell him I wanta see him."

I suppose that's how most people think of him, as the serious boy—the one who hardly ever smiles, who's always got a pencil and a pad in his hand. Mumps is constantly doing something or going someplace. He has an urgent business air about him which tacitly, but firmly, says to the world, Get out of my way. Don't play with me.

Mumps has a thief's concentration about him. He's always alert and observing everything intensely. But when he's got his eye on something that he desires to possess, nobody will ever see him looking at it. As a pattern of behavior he seems to be practically making a conscious effort not to gaze at whatever the object is he wants. He might be looking nowhere with downcast eyes as though he's in a pensive mood or staring at something else on the opposite side of the street. When you hear Mumps talk about dogs and about how deceptive the fox or the coyote can be, you think that he has patterned himself after these creatures who have to survive on instinct and a brief education. He also knows what not to do when he's out stealing. Much of this was learned from his brother before he went to jail, but some of it seems to be possibly instinctive or natural. He'll be the first to admit to you that it is "a natural thing."

Mumps tries to maintain a very low profile, and he almost succeeds most of the time, but when he's not someplace "workin'," as he calls it—out stealing or "peepin' "—he's very neatly dressed. His style of dressing isn't flashy. It's always very tasteful, and people notice him. He likes to come out in a different outfit every day. If it's on the weekend, he'll change twice a day. He wears one outfit on Saturday during the day and then another at night. When he's selling something, especially, he has on a different one. His clothes are usually fashion starters, but, of course, when he's out working he's dressed the way he's supposed to be for doing that particular number, whatever it might be. Other than his attire, he's rather quiet and seems to go through life unnoticed.

If some of the Hamites are down on the street or in a group on the stoop and everybody is making noise, Mumps won't get into it. He may say something softly to one of them, but that's the extent of it. Up in the spot, he's very outgoing, but it's not his nature to be loud, and he just doesn't get into loud scenes. He automatically tends to avoid being noticed too much.

Somebody once asked him why he's called Mumps, and he said, "I don't know, man. Well, everybody calls me Mumps because they say I look like I always have the mumps. People can't help what they look like. This is just the way my face is made. Just like my boostin' thing, you know, it's a natural. I didn't ask for a face like this. It's somethin' that comes at you, you know, and it's yours. When things happen to you in life, that's no fault of yours, like it's you and there's nothin' you can do about it, right? Well, that's how I got that jive name, Mumps. And you know what happens around here if you get a name in your childhood, man, that's you for life. It's like can you imagine people callin' Salt-Noody, Salt-Noody, you know, when he gets about thirty-five? Well, if he stays around here, his name will be Salt-Noody, like when he even gets forty-five. People stick that name on you, and it's on you for life, just like you been branded."

Mumps likes to read, and he really enjoys school. Mumps reads more textbooks than any of the Hamites, and most of them like to read. Nita likes to read everything, especially novels, and every kind of poetry and modern drama. But Mumps really gets to his textbooks. He'll "lay up in the crib," in one of the spots, with a bright light burning all night, and just "book it." He'll be getting into his business textbook, or getting into a biology textbook, and he likes to play around with mathematics, too. He's forever figuring out percentages, first arithmetically, then algebraically. That's his thing. And anybody who wants to know something about a mathematics problem will bring it to Mumps and ask him.

And he likes to play chess. Most of the Hamites do, but Mumps is extremely good at it. Mumps, Dujo, and Chips are fascinated by biology, and especially reproduction. Mumps knows how long it takes twenty different animals to reproduce. He can tell you the length of a lion's pregnancy and just how much a baby elephant will weigh when it is born, facts like that, which most youngsters his age aren't the least bit interested in. And he talks about these things with Dujo and Chips and Shaft and other Hamites who will listen.

This foursome knows more about biology and reproduction than any of the others, with the exception of Jill, who seems to know more about everything than anybody else. Sometimes Dujo, Jill, Mumps, Chips, Shaft, and Dee Dee will do an excursion bit. It's similar to a field trip when you're in grammar school and going out to the zoo. Sometimes they'll go to two zoos in a day, to Prospect Park Zoo in Brooklyn and then to the Bronx Zoo. Then they'll come back and talk about how fast a panther or cheetah will run at top speed, all kinds of "odd" things like that. Mumps says, "They're not all that strange if you're really interested in 'em." When it comes to topics like this he gets excited and will talk on and on. Somebody—Hebro, for example—will come in and say, "Hey, man, like what are you lecturin' about now?"

But he goes on, it doesn't faze him. He'll respond by saying, "Man, why don't you sit down and learn somethin' that you oughta know?"

Because Mumps is a serious fellow, he usually says he doesn't have time for the "noise" (nonsense) of a "main squeeze" (one special woman), and he says that he "wouldn't want one of these broads around here 'cause none of them are worth botherin' with, or gettin' hooked up with." He says, "All these broads are bent," meaning that they're not very bright. However, one day, of course, he'd like to hook up with a foxy broad who's "got it together." But he's not anxious. "You shouldn't try to rush because it'll show in its own time. If you rush you'll get hooked up with somethin' that ain't for real, and nobody's got that kinda time to waste."

He once had a thing for Connie, "But Connie is so, you know," and now they're just good friends. "Connie was so messed up in the mind over Chips that I just forgot about that broad and couldn't pay it too much attention."

I suspect that Mumps thinks of himself as an unattractive guy, and therefore he doesn't persist when he detects a lack of interest on the part of a girl. He's a sensitive guy with an abundance of pride, and he wouldn't want to have his feelings hurt by being rejected. That would probably hurt him more than anything else could, the feeling of being turned down after "comin' on out" and telling a girl that he really cares for her and that he wants to "hook up" with her. If he is asked about it or teased, he says he's too busy and he hasn't got time for that kind of noise. But Mumps is very fond of both Nita and Connie, especially Nita, and they both like him. He gives them things—some say it's for their favors—but nobody has any holds or claims on anyone, and they all prefer it just that way.

Dujo says that Mumps will probably end up with a kennel, training dogs instead of owning a haberdashery. And the idea doesn't appear to be too unappealing to Mumps. He gets along with dogs, maybe better than with people. He seems to talk to them more than to people, even the Hamites. He's very loyal, and he says that he likes dogs because of their loyalty. He also says there's no animal around that's as loyal as a dog. He doesn't see how people can have cats for pets because cats are not at all affectionate. "You know, dogs really get to people. They let you know when they wanta play, when they want some kind of attention for one thing or another, which makes them almost like people. And when they get tight with somebody, it's a lifelong relationship, and with a dog you have complete loyalty.

"I heard of a court case where a couple was breakin' up housekeepin', and they was in court fightin' for the different valuables, and they both wanted custody of the dog. Well, the judge didn't know what to do or who to give custody to, so he went into one of those Solomon numbers and put the dog between the two people, the husband and the wife. Then he had them both start callin' the dog at the same time. He let the dog be released, and he just gave custody to the one that the dog went to, you know. Meanin' nobody could put any flam into it, like bring any meat in there or foul stuff like that. Like he made sure everybody came empty-handed and had no appetizin' odors on 'em. It's like the judge just trusted in the dog's judgment because he knew that the dog is a loyal animal."

Perhaps Mumps has this loyalty thing going about dogs because he is so loyal himself. Jill says, "If Mumps is down with you, he's with you to the bitter end. I mean he's so faithful he gets a attitude and wants to go to war with anybody who says somethin' negative about any of his friends. It's like whenever he's crossed he always gets revenge. And it's a funny thing in the way that he does it because he ends friendships without other people or the other friend knowin' that the friendship is ended because he won't say anything. He just sort of makes a deal with himself or comes to terms with himself that such-and-such a person ain't worth him no more and he's gonna somehow put a burn on 'em in a sort of subtle way. And very often the person don't know what's bein' done on 'em or that he has been cut loose. He always gets his revenge, but the person usually deserves it because, you know, he says that he's never treated anybody foul. And I believe him."

This is true. Most people who know him can testify to it. Mumps is a guy who never wrongs anyone. If he does something to someone or hurts a person physically, which he has been known to do, the victim had it coming because Mumps never makes the first move against anyone.

I asked him if he had ever tried anything other than smoke and wine and beer, any kind of hard drugs. "No, man, I never tried any scag," he said, "if that's what you mean. I tried some coke once, you know. Everybody was snortin' a little bit of blow then. That's when I was hangin' out downtown with Al. He would tell a dude to come on in if he was dealin', you know. He'd tell 'em like this is my main man from upstate, and they'd be passin' out the blow, and I couldn't come up jive, you know, like a off dude who wasn't into nothin'. I was kinda skeptical about it, even though I never hearda anybody havin' a coke jones, but to me it was still dope, so I took it, and it felt kinda mellow. I felt a bit lighter on my feet and kinda carefree with just about nothin' on my mind. You know, it's not like when you get high offa some nice smoke. You start floatin' and, you know, your whole skull is changin' on you. When I snorted the blow, it's like I got lighter, but I just didn't feel high, I never felt any real big change-up.

"Sure, I tried it, but it just didn't turn me on that tough. Now I woulda felt better if I had some smoke and some wine, but of course you can't run that to these dudes. They're doin' their big-time thing, you know. I think scag is really a gator kinda thing, creepy people get into it in a hurry. Now I don't say you have to be a creep or a gator to cop scag jones 'cause there's a lotta pressure on most people that be out here. Everybody gonna be tellin' you how swift it is. They say scag is the nicest high there is. I never wanted to find out. I say it's for gators, dudes who just came up here from down South someplace. If you grew up in the Apple, you done seen a whole lotta dudes, some of them pretty swift dudes, too, who got stuffed around behind messin' with that scag.

"A brother of mine, he was really a swift dude, but he loved some scag and that was him. Before he knew it he was slippin'. Scag is the baddest dude in Harlem because I have seen it kick the asses of some dynamite dudes. I've never really seen nobody who could handle it. I've seen like one or two dudes who ever really gave up the jones. I've seen what it will do to you, and I know it will kick your natural ass, partner. It seems to me that anybody who's peeped what this thing can do to you knows I'm runnin' it like it is. Scag is a monster, man, like it's mean. and anybody who's peeped what it'll do to you over the years, especially if you grow up like in Harlem, it's the booger man that's waitin' in the dark for you. You know, the moment you try some of that white powdery monster you're done. I saw a whole lotta dudes who it was good to when they first started. They thought they had it under control, and they didn't seem to realize that the first time they took a nod, it had them under control, it became the master.

"I think I would rather kill myself than just be a dope fiend goin' 'round all dirty and greasy. You can't hold your head up, man, you ain't worth nothin' to nobody, you ain't even worth nothin' to yourself. I think I'd just go on and bail out, take one last big shot o' dope.

"But like the gators who just got off the bus and they scared they gonna look bad in the Big Apple and big-city life is kinda fast for 'em, and so they come on the set and they wanta show everybody how swift they are. Well, that's grief for them if that's all they can do. It's like committin' suicide to show somebody how swift they are. Say you went down South and somebody told you, 'Hey, man, go step on the rattlesnake over there,' to see if you got enough heart to do it. You wouldn't do it, right? Well, it's the same thing. You know, if you come up North, like to a big-city scene, and somebody says, 'Hey, man, you're a creep unless you go and use like some scag.' That's just like somebody sayin', 'Show me how much heart you got, and go step on that rattlesnake over there.' Scag is the rattlesnake in the city.

"Scag is the baddest dude in the whole Apple. If you don't believe it, just go downtown to 126th and Eighth Avenue, or you go down 114th Street and Eighth Avenue or 113th Street and Lenox Avenue, and you look at the corners there. Now you look at all them dudes that scag has got messed up there on the corners. Like their whole lives, seriously speakin', their lives are finished. Man, they ain't got nothin' else to look forward to, like they gave it up a long time ago.

"My moms has been on scag seems like almost since I can remember. And I see her out on the streets into her thing, like in a nod. She don't even recognize me, and she don't care. She don't know nobody but whoever's carryin' the bag. That's all she wants to know. That's one of the main reasons I wouldn't mess with it 'cause I know that scag. The city rattlesnake is just too mean for me. I know that if a rattlesnake is in front of me and he might bite me, I'm not gonna say I'm gonna bite him back. Man, I got no poison in my teeth. That's crazy. I'm just gonna get outta his way, and that's what I do with scag. I just stay outta that boy's way and just hope that it stays outta mine.

"A junkie is the most unscrupulous person alive, you know, they're fanatics. That's why those dudes like Snooky and Dujo, they call 'em the worshipers. They're just like religious fanatics because their god is scag. They worship dope, and everything else just don't matter.

"When you're stealin', you got like certain rules, you got principles, you know. You won't steal everything, and of course there're certain people that you won't steal from. I would never steal anything from any of the fellows or any of the broads in the spot. We're family. I mean I won't steal from anybody and everybody. Everybody's got some kind of principles. Anyway, I have. And I can't dig the dope fiends because, man, they steal from everybody and each other. There're very few junkies who you can trust even a little bit."

I asked him about Lee, who is an addict and is an honorary Hamite. "Lee is somethin' else. He is really a different kinda junkie. He keeps himself kinda clean. He does a thing where he's never around noddin', and only once in a while do you see him with other junkies. I mean he wouldn't bring another junkie up to the spot because he knows he'd be jeopardizin' his own thing. We'd definitely have to put him in the wind because, you know, we just don't want all those worshipers hangin' around.

"I think that one of these days, say by the time I get outta college, Harlem is gonna be a completely different place. Like they gonna clean up junkies, maybe ship 'em all off someplace, or like just let dope become a legal high where everybody can go on and get high if they wanta get high and they could stay high as long as they didn't bother anybody. Because somethin' gotta be done about 'em sooner or later 'cause people gonna get tired of all the stuff they doin'. They be goin' 'round here takin' off old ladies and doin' other foul numbers. They can't go on doin' that stuff. What might happen, we can get vigilantes goin' here, people just offin' junkies, and when they start findin' enough of 'em dead, the others will get the message and tip in the wind.

"I got what I think might be a solution to the whole junkie problem. Man, you can start puttin' bounties on their heads, just like they used to do in the Old West. Like payin', you can pay a lotta dudes around here ten dollars a head, and they would wipe out all the junkies. You know, like if somebody was to put up a bounty like fifty cents a head, I mean fifty dollars, a half a bill, a head, they'd probably all be wiped out in a month or so. And in the places where they hang out, I would go and dismember a few of them dudes and off a junkie every week. They'd find a head over here, or a leg there, or a junkie's arm, and leave his coat sleeve on it or his pants because they wear the same thing all the time. Those dudes don't change like for months. Everybody would know whose arm it is because they'd know that that's the junkie who's been wearin' that mildewed plaid coat since October or November. So you leave that on him, and every week you get another one, and I bet you those dudes would get away from there like a plague was comin' down on 'em. You wouldn't find any of 'em around in about a month. I'll bet you even the dope dealers would get in the wind. Everybody would tip.

"Well, anyway, I would want to do my thing in a cool neighborhood. It would have to be a Harlem shot, but Harlem is gonna be kinda cool in about five or six years. This can't last much longer the way it's goin'. I mean I don't even see how the junkies can last that long.

"I got a nine-year-old brother, and he's a pretty swift little dude. He's got a lotta smarts, like he's got a lot on the cap. You ask this dude what he wants to be when he grows up. You know what he'll tell you? He says, 'I wanta be a ex-junkie.' Can you dig it? I think he realizes that you gotta be a junkie first. And he's swift enough to know that there are plenty junkies out there, but very few ex-junkies, so to him that's success.

"Man, in Harlem, junkies they grow on some streets that ain't got no trees, you know. It's like the junkies might well be the city trees in Harlem. You see all them standin' in places like they could be trees. My older brother's in one o' those drug programs, that thing they got down there on 125th Street. He's been straight now for about three years. He got married, and he's holdin' down a gig [a job], and he's keepin' himself clean. I guess that's a real achievement, man, to become a real-life, straight-up ex-junkie. But it still hurt me to hear my little brother say it. Man, I was wounded. If I had some kids I wouldn't want 'em comin' up talkin' about they wanta be a ex-junkie when they grow up because, damn, that's like sayin' I wanna be a junkie, and the truth of the matter is that nobody's got time to become a junkie, even to become an ex-junkie. You gotta put in a few years at least before you can become a ex-junkie. Black dudes really can't afford it. We got too many changes to fight out there, but it's like we seem to be the main ones who do it. That's the hippest game of all, I mean that's the slickest game that the Devil came up with.

"I think the swiftest thing the Devil did to stop us in our tracks and see that we don't never go noplace was to turn that rattlesnake loose on us. I don't mean the snake faggot, because that's what they call homosexuals. Man or woman. You know, they call 'em snakes. But you remember I told you about the rattlesnake, scag. When he put scag in the black community, he did a wicked number on us. Nobody but us uses it, really. Like them white boys, they seem to have more on the cap because they mess around with that light stuff. Everybody says like LSD really puts you outta your skull, but you don't see nobody goin' 'round with no LSD jones, man, and you ain't seen nobody who got no smoke jones. And like that's about all they do, but it's like the Devil came and brought scag here. He put it in the black community.

"We go 'round talkin' all that BS about politicians run Harlem, and the police run Harlem—all that's a bunch of bullshit, man. Scag runs Harlem. If you don't believe it, you just go out there and look at them junkies and see who's got most people by their life and the strongest hold.

"Whitey just did a number on us, it's gonna take us years to get it off. It's worse than slavery. But it ain't got me. No, I'm gonna go out there, and I'm gonna open my haberdasheries in Harlem, and I'm gonna do somethin' about those junkies. Now you know I don't care about raise and what they wanna do about it, but I know I'm gonna do somethin' because I know I'm gonna live in Harlem all my life if I can, and I'm not gonna have my kids comin' off with no jones and stuff, not no scag. It might take some time. I may not be able to do anything for ten years. If you don't believe me, just watch me. It's gonna be a different scene."

Mumps has this thing about cops. He thinks they're the biggest thieves in town, and he might know. He also thinks they're pretty stupid, and he agrees with Dujo that they're racists, too. He says that if cops weren't stupid racists they would never be doing so many of the silly things that the public observes them doing so frequently. He cites the time when Snooky, who is the youngest Hamite, was arrested for stealing a car, going joyriding, and running into a police car. He says two white cops brought Snooky up to the spot, and if it were not for their particular brand of racism they would have known that nobody lived in that building, that it was a condemned building. He believes the same thing occurred when Snooky told them that Jill was his mother and Jill "cleaned it up." He says that anybody in his right mind can look at Jill and see that she was too young to be Snooky's mother.

"You know, like any broad eighteen years old—at the most, she would look like twenty-five—how could she be a mother of a dude who was already thirteen or fourteen? They came in here thinkin', Well, blacks live in garbage cans anyhow, so why not live here? They were two young white dudes who'd probably never been in a black crib before, so they didn't know. They saw all those tenement fronts in Harlem, and they didn't know what was on the other side of 'em, so they just go for anything. And they assumed that Jill could be Snooky's mother because they figure all black women start havin' babies at the age of three, anyway.

"And as far as cops bein' the biggest thieves around, like they steal from everybody. Most thieves, if they're serious thieves, they're not gonna just steal anything. They just steal certain things, and in certain places, and from a certain group of people. But the police steal from everybody, and they steal from anybody. If they run upon a dude who is hurt, busted, or sick, or dead, and if he's got any money, the raise has got it.

"Sometimes they don't make a real bust and take 'em down to the police station and book 'em because they wanna rip off the goods. It's too much of a hassle to go down there and book somebody and have people showin' for their property and sayin' that everything but a certain valuable or a certain amount o' the money was recovered, but sometimes they'll do that, too. The raise will say, 'Yeah, well, he musta dumped that before we flagged him.'

"It's like they know what their gig is all about and how to steal within the gig and not put it in jeopardy because without the job they don't get a opportunity to steal as much as they can with it. So that's what it's really all about. That's how they make their bucks.

"Police don't make a whole lotta bucks in their salary. Where they really clean up and get over is the other money. The average cop out there must make twice his salary in what he steals and in the graft he takes. I remember once I had broke into this fancy crib downtown and stole this fabulous diamond-studded gold watch that had a mahogany back on it. It was really a very expensive number with a French name—the name was somethin' like Patta Filipe. Anyway, it must have had a burglar alarm on it or somethin' because as I was about to tip I peeped twelve o'clock high [police coming]. So I went up on the roof, and when I came out I had on my delivery-boy costume, and when I showed on down the street, the raise were outta the buildin' and didn't pay too much attention to me because I was in uniform, walkin' slow and bein' cool. But then I dropped this watch outta my pocket, and he started to come over. He looked at me and started to say somethin', but he didn't. But what had happened was that he went over and scooped up the watch and just put it in his pocket and kept on lookin' around. I guess he wanted to cop before his partner showed and saw it and wanted a piece of it, you know, and he mighta stopped me if it not for the greedy fact that he wanted to scoop up that watch, which he did, and keep it for himself. Now, that's just one light example, but I'm sure that a whole lotta action like that goes down.

"They say that the police got the best dope in town. If you really wanta buy some good dope, you gotta get it from the police. You know how they get it? Everybody can't go around and break into the property clerk's office or go steal some drugs, especially now when everything is so hot there. So there's only one way they can cop. They ain't gonna go out there and buy it. They have to bust junkies and take their stuff and give it to other junkies to sell for 'em. Or it's like they'll tell dudes who dealin', like they better give 'em some good dope or they gonna flag 'em, and then they take and they give this to somebody else, you know, to another dope dealer out there, to down for them, and so their stuff has gotta be right. They tell the dudes they better not hit it, and, you know, the average dude would be scared to hit it unless he knows he can get over with some gators who won't know the difference. It's common knowledge that if you wanna find some good dope on the streets, you buy it from the police. They be shakin' down the street ladies for some blow [cocaine] and body.

"Yeah, I guess they get, you know, like the best of everything when it comes to stolen property. I bet if you were to cop a peep into the crib of the average raise, you'd probably see more stolen goods than they got down at the property office because those dudes're sho'nuff thieves. They even got a badge to help 'em steal. When they roll on somebody and the people got somethin' good, all they be thinkin' about usually is not gettin' busted, and most people will dump the goods a lotta times, you know, when the police roll up on 'em, when they hot. And the raise be layin' for it, and they gonna scoop it up, you know. As a matter of fact, those dudes will very often, especially if they know it's a dope crib, one of 'em will go down in the backyard and the other will knock on the door, go up to the crib and knock on the door and announce that it's the raise so that the people will start throwin' goods out the window. The one that's down there in the backyard is the one that's gonna scoop it up. He'll walk away with maybe two shoppin' bags full o' dope and goods if they don't flush it down the toilet because they figure the police is here to talk first, but if they hear a toilet flush, then they gonna break down the door.

"So it's like the first thing they gonna do is run for the window and try and get rid of it that way, and it's like all they doin' is tossin' it to the one that's down there. So what can the people do if they got their stuff like that? If you illegal you can't go to the police because the police is the one who came to rip you off. So they got the swiftest theft thing goin'.

"I'm tellin' you, when it comes to some boostin', ain't nobody boostin' from everybody on the set. But you know the choice of beats around is Harlem or some black neighborhood here in the city where nearly everybody's into some larceny, you know. Black folks are too poor not to be into a whole lotta larceny, so when they show into a neighborhood like Harlem, or one of the black ghettos in the city, it's like that's gettin' a choice assignment.

"Harlem, to a cop, probably means a extra twenty thousand dollars a year minimum, you know, maybe forty thousand a year. And that's for a honest raise. Now the dishonest police, they get rich, man. They be retirin' and livin' better than the president of General Motors. Like that's all they wanted is just to get them a shield so they could go on and get rich, and most of 'em do. You know, like it's only the real dumb dudes who leave the force and ain't got no bucks.

"You know, what Dujo says about 'em is right. They're racists, sho'nuff and thieves, but they're thieves before and beyond and above bein' racists because even the black cops are thieves. And it's like they might not be racists, but they all came to steal. I think the average cop, when he goes out there and joins the police force he's just a dude that's tryin' to get over. The average black raise, he just wants a gig where he can make some bucks. So here's a dude who's not too bright, usually he ain't got a whole lotta smarts, and chances are he wouldn't make much money doin' anything else. He gets himself a civil service job. Everybody knows that's a chump shot. You ain't gonna really get over doin' none o' that, so what, you work for twenty or thirty years and lay back and barely make it with some peanut pension and Social Security check. You know ain't nobody shootin' for no action like that in life. Unless they're stupid or retarded or somethin' like that. So you see these dudes are just average people who in most cases didn't go to college or barely made it through college, and you know they lookin' for a shot that's gonna get 'em over. Now, they figure if they be on the police force like, the salary ain't too tough but the gravy is mellow. The average cop, he probably don't ever take his gun outta his holster while he's on duty but maybe twice in five years, and he just layin' back, rakin' in the bucks, waitin' for the retirement day, and tryin' to be cool and not get busted, and always tryin' to cop more o' that graft money, or nut-up money. Did you see that flick *Serpico*? Yeah, well, that was a true story, man, and that probably came closer to tellin' the whole thing o' pullin' the cover off the police than anything we seen."

SEVEN

Nita

Nita's name is really Juanita, but everybody has been calling her Nita for so long that it's become shortened to just that, Nita. Nita irons for all the fellows, and they give her a couple of dollars for the service. She says with pride that she can cook. Jill does most of whatever cooking is done there, and that's not a whole lot because they usually eat hot dogs, franks and beans, and a lot of sandwiches, potato chips, cheeseburgers, etc. They drink beer and just snack most of the time.

But Nita claims that she can cook. She's tried it out on a few people, a few of the Hamites, and they liked it, and they say that she is a pretty good cook. She wants to go to college and become a lawyer, she says, because she likes to lie, "And why not get paid for it if you can? It seems to be a easy way to make a livin'." But maybe she'll go into the Army first.

Nita left home because she stabbed her mother's old man. They were dealing stuff. She said he had about a quarter-key of cocaine in the refrigerator, and her little brother had spilled some orange juice in the refrigerator, and he wet up the quarter-key of cocaine. Her mother's old man, Bruce, started beating her little brother something terrible, and she thought he was going to kill him or something. First she started pounding on him and hollering at him, but he ignored that, so she grabbed a knife and she stabbed him. She said she thinks that she was trying to kill him, but that all she did was "stick him in his back, and he had these big muscles, and they was so thick the knife didn't go all the way in."

She stopped him from beating her brother, which was her real objective, and, she said, "I was gonna stick him again, but he turned around and reached for me, and I just made it outta the door."

She ran out of the apartment because she knew that he was trying to kill her. "I knew that I couldn't go back there no more because my mother loved him more than she loved us and she really didn't care what he would do to us. She was my mother, and there wasn't much that I could do about it. I mean I couldn't go to the police or drop a dime on my own mother. I just got away from the whole scene, which was the best thing for me."

Nita has been with the group for nearly a year. She used to hang around with them before she moved into one of the spots. Nita is a nice girl, but she has something of a reputation. The other teenagers on the block used to call her Horny Nita because, they say, she used to go to the movies on Saturday, and when she was about eleven or twelve she would have boys coming at her from all over the theater. They would hear that she was in the movies, and four or five boys would converge on her to play with her body. The story is that she's actually screwed some people in the movies, right there in the seats. She likes to tease Snooky, saying that she'll give him some when he gets sixteen, and I think he's looking forward to it.

Nita says she was pregnant once, but a lady her mother knows got rid of it for her with a coat hanger. She said it was very easy, and Miss Lil was gentle and nice. She just told her open her legs and don't be scared, and went on and inserted the tube up there with a coat hanger, and the next day it came down. She was a little scared at first, but it was over before she knew it. And afterward she knew better, so she doesn't worry about getting pregnant anymore. She knows how to avoid it now.

She used to have a complex, she says, about her very dark complexion. It doesn't bother her now because she really believes the cliché, "The blacker the berry, the sweeter the juice." From time to time she's teased by Chips about this. Chips says, "Yeah, but baby, nobody wants sugar diabetes."

And she'll curse him and tell him the main reason he doesn't want it is because he can't get it. Anyhow, it's done in a very joky little fashion. She said she used to be offended when she would go places and people would call her "that black girl." It used to bother her, but after a while she got over feeling inferior because she was so dark. She knows that a lot of fellows admire her in spite of, or maybe because, she is so black.

She is very, very pretty, and she feels now that that's all that matters, not how black she is. And she has a winsome personality. She gets along well with other people, and actually there is no reason for her to be self-conscious about her blackness or to feel inferior in any way. If there is but one girl in all of creation for whom blackness is a definite asset, the girl is Nita.

Nita says that one day she'd like to go home and stay with her brothers and sisters. She doesn't want to go into the Army from anyplace but a real home. She gets mail at home,* and her younger sister brings it to her, and her brothers and sisters bring her messages from her mother from time to time. But she doesn't see her mother, and her mother doesn't seem too anxious to see her. She says that she knows where Nita is, and she knows she's all right, and that's all that matters. I think her mother isn't too concerned whether Nita is all right or not.

But to the Hamites she's like a sister. They frequently lend her money, and they never ask for it back. She gets money also from her sisters and brothers. They steal it from their mother and her mother's old man. With that money and what she earns from a job at school, she manages to keep herself looking very presentable and she dresses very tastefully.

Nita is more involved in her school life than any other member of the group. She tries to get involved in everything that's going on in her high school. She participates in more extracurricular activities in school than any of the other Hamites. And she likes it, she likes learning to do new things. She says she would like to teach people how to draw. She's a very gifted girl. Not only does she draw, but she writes poetry and dances well. She's a very sensitive girl, too. This is reflected in most of her poetry, despite her efforts to conceal it. Maybe she feels that if it should become common knowledge or people became aware of her sensitivity, she would be defenselessly exposed to a ruthless world.

Nita likes to write poetry to herself. Sometimes she composes poetry about the Hamites, and for some of the fellows. Very often her poetry is about her blackness and how beautiful she is. At other times it's just poetry to no one in particular. A sample of her poetry is as follows: "I lay there staring at the wall for a long time, and the wall

* The Hamites who have no homes other than the spots must use another member's name and address to receive mail.

stared right back at me. Until finally one of us spoke, the wall said, 'You love him, you know.' "

She's very prolific with this romantic verse. She tells the other Hamites, humorously, that if they will do something for her, not merely because she irons for them, which is usually what they're bartering for, "I'll write a poem for you." She does it in jest because most of the Hamites don't care that much for the poems, even though some of them are good. It's just that they can't spend them.

In her own way, Nita is a precious character. This is a young lady who definitely has a mind of her own and very clear-cut ideas about what she wants out of life and just how she intends to get it.

Nita can't stand Sheryl, who's the daughter of Mae, the dope peddler, because Sheryl has made advances to her. She calls Sheryl a gator because Sheryl has propositioned her at times. And Jill, who is a very good friend of Sheryl's, tells Nita that every woman has some butch in her. Nita says she doesn't believe that she has any butch in her, and if she has, "It's all right as long as it stays there and don't bother other people by comin' out uninvited."

She doesn't like Sheryl for this reason, and Sheryl is the only one who will come around and ask her to write poems for her. She usually doesn't get any reply. I asked Nita just how could she think of Sheryl as a farmer, as a gator. Sheryl has committed so many urbane deeds and has so much experience behind her, I didn't see how she could fit that description. As Nita explained it, there are two kinds of gators: the city gators and the country gators. She says, "Sheryl is just a city gator. The country gator, as soon as he gets to the city, he'll be runnin' around doin' stupid things like buyin' fancy cars, Cadillacs, Lincolns, that sort of thing, you know, and buyin' those outlandish-colored suits, and spendin' a week's pay on shoes. They gotta get somethin' to flash with. The city gator is the dude who flashes in a different way. The city gator is the guy who's already up here, but he flashes things, like a white woman. You can't tell these people that they're not livin' in the lap of luxury 'cause they got this chick, you know, white woman, or white thing to flash."

She says this is tantamount to the country gator flashing his new, shiny pair of red patent-leather shoes, or his Cadillac car. "As soon as they get up here, they want to get their hair processed, all kinds of silly things like that, and they look ridiculous and don't know it."

According to Nita, "It's the same thing with the city gators when they get some white broad. It could be the saddest, homeliest-lookin' white chick in the world. But as long as they got somethin' white to flash, they're happy. But it's all the same thing, just flashin'. Sheryl goes with this white broad, and bein' a butch who goes with a white broad, you know, she's crazy. She goes around talkin' about that's her woman like she believes it, you know, that she's really a dude or somethin'."

Nita believes that she was born to raise hell. She was born a breech baby. "You know, like I came out backward, feet first, steppin' out into the world. Anybody who's born a breech baby," she says, "has a special thing goin' for 'em. You know, like they are the natural fighters, and they've come here just to raise hell."

Now, this might very well be true in the single instance of Nita because anybody who gets Nita angry should be aware that she has both capability and the proclivity for inflicting mayhem. She has exceptionally good physical coordination and moves with confounding speed. Once Shaft infuriated Nita, and four Hamites, including Hebro, were required to dislodge her teeth from his shoulder.

There was another unusual aspect to Nita's birth. She was born addicted to heroin. Her mother was a junkie, and when she was carrying her she was taking stuff. Nita thought that she would have a natural addiction to heroin, but she didn't. She has no patience with addiction. She's repulsed by heroin, and she refuses to tolerate junkies in her presence. She says scag is destructive and sees that as the major factor in her leaving home. She says, "Dope chased me away from home, out of my house."

And she goes off into a long, almost unending sermon. It comes out pretty bitter, too, when she starts talking about addicts and thugs and people destroying themselves, but that's common to all the Hamites. Most of them have a strong aversion to drugs, especially scag, but they do other things. They don't see pot as a drug.

Nita thinks that even smoking cigarettes is a big waste of time. "If you could go and get a high, if it made you feel mellow or something the way pot does, it would be worthwhile."

Nita thinks that people who go around smoking cigarettes are substituting that for pot. "They want somethin' to happen to their head, but pot's illegal and cigarettes are legal. Of course, it doesn't do the same thing, but you won't get in trouble for smokin' it."

Dee Dee says that Nita, because she's a Gemini, is a complicated personality. "She is ambitious and sensitive, which is what Geminis are all about, and she's got all this energy that she has to release in one way or another." Dee Dee states very authoritatively: "That's what a Gemini is. A Gemini is just a body of caged energy fighting its way out."

According to Dee Dee, Geminis go through life with their souls fighting to get out. "When Nita makes something like a doily for the living-room table, this is another expression of her soul tryin' to get out." And Dee Dee says, "Yeah, Nita says it might be true 'cause she knows she can't be doin' nothing, I mean she can't sit around and not do anything 'cause she's not made that way. This constant fight for freedom of the soul goes on for like for all their lives, and finally when a Gemini dies the soul gets out. The body that's holdin' the soul prisoner in it is usually strong, but day by day it wears down.

"The worst thing that could happen to Nita would be for somebody to tie her hands and put her in a very plain and empty room where she couldn't do anything, not even sew, which she likes to do, and just keep her still." Dee Dee feels certain that such a predicament would "drive Nita right out of her skull." But Nita says that she could always find things to do. She insists that she could write even if her hands were tied. "I'd write poetry in my mind. You know, I'd still be makin' up verse, but it just wouldn't be on paper."

Nita says she has a good time just thinking to herself, talking to herself, writing poetry to herself, and she can have big fun all alone because she has learned to enjoy herself in her mind.

Dee Dee claims that most Geminis are "mental people," as she phrases it. Her conviction is that the vast majority of people are born to move, do things, and be constantly in motion in life "because that's how you know you're alive, and when you slow down, that's when you start dyin'. If you're not movin' you're dead for a while 'cause you know it's not a sign of life to be still all the time. So Geminis are more alive than the rest of us." Nita agrees with Dee Dee, and she has a related theory on elderly people.

"When old people start gettin' old, they don't move as much, and they don't move as fast. That's the beginnin' of the dyin' scene. It's like they just die little by little. They stop doin' some things as fast as they used to, and then after a while they not doin' anything, and that means that they just finished dyin'. But usually the people have been dyin' for a very long, long time. You know, it's just that it takes some people longer than others."

Nita accepts only some of Dee Dee's celestial explanations of her behavior—and even those with a healthy skepticism—but she finds them invariably stimulating and entertaining. Her verbal reaction is: "If that's what it's all about, then I enjoy being a Gemini because I like to stay in touch with all that aliveness, life makin' you move. It's like it's springtime inside you all year 'round."

And she doesn't deny what Dee Dee says about the Gemini spirit inside fighting its way out, "and all that." She always sensed that she was voracious of life and endowed with an abundance of energy and aspired to do something different and unusual. She doesn't want to be using her hands all the time or even mainly. She says, "I can be very happy watchin' television or anything like that. If my mind keeps goin', it's all right." She loves to watch people dance, all kinds of dances, and she dances rather well herself. She can sit and watch dances for hours on end because to her it's "like it's doin' something. When you watch motion and things in action, you are a part of it." She likes to go to the zoo and watch the animals.

Her grandmother seems to have been the most important person in Nita's life. They spent many mutually happy times together. Being with her grandmother for long periods of time was necessitated by her mother's frequent trips to jail. "She was always, you know, on stuff," ever since Nita can remember.

Nita's grandmother seems to have been a colorful and fascinating woman. She was suffering with cancer and eventually died, but to ease the family anguish about her impending death, she ceaselessly joked about it. Nothing was more exemplary of this woman's magnificent fortitude than the vivid memory Nita conveys of "Mama" lying in a solitary spot on a bed, being painfully devoured by mankind's most heinous disease and never faltering for one second in her role as the matriarchal tower of power for those whom she loved. The old, feisty dowager surely would have expired sooner had she not been too concerned about her family to relinquish life, despite the agony of its extension.

By the time she encountered cancer, Mama was an old veteran of life's trials and tribulations. She had been amply conditioned to cope with cancer. One of the first lessons she learned in life was to endure, so cancer was light stuff.

She had five kids, and they all became junkies, and she had to be forever chasing behind them, getting them out of trouble and into some hospital for a cure, and then taking care of her grandchildren. This was the story of her life for many years.

Nita became very sophisticated in the ways of women all too soon, as a result of living with her grandmother, sharing her plight, and empathizing with the old matron. She said she thought her grandmother was much closer to her than she'd ever been with any of her own children, and more candid in conversation when telling her things about life and about womanhood. She said her grandmother told her that nature gives a person a natural douche, and women, "If they livin' a clean life, they don't have to worry about that sorta thing 'cause nature will take care of it and clean a woman out at least once a month."

While lying in the hospital jeering at the horrid disease, Mama would be joking about the effects of the male hormones with which the doctors were treating her illness. At that time her grandmother was almost seventy years old, and she had begun to feel renewed sexual urges as an effect of the testosterone injections she'd been receiving. Nita said Mama told her that before she started "messing around" with the male hormones, she had thought that women were really more sex-driven than men because she always had trouble with Nita's mother and her sister. They had been getting into trouble with sex and boys since grade school, and getting pregnant when they were very young and before they were married. And being a woman, she knew about her own urges. But, she said, "Not until I got on this male-hormones kick did I find out that men really have some strong sex urges, and no wonder they go around rapin' people and gettin' all carried away because it's nothin' they can do to stop it."

She kept everyone's spirits buoyed until the affliction stole her voice and ultimately her life. Her grandmother told her that before the hormones she had thought men could do pretty much the same thing as a woman. When she got an urge she could handle it, sort of repress the urge for a while, by simply concentrating on something else. But once she got on the hormones, she realized that men couldn't do that. It just "isn't that easy, they got to get out and do somethin'."

And she used to joke about how lucky she was not to have been born a man. "You know, I wouldn't have time to do nothin' else." And she also felt lucky that the cancer came as late in life as it did, and she didn't get "these male hormones" when she was a young mother, because "I mighta had two sets o' quintuplets by now." As a matter of fact, she said, if she had been a younger woman, messing with hormones and getting these feelings as strong as she was getting them then, she might have "been goin' around like rapin' some man."

Nita's grandmother was quite a gal, and it's understandable why she admired her so much. She says Jill reminds her of her grandmother "because she thinks, and she's sort of wise and sort of knowin' in the same way that Mama was."

An air of respectful envy can easily be detected in the other Hamites when Nita reminisces about her grandmother.

Nita says that her grandmother looked more like her than anyone in the family. Her grandfather was a rather admirable person also. He loved all black women. She says her grandfather's controlling drive was "a need to love 'em all, and since he couldn't have 'em all, I mean bein' one man, he didn't marry any of 'em. He just kept on lovin' 'em. He serviced 'em all, or at least he tried to service all the women, it seems, in the whole world. Every black woman. I think that was his life's ambition."

She knows that he must've loved her grandmother at some time or other, and she doesn't feel bad about his not marrying her. "All people ain't cut out for that."

Nita says she'd like to have some kids, and one day she might want to get married, but she doesn't care about that so much. She says, "The marriage thing is man-made, you know, those are man-made rules and customs, but havin' kids is natural for a woman. That's nature-made, and there's just no way to get around that. I'm gonna do what comes natural. Now, the husband thing, I might do that, and I might not. And if I don't, so what? There's nothin' lost."

She sees nothing wrong about having babies without being married if a woman can handle it. And she says she knows she'll be able to handle it, and she wouldn't want to have to depend on anybody, anyhow. Nita has a strong sense of independence. You sit down and talk to this young sister, and you just know that she's going to make it. Whatever happens, Nita is going to be out there winning because that's the kind of person she is. She has this healthy sense of herself. She's got a lot of confidence, and she's got a winning personality. She's a born winner, a hell-raiser, a breech baby, fulfilling her destiny to raise hell.

EIGHT

Shaft

Shaft, who adopted his nickname from the movie hero, is the only member of the Hamites who has really been strung out or had a legitimate scag jones. He got strung out when he was fourteen. Shaft has some very interesting and almost horrifying experiences to relate about his drug experience, and he tells other members of the Hamites about them from time to time to deter them from that path of unrighteousness or certain destruction.

Shaft moved into his aunt's place on the block after his mother and father died. "My pops got offed in a stickup. My moms died two years later from a methadone-and-wine mix. She took a whole tab and a half a tab, and she was drinkin' a lotta wine, you know, and just went to sleep for the last time. That was about a hundred and fifty milligrams of methadone and wine."

His jones almost led him to the same fate, but he says he first took scag by mistake. A partner of his had brought some blow (cocaine) to school and given him some. "And I dug it." Then, about a week later, "We went to a party, and he slipped me a piece of tinfoil, and I thought it was some more blow, but it turned out to be scag, and I liked that more than the blow. It made me feel hipper than I'd ever felt in my life. I had to try it again and again. It gave me a real mellow feelin'. At that time there was a lotta quinine in the heroin, and it had me stranglin' when I snorted it, and that was cool, too. I mean, I dug that, too. That was maybe the big part of the whole scag cool, you know, always havin' to draw the stuff down from your nose and all that. It was kinda cool, like somebody who had a permanent cold. I dug it, so I kept on snortin', but I had every intention of makin' it a weekend thing."

He did limit it to the weekends for about three weeks. Then, he says, he began to cut classes and to play hooky, at which times he and the other fellows would chip in and buy some dope. "I had a snortin' jones," he said. "I had to snort three or four bags to get high, and that was becomin' sorta expensive."

Next, Shaft was introduced to skin-popping. "One Friday night I was goin' to a dance with a partner o' mine. We stopped in a hallway, and he pulls out a bag o' scag and says, 'Let's get high.' I said, 'Man, that one bag wouldn't be half enough for me.'

"He said, 'Yes it will, if you skin-pop it.'

"I said, 'No, man, I don't put no kinda needles in my arm.'

"He said, 'It ain't goin' hurt you. Ain't nothin' to be scared of. You'll hardly feel it, and the high will be like you snorted nine or ten bags.'

"The last sales pitch made me feel that I should at least try it. I let him give me my first skin-pop. When I saw that he had only a 'G-shot' in the dropper, you know, just that little bit around the needle's nose, I said, 'Man, that ain't enough to get nobody high.'

"He went on and fired me up, and that was the best high I ever had. So from then on, I was skin-poppin' for about three months. I felt like a fool because I'd been spendin' all that money for so long, but all I had to do was cop one three-dollar bag and skin-pop it. I wanted to kick myself in the ass with a iron boot.

"But soon I needed more and more bags of scag to get high by skin-poppin', so I went to mainlinin'. I was in Philly with some fellows, and we only had two bags to split up among four of us. We was goin' to a party and wanted to get high first, so, like before, I started complainin' that the two bags wouldn't get all of us high. And my partner said, 'Yes, it will, we gonna mainline.'

"I was a little scared when I first heard this remark because all the while I was usin' stuff I had not yet come to see myself as a bona fide junkie. To me I was just a dabbler, and mainlinin' was a serious junkie act. And at that time I didn't want to be a junkie, I mean because junkies was always dirty, always dirty and greasy, and they looked bad. I didn't wanna be lookin' like a junkie. But after watchin' two of the fellows mainline and seein' how good they seemed to be feelin', the fear left me, and I couldn't wait to try it. I tried it, and it was outta sight. Then it became like a everyday thing. It was impossible to go back to skin-poppin, because mainlinin' was a deeper high and it lasted longer than the skin-poppin'.

"As time went by, I had to face the fact that I was a junkie. I saw myself gettin' dirtier and dirtier with people, not the way I was lookin', but the things I was doin'. I was runnin' some real low stuff up under people. I was doin' some foul acts, man. I once gave a partner of mine a water shot and insisted it was scag. When he dug it and started squawkin', that was the day I admitted to myself I was a junkie, you know, a straight-up, unmitigated, certified grade A-one dope fiend.

"I got my first dope-cravin' sickness and thought I'd come down with a cold or a virus. There I was, wishin' that this cold and other misery would go away, and somehow I just knew that if I could get a shot of dope I'd be okay. I got the shot, it cured the misery, and I knew that I had a jones. And I knew that each time the sickness came it would be worse than it was before. I had heard about it. And sho'-nuff, it was.

"It wasn't until much later that I found out all dope fiends, when they first get a jones, refuse to believe that they have a habit. We tell ourselves we have a cold, a virus, flu—everything but the truth. You have to give yourself a story, the truth is too hard to live with. Usually we really believe it until somebody who knows runs it down to you that you don't really have the flu and a shot of dope would straighten you out. You know, like I was in bed takin' everything possible for the flu. Even went to the doctor. My doctor prescribed some flu medicine for me, after examinin' me, too. Maybe he wasn't hip to it, or maybe he just went to nut city on me and didn't want to get involved and just gave me some other stuff. But he prescribed somethin' for flu.

"No doubt about it, scag is the best high in the world. If it was not for the fact that you always get a jones, and it's so expensive, it would be great. But the jones makes you such a dirty dude, it makes you just a foul person. You start hatin' yourself behind some of the numbers you do. I hate to think about some of the things I did when I was jonesin'. I once beat up a crippled old man and took his watch, but I didn't care if I hurt him or killed him. I had to get me some bucks. The old man was black, too, but you know how that is, nobody means nothin' to a dope fiend.

"If I had the bucks, I mean if I was rich, I'd stay high all the time. And I wouldn't look bad. I wouldn't have the scars that junkies have and wouldn't be all swollen 'cause I wouldn't even be hittin' myself. I'd have a doctor who would be paid just to hit me when I want it. The sores and the swellin', that comes from junkies bein' so anxious they usually miss the vein. If you had a doctor who was a professional dude with a needle, you wouldn't have to worry 'bout that action. Everything would be cool. For me that would be the only sensible way to get high, or the only way that any dude should wanta mess with scag, I mean if he feels that he has to. And a very few dudes are in a position to mess with it like that. So that's why I don't bother with it no more myself.

"I coulda stopped before 'cause I knew how dangerous it was. I got messed around. I had a brother on stuff. And the reason I started messin' with scag, and methadone, I mean once I tasted it or tried it and knew what it was all about, that's what the crowd that I was in was doin'. I wanted to be with the in crowd. I just came up from down South and was hangin' out with Mae's daughter Sheryl, and her crowd was into it and they used to put me down for not bein' hip. You know, they called me a gator and all that. I wanted to be as swift as everybody else was, you know. I was born up here in New York City, but when I was real young I went down South, and I was down there for ten years, since I was three or somethin' like that. So I really didn't know anything about drugs. I just wanted to be down with the crowd. So everything they did, I did it, too. I thought it was beautiful, and everybody else seemed to dig it, so I guess eventually I just did it, too. I mean who knew anything about a habit or narcotics? Not me! I just got off the bus from Georgia.

"I started out my dope-fiend career like most people, standin' around a lot and peepin' in, and one day like just sort of sneakin' up on it. The people I was hangin' out with was just doin' it. I knew it was comin' one day, even though I was a little leery about it, when I couldn't back out when they offered me some. Besides, it woulda looked like I was scared of a needle. And that'd be a real jive thing to have to live down. So, I got righteously messed up. The first time I ever tried scag, I fell madly in love with 'the white boy,' and been faithfully devoted to him ever since.

"Of course, as time went on, I had to use more and more. That's the way the thing goes. The need had me doin' fool stuff, stealin', burglarizin', takin' off places, people, in a matter of months. Before I realized it, I had stopped carin' about anything, anybody. Family, sister, brother—nothin' mattered but scag. If I knew where anybody had some money, I would steal it in a minute. Scag had become my god, and I would do anything to get it. You know, it's like heroin casts a spell over you and makes you a dirty, triflin' kinda dude. You don't care 'bout nobody, not even yourself. I had become a dog, man, a sho'nuff, sho'nuff dog. I shoulda known better because my older brother was a dope fiend, and my aunt was always sayin', 'Don't be like yo' brother.'

"I dug my brother, even though he had a monstrous jones. But when I started usin' dope I wasn't tryin' to be like my brother or anybody else. I liked it, that's all. I always had my aunt's sermon in the back of my mind, you know, 'Don't be like yo' brother.' And I was determined not to be like him 'cause even though I dug him the most, I knew that the dude was wrong. I mean sho'nuff foul."

"How did you kick?" I asked him. "Did you go to a drug-rehabilitation program of some kind at that young age, or how?"

"No, I went back down South. I stayed down there about three months and got sick. I knew I had to get away from that stuff. I figured that bein' down there I wouldn't be able to get none 'cause nobody knew what it was. After I had got sick and was goin' around actin' funny, like I be walkin' past people who knew me. They'd see me in the town, and I be sick and messed up. I was in such deep misery I'd just say, 'Hey.' I didn't have time to stop or couldn't bring myself to stop and say anything to anybody. Some of the people who had heard that I'd gotten back would come by the house, and I wouldn't even say anything to 'em. I just told 'em that I was sick, and nobody knew what was really comin' off. So after three days I got cool. I went out, and I talked to the people 'round there, and everybody accepted the story that I was sick, but things had gotten back to normal and it was cool.

"About a month later I found out that they had the stuff in the town, but I just wasn't ready, and I couldn't get that much money down there. I just wasn't ready to get caught by that monster again. And when I came back to the Apple, I was determined to go back to school and get that thing cooled out. You know, like I saw some of the fellows that I used to get high with, and I'd just tell 'em, 'No, man, I'm straight now, I cleaned up. I don't mess with that scag no more."

"And once in a while I would be tempted, but then I was hangin' out with the fellows here in the spot, and we used to do a different scene, and that real good smoke was around, the monster. There was really no need to, and every time I thought about it, I thought about all that money, and I didn't want to take my aunt through no more changes.

"It's like I just made up my mind, and I haven't touched any of it since. But I know that's the most mellow high out there, and if I could afford it I'd probably just go on and do that. But since I know what it's gonna do to me, I can't take that greasy thing 'cause I got a lotta pride. It hurts me to be hangin' out like those dope fiends out there, you know, dirty, sick, lookin' pitiful, and waitin' to cop, and everybody feelin' sorry for you. I couldn't go through those kind of changes, man, not anymore. It wasn't really hard for me to kick, but if I hadn't gone down South, I probably never woulda done it. I woulda stayed here and kept on doin' the things that I was doin'."

"You don't think that you'll ever backslide or start dabbling again?"

"Not unless I was to get rich. If I was rich, I would go on and do it because I could afford it, not like the average dude out there on the street, with a job, say, makin' a couple a hundred dollars a week. I wouldn't try it then because your BR [bankroll] can't handle it. Maybe you could handle it that way for about a year, but it keeps on makin' more and more demands on you financially. You gotta lose if you lay with it long enough. No, I wouldn't try it unless I got rich, I mean filthy rich.

"Besides, let me tell you another thing. Like when you're livin' in Harlem, like you gotta be careful because it's so easy to go to jail in Harlem. Practically everybody goes to jail here sooner or later for somethin' or other because it's so much temptation out there. Just about anything that ordinary people do, you can get busted for in Harlem.

"You know, people probably smoke as much herb downtown in ritzy neighborhoods as they do in Harlem—and probably more because they can afford more down there—but nobody goes down there makin' any kind of busts. But you get busted in Harlem for it. And you probably sure to get busted here for things that maybe the police think is more serious than some herbs. Like if you snortin' blow or something, you can get busted. They just stop you on the street here because I've had it happen to me a whole lotta times, and search you, ask you where you been, and talk some garbage about a stickup or somethin', or somethin' went down someplace and somethin' criminal came off. They just say somebody looked like you. If you clean, they say, 'Go on, it wasn't you.' You supposed to be grateful. If you go somethin' on you like a little bit of stuff, like some scag, or some blow like for your own use, it's like you gotta pop just for that.

"If you were one of them rich dudes who live in the rich neighborhoods downtown, ain't nobody gonna stop you, talkin' about somethin' came off, some kinda takeoff or somethin'. You could be walkin' 'round with a quarter-pound of stuff or half a key in your pocket, and the raise ain't gonna be messin' with you or takin' you through changes like they would up here. It's like just livin' in a place like Harlem you gotta be extra careful 'cause this is where the raise gonna come when they wanta make busts.

"Yeah, this is the huntin' ground for busts. Like when they wanna pop somebody on somethin' that's jive, they don't go downtown. They come up to Harlem 'cause this is the place they make their busts. It's like just goin' huntin'. Police got a license to hunt everybody in Harlem, and it's always open season. You gotta be extra careful livin' here not to be flagged, especially if you doin' somethin'. You know how it is and how bad they wanta flag somebody here.

"We don't have any static here in the spots, ain't too many people comin' in here. Somebody can boost somethin', take somebody off, and run in here. The raise is always runnin' past the buildin' and tryin' to make like they didn't see where the dude ran because they know it's dangerous to come in here. The lights is out, and probably all the raise around here know that those two steps are missin'. The police don't know where the stairs is exactly, and if they come up in the dark, somebody could just take 'em off, 'cause we got no lights. If they get up on the second floor here and they miss one o' them steps, they gonna be in the hospital and they sex life is gonna be finished. So they ain't too anxious to come in here.

"The spots are kinda cool, this buildin' bein' as treacherous as it is, and they hip to it. They don't wanna come in anyplace where it's dark and dangerous. The raise who're hip to it don't come in here, even if somebody tells 'em that some dude did somethin' and ran into this buildin'. They gonna try to nut it off because they know that the buildin's not supposed to be gone into by anybody who is a stranger.

"So we sit in here and do our thing. We usually don't have to worry about nothin' 'cause we got that big cowbell on the door downstairs anyhow. If people like come in and don't jingle it twice, we know that's the wrong people, and by the time they would get up here to the second floor, if they could make it, we can clean up anything that we doin'. They could smell some herbs, but they couldn't say that anybody wasn't burnin' tea in here, smokin' asthma cigarettes, you know. This place has been pretty cool.

"If you had dope fiends hangin' 'round, you couldn't keep it cool 'cause junkies don't know how to keep a cool. When you use stuff, you may think you cool, but if you standin' on the outside peepin' somebody who is usin' it, you know, he ain't cool. You seein' somebody noddin', and half the time he don't even know where he's at. And the dude could take off if he's jonesin', he could take off if he's got some of that dyno scag, he could have fifteen decks, three-dollar bags of scag, in his hand and take off, go into one o' them five-minute nods, and that's like askin' the police to come on in here and get you.

"That's another reason we don't want any o' them junkies in here. They'd probably blow the whole thing, not to mention that they steal everything. They take all the pipes, plumbin', and stuff out, and down it. We still got runnin' water in here, and this is one of the few condemned buildin's on the block where there's still runnin' water 'cause like the junkies took the pipes from the other joints and they downed 'em. If we ever let 'em get in here, they'd do the same thing. They was tryin' at first, for a while. You heard about the static we had when we first took over and had to get 'em out. But now they know where it's at. They know if they come in here and try to rip somethin' off, what's gonna happen. Like we'd probably throw them out the window, and they don't wanna go through that. So they stay clear. We sort of got a understandin' goin'."

Shaft likes to say that Sheryl turned him out, that is, put him on the corner like a prostitute or something, made him prostitute himself. Of course, Sheryl never did this to Shaft, but that's how he refers to it. He says Sheryl turned him on to scag. But Sheryl turned many people on to scag because she had so much. She was dealing it for her mother, and it was always around the crib. She felt that she could give it to anybody she wanted to, and she seemed to feel during those times before she'd really got strung out tough, before she had a heavy jones that had become a problem to her, that anybody who hadn't tried scag hadn't lived. And so she was always pressuring people around her, anybody she knew who wasn't on stuff, to try it at least once. "You know, fly, and see how high you can go, and see what life is really all about. She really thought that life was all about scag or bein' high on it."

Now, Shaft believes that the Devil is a woman, and the woman is Sheryl. He said he'd never met, in his entire life, a young girl who was quite as daring as Sheryl. "Sheryl would try anything at least once. She did all kinds of crazy acts, and she wanted other people to do nut numbers with her. When she was fourteen, fifteen, she was always doin' things that most of the fellows wouldn't do, didn't have enough heart to do, and she would get out there and start agitatin' people into doin' things that they didn't want to do, tellin' 'em that they didn't have any heart. She had some dudes doin' some heavy stuff. Her regular mix was speed and coke and scag when other people was scared to even shoot up. She would tell 'em, 'Oh, you ain't got no real high, you know, until you had a speed mix, with some scag and with some coke, you know, gettin' those rushes both ways, downers and the uppers.'

"She wasn't scared o' nothin', and she'd make it seem like a sin for anybody else to be scared. Like yeah, man, I know that broad, I guess she turned a whole lotta people onto the fast life. She turned a lotta people onto scag who would never have messed with it in they lives, especially if they had to pay for it. But because she was out there with so much, and givin' it away, I guess some people who didn't know what to do with themselves anyway, said, 'Why not? Come on, let's get high.'

"She used to like to mess with people like that, get 'em sort of dependent on her for the high, and then she'd cut 'em loose. She wasn't gonna give 'em nothin' no more, and they'd have to start throwin' rocks to support the jones Sheryl gave to them.

"Sheryl did all kinds of weird and strange numbers. Remember that time when her brother got busted for the ride? Well, it was actually Sheryl's car. About a year ago Sheryl had just came outta jail. That's where she started goin' with this white broad. You know, I think Sheryl always had some butch in her. Or it might have just beein somethin' new for her to try. So, anyway, while she was in jail, she'd tighten up with this white girl, so when she came out it's like Sheryl and the white broad, they started like butchin' around in Harlem. And needless to say, they both had a jones. Sheryl's done had like two or three cures, supposedly. I mean she's kicked it a couple of times, but she digs it, and she wants to keep goin'. She and this white girl, her name was Cindy, they used to always be stealin' things and doin' crazy dope numbers and sellin' garbage drugs and jive hot goods, gettin' into fights with dudes. It's like they was really hooked up, they was married. Sheryl's mom, Miss Mae, just accepted them bein' as tight as they was. She was into so much larceny, I guess she could just accept anything. Well, that's how the crib got busted that time, you know, the crib that they had on 148th Street. It got busted behind Sheryl and her numbers.

"This crazy white broad stole a ride, brought it uptown from where she stole it in some white neighborhood. She let whatchama-callum, Manny, Sheryl's brother, borrow the car, Manny and his stuff, Elaine. He's all banged up, you know, like he was on that methadone, scag, and wine, and he was just sort o' swervin' all out in the street. The raise sort of pinned him for a while, drivin' in a crazy fashion, lookin' like he was drunk, and when he stopped, the raise pulled up in front of him, stuck a gun into the driver side of the car, and told him to get outta the car slow, with his hands in front o' him.

"The dude jumps outta the car, and he's just so messed up he could hardly stand. And the raise asked him for his driver's license and registration, and he says he left them upstairs. He told 'em like he'd go up there and get it, and they said okay, because they knew he'd come back for his stuff. Elaine was his main squeeze, you know, but the cat was just so messed up that he went upstairs. He knocked on the door, and they opened the gates and the door and all. You remember, they had gates on all the apartments. You know, every time Miss Mae would set up her dope shop someplace, one of the first things she'd put up was the gates.

"Well, anyway, it seems that he forgot that he'd left his stuff, Elaine, down in the car. He just wanted to get away from the raise, so he goes into a bedroom and out the fire-escape window. Maybe he was gonna go over the roof or somethin', I don't know. But I think he was too high to make it to the top fire-escape landin', so he got up there, fell out, and went to sleep.'

"Now the raise is waitin' and they puttin' pressure on, takin' Elaine through some changes and askin' her, 'Well, look, where did he go?' They all went up there and knocked on the door, but nobody would let 'em in, and so they outside makin' all that noise about bein' the law, like open up the door in the name of the law, and Miss Mae was cleanin' up, tryin' to get rid of some of the hot goods that look like hot goods, and all the stuff she had around that she couldn't flush down the toilet at one time.

"So she put it all in the shoppin' bag, and she'd just open the back window and throw the stuff out in the backyard. When things got cool later on, she could go down there and get it. Or she'd try and throw it down on the fire escape a couple of floors below, so she could run out there and get it once the police had split.

"The raise looked like two fools out there makin' all that noise, so they got mad, got a ax outta the trunk o' they car, and came up and tore down the gates and the door. They went lookin' for Manny, and they saw a whole lotta stuff that didn't look too cool, like she couldn't get rid of everything. It never looked like an apartment, you know, it looked like a variety wholesale house. She had some of everything in that crib. She had everything in there but a Cadillac.

"Anyway, it's like when the raise couldn't find him, they arrested Mae, you know, for helpin' him get in the wind, but then some woman who lived up on the top floor told the police that there was a man outside on her fire escape, sleepin'.

"When they got in the crib, Elaine told the raise it was Cindy's ride, and they started hasslin' her. Sheryl went into her act and started gettin' stupid, she's goin' to war because they all high and everything. Sheryl is there, comin' out her mouth, tellin' the raise, you know, like what they not gonna do to her woman, meanin' Cindy, and the raise got mad because they white police and here's this black broad talkin' about this white broad is her woman.

"Well, it came off that the raise beat Sheryl and Cindy's asses and arrested 'em, and they also arrested Miss Mae about the apartment, and then they went out on the fire escape and arrested Manny. Everybody got busted, but it didn't matter too much to Manny because he didn't know what was goin' on. When he did get his head back together several days later, he started blamin' the whole scene on Sheryl, and it probably was Sheryl's fault for bringin' that crazy ol' white broad around there.

"Sheryl's turned a whole lotta people on to scag, you know, and they've gone on to some real mean scenes. Some people have OD'd, you know, people have been messed up in all kinds o' ways.

"This friend of Sheryl's, Pearl, had a stroke, and she was only about seventeen, but she used to shoot so much scag and blow and take so much methadone—she was tryin' to keep up with Sheryl —that she couldn't last long. Sheryl has been usin' stuff since she was thirteen, and she's got a drug tolerance of ten horses. Nobody can keep up with her, but everybody is always tryin'. It's a wonder that this broad ain't killed herself.

"Sheryl tried to turn Chips on, but Chips was too swift. He just went for the bucks. She was always givin' Jill some dope when she wanted it. She would like to see Jill get back on the stuff so she could have a runnin' partner again. You know, one who's out there and who's swift and who really digs her. Broads don't dig her too tough. And she knows that she can trust Jill, like farther than she can trust anybody else. Because there ain't a whole lotta people around who really dig Sheryl for herself 'cause Sheryl can be a wrong and vicious and foul sorta broad mosta the time. I've seen her get so catty with broads that I can't see how any broad can really dig her.

"Sheryl's in big trouble. She's got this sort of ego trip goin'. She's on a ego trip where she wants to run every show, you know, and be tellin' everybody what to do. A whole lotta people go for it just for the drugs, and dudes will go along with it because, you know, they can always get some bucks if they hangin' out with her, and she'd always be supportin' they jones.

"I hung out with her when I first came back here, and I was only fourteen when I showed back from down South. It was somethin' big for me to be hangin' out with Sheryl, as swift as she was, and she always had a whole lotta money and she was always givin' you things.

"The broad really taught me how to dress, what kinda threads to wear. And not only that, I knew what kinda threads I liked, but I couldn't afford 'em. But Sheryl could afford 'em. She always wanted the dudes who was hangin' around her to look kinda swift, too. She she would say, 'Here, I thought you'd like this, so why don't you try wearin' it?' And of course I'd go along with the program, especially after I started like messin' with scag because it's like then I sorta had to depend on her to keep my head right.

"Sheryl liked to make people dependent on her. She would just give you a little bit to hang you up anytime you needed some drugs, and you thought you had a gold mine. You'd found a slave and a servant, but before you knew it you were her slave and her servant. You know, anytime she snapped her fingers you was jumpin' because she was holdin' the golden bag, the scag bag. And everybody was gonna jump for that, everybody who had a jones.

"The broad is really a witch. She had a kid, and she never was much of a mother. She'd been through a whole lotta stuff. She was screwin' grown men since she was about ten years old. The truth is that Sheryl is the Devil, and you know what they say about the Devil. It's like fire don't burn him. Any other broad Sheryl's age who had gone through half of the stuff that Sheryl's been through would be dead by now.

"Lemme tell you what this broad did to me, man. It's like she used to go to this beauty parlor, you know, 'round there on Eighth Avenue, that this snake owned—yeah, that tall, ugly faggot. Anyway, she shot on me about this snake had a thing for me, and I'm sayin', 'Yeah, well, you know that ain't my shot, baby.'

"I wasn't payin' no attention to it at first, and I just figures there goes Sheryl on another one of her excitement trips. Like sometimes life just gets too slow for her, and she does a whole lotta crazy things just, you know, to make life become a little more excitin'. A week after she shot on me about the snake, she told me to meet her at the beauty parlor. Sheryl wasn't there, but the snake was there, and he was doin' another broad. He told me that Sheryl had said she was goin' to be there and that he should tell me to wait for her. So I said that's cool. I just sat there, and he started talkin', tryin' to get into my business. I'm nuttin' on him, just tellin' him no more than I have to. He finished the customer's hair, and she left. After a while he just came on out with it, brought it down front, and said, 'Now, you know she's not comin'. You not really expectin' Sheryl anymore, are you? Don't you know that she did this for me?'

"I said, 'Man, ain't this a damn shame?'

"I told the dude I didn't have anything against him, but snakes just wasn't my thing. I was really mad at that broad. I said, 'When I see her I'm gonna beat her ass, I'm gonna put somethin' on her behind.' I didn't see her for two days. She'd gone someplace and was shackin' up with somebody and gettin' high. But it turned out that the whole thing was over.

"You can't say that you was in love with Sheryl or anything like that, or that Sheryl was in love with somebody else, because you know the broad just ain't made that way. She don't fall in love with nobody. She likes to run through as many dudes as she can, you know, see what everybody is all about. It's like she just always liked a new bag, like new toys until she played 'em out. I guess she dug me, you know, and wanted to shove me aside as gentle as she could, and maybe that's the way she saw as the easiest way to do it. What she had done was gave me to her beautician, who was a snake, ain't that somethin'? The broad got tired of me and gave me to a faggot.

"But when I ran up on her a few days later, my jones was down on me, and I couldn't think about whippin' her ass or anything. I was lookin' for her to get some dope. I had gotten kind of lazy and everything because I didn't have to hustle. That's like takin' a animal out of the jungle, a lion or a tiger or somethin' who has to hunt for his food all the time, and you take him out and you start feedin' him, put him in a zoo or someplace where he don't have to hunt for food, he's not in the jungle and he don't have to sweat nothin'. It's all comin' to him three times a day even if he don't move durin' the whole day. He gets fat and lazy, and after a while he loses his huntin' ability. And that's what happened to me.

"I'm there beggin' her and all that noise, sick as I can be, and she said no, she can't do it 'cause she ain't got none, and she can't be givin' me anybody else's. So I knew our thing, whatever it was, was over. But then I got scared because I knew that by that time I had a sho'nuff, sho'nuff jones. I mean my jones was serious by then. It's like I was doin' about forty dollars a day, and I was scared because I knew that I'd lost my survival ability out there on the street. It had been about a year since I'd been out there hustlin' to keep that sickness away, and I didn't know what I was gonna do. I almost panicked. I begged her and begged her, but, you know, she's a pretty cold broad, and she just kept sayin' no, she couldn't do it. I hadn't been chasin' the bag for so long or out there scroungin' to get that sickness off, and I really didn't know where to start.

"My sickness was gettin' meaner and meaner all the time. I had to come up with somethin', and quick. It took me about a hour, and all I had was four dollars, so I saw this old man comin' up the hall stairs, and, you know, I just hit him. I knocked him down, went through his pockets, took his watch, like real fast.

"Yeah, but the broad was so cold, man. It's hard to imagine a woman as young as her bein' as cold as she is. It's like she's got a lotta Miss Mae in her. If she wasn't on stuff, she could be a dynamite businesswoman, and if any one of them should take over Miss Mae's business one day, it'll probably be Sheryl because Sheryl's the swiftest thing out there.

"My whole life woulda been different, much different, if I had never met Sheryl. I was just dabblin' in stuff a little bit when I met her, and she kept sayin' how much of a creep I was because I didn't do anythin' but smoke pot. She'd say, 'Oh, you still on that pot, huh?' Make it sound like, 'Oh, you still usin' that greasy kid stuff?' And it was a put-down, so actually I had to come on in, and I guess I fell victim to the Devil, too. The chick made me do a whole lotta things that I know I never woulda done had I never met her. But she taught a lot, too. She just might be one of the swiftest broads out there, in this neighborhood, next to Jill.

"Jill is one swift sister, too. I'm not puttin' nothin' on her, but she's probably much swifter than Sheryl is. Jill had enough sense to get up off stuff. She don't mess with nothin', she don't even mess with any methadone now, and Jill said she used to really dig methadone. It might be a toss-up between Jill and Sheryl as to who knows the most about life, about dudes, about dope, about hustlin', about everything connected with the street. Jill would probably know a little bit more. Jill's been out there on her own in the street for a long time, and the truth is that Sheryl ain't never been all the way out there. Miss Mae gets mad at her sometimes and puts her out, but that's her daughter and she's never gonna see her fall but so low. She'll always have a change of heart, soften up a little bit, you know, and let Sheryl come home. She does the same thing with Maggie and Manny, too. Those are her kids, and she ain't gonna be but so hard on 'em.

"Maybe you can't call 'em the real street dope fiends because they never had it as hard. Sometimes Miss Mae gets mad at 'em and they have to get out and hustle just like everybody else, be boostin' and takin' off people, doin' all kinds of real street action to get some dope, because they moms is a businesswoman and she ain't gonna let them put her outta business by usin' up all her stuff and beatin' her for all her money. But she is a mother, I mean she digs 'em and she ain't gonna let nothin' that she can help happen to 'em. So they've never had the real things go down with them that most junkies would have to suffer.

"I learned a whole lot of things from Sheryl. I learned a lot about women and the schemes they scheme and how they game on people from just layin' back, by pinnin' this broad when she be goin' through her games with people. She is a swift broad. You know, before she started lookin' so much older than she is and drug-worn, she was into a whole lotta things, and she used to get all kindsa offers, propositions, and opportunities to do things and to get into things that very few women got into.

"As a matter o' fact, I learned about addiction from Sheryl, not just scag addiction, but all kinds. It's like I could be with people whose jones was gettin' next to 'em and they'd be goin' through changes, too, but I'd be halfway up there, she would slip me somethin', just a little bit to get the pain away, and she would say, 'Look, why don't you sit back and peep these people, make believe that you still as sick as they are?'

"I would do it, and I would see what it was, you know, what the whole thing was about. I would see that bein' a alcoholic is just like bein' a junkie. It's just like bein' strung out on cigarettes, gotta have one, where you gonna really go into the jitters with what they call havin' a smokin' fit and all that sorta thing.

"All addiction is the same, if it's really addiction. When you can't get it, your mind goes off. You can't think like you would ordinarily think. If you on anything that you need, that you have to have because your system, you know, your biological system has gotten used to it, it sort of functions on that just as much as it functions on food. And with some things like scag, it becomes more dependent on that than it does on food. Needs it more. It really comes on you when you're addicted. You know, that's a thing that shows when you're not drinkin', when you're not smokin', when you're not usin' some stuff, when you're not high. That's what addictions is all about. It's when you're not usin' anything, and you need it, and you goin' through the jitters or you goin' through all kindsa pain, sickness, hallucinatin', or havin' tremors. It's like then you know that you're a junkie.

"Alcohol is just another drug, but so is nicotine, man. I learned that whole thing from Sheryl. And I learned a whole lotta other things from her, you know, like how broads get tired of people and how there's some broads who's always gotta try somethin' new to keep their interest goin'. I'd see other dudes that she was tight with would always be bringin' new dudes around to cut into her because they was swift enough to realize that when Sheryl was gettin' tired of 'em she was gonna be lookin' for new stuff somewhere, and if they didn't go out and provide it for her, bring somebody in, well, she was gonna split from 'em and get tired and find it herself.

"So what a whole lotta cats was doin', other dudes would beat her to the punch o' throwin' 'em aside or droppin' 'em by runnin' out and gettin', you know, like snatchin' up some dude for her and sayin' like, 'Here, here's your next squeeze. He's a friend of mine, and you know you got 'em through me.'

"They knew what kinda dudes she dug, like swift dudes, you know, and especially if it was a dude who wasn't on stuff, like she couldn't get him right away, so it's like she had to use the middleman for a while. That was the dude that cut her into the new one, or whoever she was hooked up with before. So what he was doin', in fact, was keepin' his thing with her together. Like she became dependent on him for gettin' to this new thing. And bein' the Devil that she was, you know, she always wanted to conquer another soul.

"She was a broad that never was happy just goin' to bed with somebody. And she pulled my coat on what was happenin' with the real people-to-people relationships. It's like for you to really be of value to people out there in that street life, they gotta have some kinda need for you. They gotta be dependent on you one way or another. It's gotta be somethin' that you know that you can provide for them—that only you can provide, yeah. Well, then you really got somebody uptight.

"She was really a schemer and a game player, and she used to like to get a whole lotta people in a room and play one off against the other. She was good at it. You had to admire the broad for it, for bein' able to do it and to teach people things.

"She taught me about how to whack scag, how to cut it, how much you needed to put with how much dextrose, and how to make a nice speed fix and shoot up. But more than that, she taught me how, when it came to cuttin' cocaine, how to put coke with some bakin' soda, and it would really be a thing for people who dug freezes and all that and was always tryin' to judge where the coke was at by the freeze.

"She said, 'Yeah, you can cut some coke that'll take a three if you were to cut it with some lactose. If you cut it with some bakin' soda, it'll take a four and a half and have people swearin' that they got some dynamite blow in their heads when they snort it, when they shoot it, too.'

"She taught me a whole lotta other little things, little halfway slick money games and how to look at stolen goods and all. It's like the broad is a teacher for anybody who's unfortunate enough to go to her school. But the whole thing is that you may not last the course out. I don't regret havin' known her, but I wouldn't wanna go through that sorta scene again, man, because like I said, that broad is the Devil.

"What I want to do now, you know, it's like I spent some time down on the farm, and I dug it. Everybody talks about the farm, like it's somethin' terrible, man, unhealthy or somethin', like it was diseased. But you know, when I was down on the farm, I dug it, and I had a whole lotta peace down there, and quiet, and it was a healthy life. You even breathe different. You feel better. So what I'd like to do one day, when things get right, when I'm through with school and everything, I'd like to go on and hook up with Dee Dee. I mean like hook up legally and buy a farm one day. Yeah, we'd go back down the way and live on the farm. We just might take Salt-Noody with us and let him grow a whole lotta mean smoke down there. He would dig that, too. It'd be a groovy thing because actually he ain't got no business in someplace like New York City. That dude is like as out of place in New York City as a barber pole is in a bathtub. It's just not him."

"Shaft, you say you're in love with Dee Dee, right?" I asked. "And you're planning on marrying her as soon as both of you finish school and you can get a place, right?"

"Yeah, man, like me and this woman, we got somethin' beautiful. Somethin' tight and real beautiful goin', and we gonna tighten it up all the way the first chance we get."

"Wasn't Dujo in love with her once, too?"

"Wait a minute, wait a minute, let me tell you about that. Dujo mighta thought he was in love with her, but the truth is that this girl is too deep for any of these dudes around here. They ain't swift enough to peep how deep she is. Dujo is a pretty swift dude as it goes, but Dujo is still in that stage where he's in love with sex and lotsa women, and he just don't know the difference. I mean that's all that was really happenin' with her and Dujo. I used to peep it when she and Dujo was into it. It's like sometimes he'd be draggin' her out to places, and she didn't wanta go. She wanted to be with him, and he be makin' her go out and hang out with the fellows. And I guess that's where she really got that habit from, the hangin'-out-with-the-fellows jones, bein' Dujo's woman for so long. He was treatin' her like almost one of the fellows, and she wasn't. He wasn't really that hip to what was goin' on with the broad.

"I mean like how sensitive she was and what her needs was all about. You know, that's somethin' that I peeped, and that's really how we got tight, because when Dee Dee'd be feelin' bad sometimes about some funny stuff that went down at the crib or somethin' that happened with one of her family like her brother, one of her brothers or sisters, like she be worryin' about 'em and feelin' low, you know, that dude really couldn't come on and get down with this. Like he be up there treatin' the broad just like all it was to her was the sex thing. And they'd be takin' it that way when sometimes the broad didn't need sex. What she needed was some understandin'.

"When I came on the set with her and we got tight, I mean I was just givin' her a understandin' thing. It's like she and Dujo, they thing was over by that time, but she wanted to hang out with me 'cause I wasn't comin' at her with a sex thing all the time. With me it was understandin', and she needed somebody to talk to, somebody who she could lay her head on his shoulder when the pressures come down on her. I guess Dujo really didn't wanta deal with it.

"You know, a whole lotta dudes are just like that. They dig a broad, I mean they dig the woman, but they don't wanta deal with her woman thing that women go through sometimes. They get into themselves, and things be botherin' them that they really can't talk to nobody about, and you gotta sorta like coax it out of 'em. And they wanta talk to somebody, but they don't feel right about it unless it's one of those broads who're always cryin' about somethin' anyhow, like them old jive broads who like to be complainin' all the time.

"Most broads don't wanna be layin' that on somebody all the time because they know the average dude's got his troubles, too, and he ain't got time to be just hearin' what's wrong with her because it's like she's always got somethin' wrong. Especially if the broad is kinda sensitive she's gonna try to keep that away from the dude, right? I mean if she digs him she don't wanna add to his problems. A broad like that, you gotta coax her out of it when she needs something. And when she goes out on a limb, you know, through that silent thing, and you can see she's kinda sad, it's like she needs somethin'. She needs a man to come in and say somethin' nice to her, to be sweet and gentle.

"Dujo just wasn't givin' the broad enough of that. She's not one o' them cryin' broads who's always got somethin' wrong with her or one of them broads who thinks she's a superfox and all that, you know, and she's always got some problems on 'cause that's all she wants to be. You know, just a walkin' problem. It that's where she was comin' from, I wouldn't be interested in her myself. But the broad, you can see the stuff that she is now. She's probably the downest member o' the group, or the swiftest member o' the family next to Jill. She'll do things for everybody, take care of everybody's problems, try and help everybody when they got some problems. The rest of these dudes around here, they can't peep that sometimes the broad might have problems, too. But they just go on off into they thing and always comin' out they mouths with some garbage or somethin' like she ain't really a person. Like she's just in here, one o' the things, and like she's almost one o' the dudes to them. Like they don't know.

"Dujo is swifter than most of the dudes here, but he wasn't swift enough to peep that Dee Dee had some needs and her needs're kinda deep. I was just interested in the broad. She knew it, and that's what it was all about. That's what she responded to.

"And if anybody really got to know her, just like I'm tellin' you these dudes really ain't that swift, I don't see how they could fail to be interested in this woman.

"Dee Dee can dress and keep herself together when she wants to, but she didn't care too much about that all the time she was goin' with Dujo, or before we hooked up. It's like all she was doin' was just throwin' on anything and actin' like she was supposed to act, like they were treatin' her, they gave her a role and she played it to the bust.

"But then, when we hooked up, she started carin' more about herself, I mean more about herself as a woman, and started tryin' to look like one and actin' more like one because she knew that there was somebody who saw her as a woman, I mean as opposed to just one o' the dudes who you might like to jam sometimes when your sex jones came down. And it did a whole lot for me, too, because I had never met a broad who was as together as Dee Dee is before we got into it. Yeah, I'd like to marry her.

"The way I look at this thing, it's like we got such a mellow thing going, why shouldn't I spend the rest of my life with her? I have never been as tight with a broad as I am with this girl now. I have never cared that much about any broad that I know, and I know a few broads. I don't claim to no straight-up dyno lover or somethin' like that. I been tight with some broads before, but I've never been like in this thing or as tight in this way with any broad because none of 'em ever had enough womanness in 'em to bring my thing out and make me wanna do somethin' for 'em or treat 'em as nice as I wanna treat Dee Dee. She makes me really worry about her and be concerned, be as much concerned as I am about myself. And if she wasn't the type of woman she is, like I couldn't have this feelin' comin' outta me, this feelin' for her, because it's like nobody else ever could do it to me, you know. And some of the broads I had, you know, I thought they was mellow.

"Like me and Connie was tight at one time, but Connie is like tighter with herself than she is with anybody else, and she really can't give as much as Dee Dee can. And so she don't make nobody wanna give to her. I think Connie is mellow people, and she's gonna be like a dynamite broad when she gets a couple of years older. She's gonna be too swift for all those dudes who know her now. We gonna look around, peep that girl, and say, 'Wow, is that the same broad?' But she just got a little growin' to do. She ain't got a whole lot goin' for her now, but I mean you could see it, the seed is there. You could see that the makin' is there, and maybe all she needs is the right dude. Not like me, I didn't have that much patience. With a girl like Dee Dee, you don't need that much patience. With Dee it's there but it's out in the open. You know, I mean she's, she's just really the best people you wanna meet. Of course I'm gonna marry her. I'm gonna marry her as soon as I can because I'll never meet a broad that mellow in my life again. Yeah, she is a once-in-a-lifetime stuff."

NINE

Connie

Connie is sixteen years old, unafraid of anything but the Hamites, and a little bit cynical. Her father is in jail in Pennsylvania, and the group consensus is that he's doing life because if you ask Connie how much time her father has, she answers, "Forever." Her mother keeps threatening to have her put away if she doesn't come home, but she's never taken any definite steps to carry out the threats, and Connie suspects that her mother is happy that she isn't at home.

She'd like to go to college far away from New York. "People in New York," or the people she knows in Harlem, as she puts it, "don't want to see anybody make it."

Connie thinks her whole family fell apart when her father went to jail. Up until that time, her mother and father used to take her and her two younger sisters to the national parks and other places on holidays. Not many people in Harlem, or at least in this neighborhood, do that sort of thing. It seems that she had a semblance of an average, normal American childhood, whatever that is. She thinks that it was a "freak thing that's not supposed to happen in Harlem," and having it happen for a little while does people more harm than good because you know it's something that's not coming again, and it leaves you sad for a long time. If she should ever have some children, she wants to do just what her mother and father used to do with them, all the same.

She remembers her father as a hardworking man who was really concerned about his family and proud of his daughters. She says she knows that he loved her and the rest of the family. He was the pillar of stability. When her father was at home her mother didn't drink, and after he went away she started and the family life began to erode. Her mother had a couple of other dudes come in and live with her for a while, but everything was not the same as when her father was there.

She doesn't know exactly what her father went to jail for. She knows that he killed somebody. Nobody would ever tell her exactly how it happened, and, knowing that her father was really a good man, she just assumed that somebody must have tried to rob him or wrong him and that he didn't have any other choice but to kill him. Some people have told her that if you have to kill somebody in self-defense, they usually don't give you life in any place, even Pennsylvania, but she doesn't listen to such logic.

Some of the Hamites say that Chips was the reason for Connie's becoming a cynic. She came into the group because she was in love with Chips. She was also a close friend of Nita, who introduced her to the family. That was shortly after Chips had gotten burned out of the other place he was staying. He used to be embarrassed about Connie because "She is so naive, even though she's sixteen, not just about the thing wit' her father bein' in jail forever in Pennsylvania, but she would say things like that her oldest sister who is twenty-two is still a virgin."

Members of the family would make fun of her because they were always trying to appear sophisticated. They would laugh. Chips started putting her down in front of the others, also. He said, "Hey, did you hear this broad? She said her sister is a twenty-two-year-old virgin. Man, even nuns ain't virgins by the time they hit twenty-three."

She felt hurt about it for a long while and became self-conscious of the things she was saying around the spot. But most of the members seemed to be pretty sensitive to the others and what their sensitive areas are all about. The other Hamites passed over it when they saw that she was feeling bad about it, and tried to make her feel that she hadn't said anything that was so wrong.

One of the few people she can really empathize with is Jill, and I suspect that's why she admires Jill so much. She thinks Jill is the swiftest person she's ever known. Jill told her that when she was younger, people thought she was naive or silly or stupid, and would not give her any respect or take her questions seriously when she asked about things. Now Connie is sort of in the same position.

When Connie wants to know something, she doesn't dare ask one of the fellows. She always goes to Jill. Jill is very protective of Connie. Jill knows that all the Hamites are hiding something about home life and all the family members are too tactful to try and dig it out. Everybody just waits and lets the various members tell what they want to tell, and nobody asks anything.

Connie is rather good in school, and she likes school. As a matter of fact, it's something of a puzzle as to why she does not want to go home, more so than any of the others, because she does have a mother nearby who expresses some concern for her from time to time, which is more than can be said for the others. The suspicion is that something more happened at home than she's told anybody about, but nobody pries into her affairs. Connie will do things for the group or for the members that the others won't do, or nobody else can do. She's got a lot of patience, and she's really the person best qualified to help with homework. Salt-Noody comes to her for help with his spelling.

Connie is proud of the fact that she can type forty-five words per minute. She is determined to teach Salt-Noody how to type before the year is out. All she needs is a typewriter, and Mumps has promised to get her one, for a price. Nobody knows exactly what the price is, but there are educated guesses being circulated.

Connie does favors for various members of the group. When it comes to making signs or writing somebody a birthday card or making a special birthday card or doing the Christmas card thing around the spot, she is ready.

Connie and Salt-Noody are the two picture people. Dujo and Salt-Noody brought the pictures of Malcolm X. She brought in Kennedy and Martin Luther King, the great men and martyrs. Some of the Hamites didn't want her putting these two in the best spot in the living room. They only wanted Malcolm X's picture. But she stood her ground. She put the three martyrs' pictures in the living room, and she's very proud of that. "Just one picture," she says, "would look like this is one of those militant places, especially if it was just one black picture."

She reads a lot and says the others should read, too, and get to know something about what's really happening in the country other than what they see in the movies and what they hear. She can read all day and all night. Sometimes the other members give her a hard time about it, but when she tells about what she's read they become attentive and listen. Connie is an excellent storyteller. And sometimes she writes book reports and essays. As a matter of fact, she does book reports for everybody in the group. She reads what they're supposed to read because she likes to do it, and that makes them refrain from teasing her for a while.

She has a definite place in the group. It's just that she hasn't learned yet to do the give-and-take exchange as well and as agressively as the others. But she's getting there, and in time she'll be holding her own and won't be having the trouble that she's had in the past by being so passive. It's just a matter of time. In the meantime, she has her good moments when she's really at home and knows that that's the place where she belongs. It's more than she's likely to get anyplace else, and she has decided to settle for it.

Nobody has a claim on Connie, and she doesn't have a claim on anyone. She's gone with a couple of the fellows, or been committed from time to time, but now she is sort of a free agent. She doesn't want to be committed to anyone, and nobody, apparently, wants to be committed to her. She accepts the fact now that Chips is not as interested in her as she once thought he was. Most of the Hamites like the idea of being uncommitted and everybody having the freedom to do whatever they might like to do at any given moment without having to answer to anyone or somebody having any kind of hold on them. It's just possible that's one of the reasons why they are not at home—not having to answer to anyone for anything. At the same time, the fellows are not tolerant of nonmembers getting too close to the girls in the group.

Connie once "hooked up" with a guy in the neighborhood who was not a member of the group. "Nobody really knew him well because he never hung out with us, but when he came around it's like the fellows would freeze him and let him know in no uncertain terms that he wasn't all that welcome. And he wouldn't come around after a while. He was always havin' some static with one of the fellows whenever he showed."

I think Connie knew that they were indirectly laying down some rules, like don't bring strangers in. Some of the fellows have girls who are not Hamites, but they don't bring them around. They don't hang out with them at the spots, and the girls don't come there to see them because the female Hamites can be quite cold, too, toward girls who are nonmembers. So they just don't bring them around. They see them on the outside.

For some old-fashioned reasons that she was not certain of, Connie's guy that she'd gotten tight with didn't want to take her home and have her around his house too often because his mother didn't approve of her, and they had trouble getting together.

She was gradually pulling away from the group, and after a while somebody "came out of his mouth" on her about it and said maybe she didn't want to stay at the spot anymore. Or maybe she was putting them down. But she didn't want to do anything to alienate the Hamites. None of them will do anything intentionally to offend or alienate the others. That's what keeps the family tie so strong, and it is very strong. Therefore, she gave up the other fellow, who could have been a ruse to begin with to show Chips, for instance, that somebody else wanted her.

It's different with Jill, Jill has more freedom than any other member in the group because she takes it. I'm sure most of the Hamites wouldn't dare say anything about it. She hooks up with other fellows at will. She was going with Brown Brother down the street, but she wouldn't bring him around the Hamites too often. Most of the time he would call up to the window or whistle, and she would come down, and they would go someplace. But she never tried to bring him into the spot or to the family.

Most of the Hamites have known each other for a very long time. Anybody who just comes along all of a sudden and tries to gain entrance is trespassing and is resented right from the outset. Every member has known one or two of the other members, or even more, for many years. Most of them grew up on the block or near the block, like around the corner or someplace. They weren't necessarily running partners or chummy, but they knew each other. The group is very similar to a provincial clique. They don't go around offering family membership too often. This is usually something one grows into or is born into. They had something, a strong bond, even before they decided to establish a common residence.

Connie has her place in the family, but she's a slight misfit. She is more or less the most outside member of the family. She doesn't demand any more rights than they give her.

Everybody knows that she's got a strong thing going, a sometimes really painful thing, for Chips. He knows it, too, but he takes it very casually, as though that's the way life's supposed to be. Jill has often talked to her about it and told her, "Look, why don't you show the dude that you're not interested in him, pay more attention to some of the other fellows, and don't be always at his beck and call?"

Connie has tried that. She would like to be a strong, assertive, and freewheeling girl, but it's just not her style. Every time she has tried it, she blew it from the very beginning. She keeps saying that she doesn't really care about him that much, but everything she does contradicts what she says.

When Chips was living at Mae's, he used to take packages to and from the "factory," and he used to pick up packages from the supplier and pay off the cops and the whole bit. So I asked Connie if during this time Chips had asked her to get down on some scag with him, would she have done it. And she said she doesn't know for sure. He never asked her, and that test never really came about. She thinks that she might have done it because he really had her nose open "at that time." He had her "under a spell." She thinks she would have done anything that he asked her to do.

Actually, she was almost sorry that he didn't because if he had she would have known for sure just how little he cared about her. And she says that one day soon—and she's been saying this for some time now—he's going to call for her, and she's not going to answer, and that's really when he's going to miss her. "That's how all the dudes who think they so fly wake up and see what they've been missin'."

Her story is that she was always waiting and biding her time. Well, she's been waiting a long time, and it could have happened, but I don't think anybody believes it will, not even Connie.

I asked Connie how she happened to meet Chips. She said she'd seen him around for a long time but didn't really know him. They weren't tight or anything. Until one day he beat up a friend of hers, and Connie reprimanded him about it, and he beat her up, too. The next day she saw him, and he apologized and said he didn't mean to beat her up, and asked her to take a walk in the park. He said he was truly sorry about hitting her, but she shouldn't have gotten into his business. She said that it was all right, and they got tight, and then the other girl whom he had beaten up accused Connie of trying to steal her boyfriend, but Connie said he really didn't like her anymore, so there was nothing really to steal. Whether it's true or not, that's how it turned out. She used to see him when he was out on the street. He used to "walk so cool, and he was always movin' fast, as though he had somethin' to do. He was always out there with the swift people, movin' right up fast street."

She never really expected to get hooked up with him, but when it started happening she didn't bother to fight it, she says. Connie wasn't mad at him for beating her up because she figured he was right and she should not have gone and butted into his and Gail's business. "Besides, if he hadn't beat me up, there would've never been anything to apologize for, and we might never have gotten tight."

Her mother didn't trust him because she thought that he was too old for Connie and that he was trying to take advantage of her tender years. He tried to "take her off in the house, and Moms wasn't going for that."

She wasn't going to bed and leave them up. She used to tell him it was time to go, so he started keeping Connie out late, and he would just take her panties off in the hallway and they'd "take care of business" there before he would let her go into the apartment. She thinks "Moms got hip to that because she began telling me to stay away from him because he's no good."

She was constantly protesting to her moms, "He doesn't mess with dope and he goes to school and does everything the way he's supposed to. He's always clean, and he dresses nicely, and you don't ever see him high."

She said Chips never made her feel uncomfortable like other dudes can do. They wouldn't know what to say or how to say it or how to make a move if they wanted to go into her panties or something like that. "He did all that like it was real natural and wasn't fumbling or anything like that. The dude could open my bra with one hand without fumbling. He just went right to it, and *snap,* it just jumped open, and before I knew anything, he was playin' with my titties like he knew what he was doin'. That made me feel at ease."

Chips treated her right for a few months, but sometimes he'd get in his moods and would be mean to her. He'd slap her once in a while, but then he would always apologize, and Connie claims that she could understand why he beat her sometimes. Once he told her that when he was a little boy he saw his father knock his moms down and kick her a couple of times, and he said he always hated the dude after that, and he wanted to kill him. He promised himself that he was going to kill him behind what he saw him do to his moms. But he said when he got older, old enough to understand what was really going on, he saw the numbers his moms was doing on his pops, who was a rather righteous guy, "one of them hardworking dudes."

He said after a while he began to appreciate his father. He saw the changes that his moms was putting him through, and he thought about how he felt when he was a little boy and saw his pops knock his moms down. He said to himself, If that was me, I woulda killed that broad.

Connie figured that he takes the hostility he had toward his moms out on all the girls that he knows. She believes that deep down inside he really loved her. She thinks that if he didn't love her, he wouldn't bother to hit her, or he wouldn't get angry enough to hit her.

Chips doesn't hit Connie in the presence of the group because the family just can't go for that. Everybody in the family has to get along with everyone else. If any kind of real static arises, nobody knows which side to take, and if anything should get serious enough that somebody might be moved to get the police and bring them to the spot, that would jeopardize everybody's freedom. Nobody would have a place to stay. So when any kind of static occurs, when Chips gets mad or he wants to hit her, everybody has to remind him that she's not his stuff and that she's everybody's sister and that's wrong.

Hebro's going to be the main one to let him know that what he's doing isn't right. "Matter of fact, it's foul to be hittin' on a nice broad like Connie."

This is one of the things that Connie mostly appreciates about the family arrangement. None of the Hamites is going to permit any of the others to be abused too much, especially physically, by any of the other family members, or anybody else for that matter.

Connie says that all Chips is doing when he hits her or gives her a hard time is really expressing how much he cares for her, the only way he knows how to express it. But the others don't want any static in the place. So she can get away with more in the spots. She can talk back and get "sho'nuff mouthy" with Chips there. And all he's going to do, and she knows this, is walk out, which is the best thing to do.

It seems it's almost like a husband-wife relationship with Connie and Chips. She gets mad when she hears about other girls that he's into something with. The girl around the corner who had a baby, and it's supposed to be from Chips, the girl would say hello. She tried it a couple of times, but Connie would just "nut on her" and walk away like she wasn't even there.

Connie is sort of like the sufferer of the group, but everybody likes her because she suffers in a way that doesn't bother anybody. If she gets truly upset and disappears like she did a couple of times, for a day or two, everybody gets worried. The only person who doesn't get worried is Chips. That's Connie's lot. She bought it of her own free will, and everybody lives with it. Nobody tries to get her out of it. Only Jill tries.

Dee Dee says that Connie's problem is that she is a Libra and that Libras live inside themselves. They don't do too much relating to the outside world. They're more ideas people than anything else. Dee Dee says Connie wants to relate to people or she wants to get out and be closer to people, but she can't get outside of herself to touch anybody. She's not really introverted, but everything about her is so guarded she can't let down her guard long enough with anybody to really get out and reach. According to Dee Dee, "She's the type of girl who could go through, I mean run through, a million guys, you know, live with them, or with a hundred dudes in ten years, and never be close to any man, or anybody else for that matter. It's like her whole existence is turned inside herself and she does most of her living in there." According to Dee Dee, Connie's been buried in herself so long she doesn't know how to really get out and touch somebody or "touch somebody's soul with the finger of her soul. And maybe it's something that'll wear off. Maybe she has to become really close to one person at a time. She probably had some bad experiences that they don't talk about and that she isn't even aware of herself."

All the Hamites have their opinions about Connie. Of course, she says that she wouldn't be bothered with any of the dudes around here in the neighborhood because they're not worth anything, including Chips. But she likes Mumps. She says, "Mumps is a pretty mellow dude because he's serious, like real in what he's doing." She describes Mumps as "beautiful and serious people." He thinks she's all right, too. He gives her things from time to time, but he doesn't seem to be too anxious to get involved in anything serious or even semiserious with Connie.

Shaft says, "Connie frightens dudes away because she looks like she's in heat all the time. She looks a little bit like a sex junkie, I think. She's got this real quiet thing. I mean they're a lotta girls like that, grown women, too, who don't even know how to look at a man. They can't look 'em straight in the eye, and when they finally do, it's like the whole sex thing comes through, and that's all."

Connie just says, "Well, it's not my fault. It's probably something that's in the minds of other people. These dudes be lookin' at me, they probably look at all women with the same thing on their feeble minds. And it's got nothin' to do with any woman, it's just them. And even if there is some truth to it, I can't help it if I look sexy. So what?" She adds sort of jokingly, "Soon my prince will come."

Connie says she once thought she was going to become a butch. And I asked, "Why'd you think that?" She said she had a traumatic experience when she was eleven. A man raped her, and for a long time after that she hated men. She said she knew that it did something to her mind because after she was raped she started walking like a boy. She became "very boyish and had that sort of dippity-doo or bopish walk that the boys have where they dip a little with every other step they take." She said it stuck with her for a couple of years.

The man who raped her caught her in the hallway and beat her. She wasn't hurt by the beating. She remembered she'd been beaten by her stepfather, who used to tie her to the bed and beat her. She said she could take the physical beating, "but it was the pain of that man between my legs that wouldn't go away for days." She didn't tell her mother, she never told anyone about it, but she never forgot it. She never went to a psychiatrist or anything, or sat down and talked about it, but she knew that it had put her through some changes.

For a while she thought "Boys were strange and dirty and nasty and, you know, and crude, always wanted to hurt somebody," because that's what she associated sex with.

She never thought she would become a real butch like having eyes for girls or anything like that because that never was her thing. But she wanted nothing to do with fellows. She said once she was approached by a girl, but that "the idea of rubbing pussies with some girl just seemed perverted and dirty." Then she met this dude Rufo, "a big, bad, and mean dude, I mean he was terrible and everybody feared him. He was wicked."

She said she was scared of him at first, too, just like everybody else, but more so, and then when she stopped and let him talk to her one day, "He just seemed to be a real nice person." She never believed all those things that people said about him, even after he went to jail—he's doing a nickel. They might have been true, but she knows that he wasn't like that with her.

"He started me to likin' dudes again. I really started diggin' men then, and I saw how nice sex could be and got over the fear. Yeah, I always think of Rufo as my cure. It's really hard to tell whether you're in love with somebody or not who's in jail because you can't see him and you can't touch him," Connie says. "He's a mellow dude and a beautiful person to be around, but, you know, like I just haven't seen him in a long time."

The letters sound good and all that, and if she were to see him and have him touch her, she says, she might still be in love with him and she might not, but she would have to see him to know about it. And next came Chips. He almost started her hating men again.

When Connie first left home she tried to turn a trick to get some money. Jill told her how to do it. She went out, and she tried. She was down on Thirty-fourth Street someplace, and the prospective trick was coming out of a hotel. She was nervous. When she went up to him and asked him if he wanted to have some fun with her, "The dude sort of smiled like he thought there was somethin' funny about it, but he stopped. He asked how much did I want, and I told him it was twenty dollars and ten dollars, twenty dollars for me and ten dollars for the room."

That's what Jill had told her to say, and the dude laughed, so she asked him what was so funny. The dude said, "You are. You are, little girl. Don't you know that there ain't thirty dollars' worth of ass in the whole world?"

She turned around and ran to the subway, got on the train, came back uptown, and never tried that again. She said she didn't think she would have made out too good anyway, "sellin' it." She could never imagine herself just going and sleeping with strangers, people she didn't know and didn't like. She "wasn't sure, but something about that wasn't right." She was afraid she might lose all feeling, "you know, all sexual feelin'. Maybe I would never again be able to really enjoy somebody I really dug. It's like they all just might become the same."

That was the main thing that turned her against the idea. That and feeling so foolish after the man laughed at her.

Connie said she'd like to get married one day, but she's in no hurry. She says she's young and can afford to wait. She resents the fact that people think girls—and just girls—should want to get married, "especially when there're so few dudes around anybody would wanta marry unless she wants to marry a dopey or somebody else who's just as messed up in the mind."

She says, "Before I met Chips I used to think everybody that lived in this block was crazy, or at best had very poor minds. The young girls all wanted to be dynamite whores or something. They were all tryin' to be hookers even before they got to high school. All the young boys wanted to be junkies or pimps or somethin' crazy like that. And these were their dreams, the goals they had set for themselves in life. People who can't afford even healthy dreams, they are poor. That's real poverty.

"I used to try and stay away from this block. I guess a lot of people used to think I was stuck-up, or I thought I was better than everybody else, livin' over there in Esplanade Gardens, but that's not what it was. It's just that the way I saw it is they had nothin' in common with me. I had some dreams. Now I spend a whole lotta time in school, just to be away from all the madness of this block. I think salvation to a lotta people in Harlem would be gettin' away from Harlem. Harlem seems to me to be like a big prison without bars—I'm not sure maybe the bars are invisible—where they let the people out to work for the white rulers during the day and put them on the subway and take them back to their cells at night.

"In the mornin' you get on the train, and you see a whole lotta black workers goin' downtown, and then, in the evenin', a whole lotta black workers goin' back uptown. They just keep shufflin' 'em back and forth. It's like a mass transferrin' of prisoners. It looks inhuman. The only place they could keep these people is up in Harlem, where they keep 'em ready and waitin' while they get the next chores ready for them.

"Maybe Harlem is like it was in the Old South, where the slaves stayed in the slave quarters. This is where they keep the slaves until they're ready for 'em to come out and pick cotton. They let 'em come out in the mornin'. That's almost the only time they get to see the outside world. They go underground in Harlem and they come out from under the ground downtown where they work.

"You know, it's like Jill was tellin' me. In jail they keep you walkin' in line and tell you, Don't look this way or don't look that way, keep your eyes in front of you. You not supposed to see nothin', just go to where you goin' and back. It's pretty much the same thing in Harlem, even though there's nobody watchin' 'em, but the guard is the clock that's tickin' time away. The clock tells these people when to go to work every mornin'. It tells them to keep their eyes in front of them and when to go back to their cells.

"And it's almost like marchin', too, the same as people in jail bein' in line. These people are almost in line, too, a sort of raggedy line. It's just not a neat line. They all rushin' up outta the subway at the same time or down into the subway, and they're all headin' pretty much the same way. And everybody knows they gotta squeeze through those narrow little subway openings. There's somethin' about it that's very much like a prison, just the way people are controllin' you."

I said to her that many people love Harlem and don't think it's a prison. "Yeah, I know that," she said, "but those are just some prisoners who have special privileges, the trusties, and can deceive themselves—people like doctors, lawyers, preachers, politicians —they just upper-class prisoners who tell themselves that they're not in jail because whitey lets them exploit the other jailbirds. But you know, this goes on in all prisons, I guess in every system. Like in a school classroom there're gonna be some students in there who will have special privileges. Or workin' in a place of business, if the boss likes you or if you're a pretty girl and you let him do what he wants to do with you, you can get special privileges, too, but you're still gonna be just another employee who's workin' for that man. If you ain't got enough sense to realize it, you're gonna really make a fool of yourself. It's the same way with those people who go around talkin' about they in love with Harlem, they just kiddin' themselves. I mean it's a game they're playin' on themselves. They know they can't really get out of it, so they might as well tell themselves everything is wonderful. I mean what is there to love about Harlem?

"But for anybody, you know, who is not one of the trusties or privileged prisoners, for him to be goin' around tellin' himself how wonderful Harlem is, you know, he's gotta be sick, completely outta touch with what's really comin' off. Either that or the pressures of this prison have blown his mind. He's still gonna be in the same trick when he wakes up. Because somebody lives on another street in, let's say, Esplanade Gardens, you can't say that they're not in Harlem.

Now, maybe they don't have to be bothered with the roaches and the rats—and that's just maybe—maybe they don't have to be worried about not havin' heat and hot water in the mornin', but they have other problems.

"It's very difficult to get out. Most of the prisoners don't make enough money, and you've gotta buy your way outta this jail, too. I think that's true in all jails, you've gotta buy your way out. If most people had the right lawyers, they wouldn't be there to begin with. People who live in places like Esplanade Gardens or Lenox Terrace, it's easier for them to tell themselves that they're not prisoners.

"And you always hear a lotta the politicians and the doctors and the lawyers talkin' about how nice Harlem is. That's because they don't live here anyway. They might have a office or somethin' and a paper address, but they live someplace else. They can go on and holler about how wonderful Harlem is because they know they've been saved. Salvation is gettin' outta Harlem. It's easy to stand outside the fire and talk about how cool it is from the outside when the people who are in it are burnin' up. Once you get out you can breathe, and you don't have to be goin' through all those jailhouse changes anymore. But there's nobody livin' up here in his right mind who can honestly say that this is good and this is where it's at.

"When they come out of the Esplanade Gardens or Lenox Terrace or off the Strivers Row, they've gotta get in the house before it's too late at night. And they've gotta carry a gun when they go out so as not to be mugged by these wonderful people in this wonderful place called Harlem. They been goin' around all their lives tryin' to be better than everybody else or tryin' to make themselves feel that they weren't really as bad off as most black folks are when they know that's a lie. They've gotta go through all the same changes. You can't get a pistol permit by sayin' I'm in jail, and of course when people get killed in this jail called Harlem, nobody worries about it too much. The police don't worry about it. They know that's gonna happen when you get a whole lot of enraged people together. They liable to do anything. And whitey knows that Harlem is a jail.

"What're you gonna do when a prisoner kills another one? You just add onto his time, right? Or you transfer him to a tougher prison. Well, they do that in Harlem. And most of the people who live in Harlem are gonna be doin' life here anyhow. To take somebody from Harlem and put him in jail, it's a joke, because they just takin' him outta one jail and puttin' him in another one. Privileged prisoners sometimes get off with a warning or a fine or will be put on probation, but even if they kill somebody they don't have to be too concerned because it's just gonna be another prisoner. The people who run the system expect some of these prisoners to kill each other from time to time. They'll just say, Well, it's one less prisoner we have to deal with.

"And when people start gettin' laid off and can't find jobs anymore, they're deepest in prison. They don't have that much to lose, so they might as well go out and commit some kinda crime. They say they gonna throw me in jail, I'm gonna be in a real prison, but I'm in a real prison anyhow. I have to worry about how I'm gonna eat, how I'm gonna pay the rent, the electric bill, and the phone bill. You gotta pay these exorbitant prices to live in this prison. And if I go out and commit a crime and get flagged, I'm gonna go to the other prison and somebody else is gonna pay. I don't have to worry about eatin', I don't have to worry about room and board, and I don't have to worry about clothes. I don't have to worry about light bills, I don't have to worry about rent, I don't have to worry about nothin'. All I have to do is face up to it, that I'm in prison.

"Well, what's happenin' now is that all of New York is becomin' one big prison because white people can't go out and do what they want to do, either. Maybe they used to go downtown and see a Broadway play, but they can't do that anymore because this whole city is becomin' the prison. I'm just hopin' that I can get outta this prison before I bug out. All I wanta do is find someplace where everybody is not spaced way out on a one-way trip and not likely to get back.

"You go down to the bookstore on 125th Street, the black bookstore down there, and get that *Harlem on My Mind* that's on sale now for one dollar, and read about how beautiful Harlem was and how great it was, and I say, Wonder what happened? I'm not that old, but I don't know one person who remembers it bein' all that beautiful."

TEN

Stretch

Stretch is one of the closest friends of the Hamites. He is the neighborhood carpenter and electrician and general fixit man. He fixes everything—radios, television, refrigerators, chairs and tables, and just about anything that might break or break down. You even sometimes see him out on the block working on cars. He's always helping the Hamites get their spots together.

Stretch is tall and lean. He's about fifty years old, but he looks no older than thirty-five. He has been warned by the doctors not to drink or smoke anymore because he has a heart condition which twice required open-heart surgery. Stretch just laughs at the doctors and their advice. He says that he might as well not live if he's not enjoying life, and life without any liquor or cigarettes "is a lot like being dead anyhow." What they're trying to do is rush him into heaven, he says, and he's not "gonna go for that trip."

He will tell anyone who'll listen that the doctors don't know anything about when somebody's going to die or what smoking cigarettes is going to do to him. He says they've been telling him that he's going to die from smoking and drinking for six or seven years, and he's still going strong. "They was tellin' Winston Churchill the same story for twenty years. They tell everybody that, and they know that eventually everybody's gonna die, and the drinkin' and the cigarettes have nothin' to do with it." But, he says, the doctors can always point and say, Yeah, you see, I told you that dude was goin' die.

According to Stretch, "They gotta be right because everybody's goin' die one day."

Stretch doesn't act like a person with a serious heart condition.

He smokes those strong cigarettes with no filters, and you'll see him go to the bar across the street three or four times a day and stay for about fifteen minutes. He may have two or three or more drinks, but he never gets drunk.

He's got an enormous amount of energy for a man of his age in his condition, or in what he says is his doctor's "made-up condition." He's always doing strenuous jobs, carrying heavy boards and equipment. And he's always running back and forth from his car to the shop, across the street, upstairs and downstairs. On top of all that, he lives on the sixth floor, and he runs up and down at least five or six times a day.

Stretch has to wear very soft shoes with crepe on the outside and a cushion on the inside. They are custom-made because Stretch has what must be the worst feet in all of New York City. When he has his special shoes on, he walks with his head tilted way back and moving in a big stride, like a tall drunk leaning way back because he's afraid that if he tries to straighten up he'll topple over forward. But it has nothing to do with being drunk. It's just the comfortable way for him to walk.

But when he doesn't have his special shoes, he has to walk very slowly. He takes about one step a minute, or every thirty seconds at most, like somebody barefoot trying to walk over a spot where he knows there's broken glass but he can't see it. He's also careful not to step on headless paper matches. He tells the Hamites that his feet got so sensitive "from standin' on too many corners."

Stretch was in the Army during World War II, and he says, "All that marchin' wasn't good for me, and they never had shoes that could fit me." Stretch wears something like a size 15.

According to Stretch, he has had all kinds of money problems because of his feet. He says that there was a time when all of his money went into his feet. He says that one year he thinks he spent more money on his feet than he made. Stretch says that sometimes his feet ache so much that he's tempted to rob a bank to get some money to solve the problem.

Stretch was born and raised in the building next to his shop. It's an old five-story tenement just like the condemned building adjacent to it in which the Hamites live. He says that when he was born there, Harlem was still inhabited by 65 percent white folks.

Stretch is genuinely fond of all the Hamites, and he thinks it's a curse that they have to grow up on this block. He thinks it's a curse that anybody has to grow up on this block, even though he raised his own kids here. He says, "Children shouldn't have to be condemned to this block just because they didn't have the right to choose their parents."

Stretch is generally protective of all the kids on the block. He gives them advice, and he scolds them as though he's the block father. He's without a doubt the best and most valuable friend the Hamites have. If anything happens to their electricity or plumbing, if they need somebody to put in a window or plug up a rat hole, they will either get Stretch to do it or ask him for the use of his tools. Usually he'll lend them with a warning, "If you hit anybody in the head, don't ever come and ask for anything again. And I'ma be lookin' for you to hit you in your head."

Nobody's done that but Salt-Noody, and he felt so bad about having betrayed Stretch's trust that he kept coming around and giving him things and offering to help in order to atone for what he had done. So Stretch finally forgave him and let him borrow his tools again. Of all the Hamites, Salt-Noody is Stretch's favorite because he has a special aptitude for fixing things.

Mumps frequently finds useful tools in his line of business—stealing—and he'll promise them to Stretch. All the Hamites like him, and they know they can always get Stretch to do something for them or help them, even if it's not in his line of work.

Sometimes he'll tell the junkies to "get away from the buildin' and don't be harassin' those kids." He's a big guy, so they move along.

Stretch says he was dealing heroin and cocaine on this block in 1946, "when hardly anybody in my generation knew what it was and when you could buy a shiny, brand-new Buick for fifteen hundred dollars." He got flagged, and he did every day of a dime—ten years —and walked out not owing anybody a day of time.

Stretch lives in a city-owned building that should have been condemned years ago. There hadn't been any hot water for a long time, and one day the cold water was turned off, too. Stretch was the one who organized the tenants in the building to tap the fire hydrant. He had a wrench, and he had pails that he rented out to everyone.

Stretch keeps an eye on Salt-Noody with his spray can and tells him what various janitors are going to do to him if he keeps messing up their buildings. He understands that Salt-Noody has to have his spray cans, and he won't let anybody bother him because he knows that Salt might do serious harm to someone.

Stretch feels that most people don't realize Salt-Noody's talent because he just prefers to keep all the "bullshit" out of his personality. In trying to explain why Salt-Noody is not so strange, Stretch will tell you how one of his own kids didn't talk until he was about four years old. "It's not that he didn't have anything to say—it's just that he realized, you know, before he started talkin', that people were usually bullshittin' away, and he didn't want to get into that. He was such a real and sincere person he wasn't gonna bother gettin' into a whole lotta bullshit, and he wasn't gonna talk until he had somethin' to say. Salt-Noody is the type of kid who could talk and say a whole lot more than he says if he had a mind to do it or if he felt that there was any reason to do it. But he's just so far out of all the bullshit in life that he just goes on doin' his thing, what he wants to do."

Because he does understand him, Stretch is more tolerant of Salt than most people are. He got angry and started to go to war with the janitor down the street because the janitor threw a brick at Salt-Noody for spraying the entrance of his building. Stretch figures, "Here's a stupid old fool who's gonna hurt this kid who's just doin' his thing, somethin' that comes naturally, not because he's doin' something to anything of his, but because he's worryin' about the property of some slumlord."

He told him, "If I ever see you tryin' to hurt that kid again or throwin' at that kid again, I'm gonna break your ass in five different places."

The janitor wolfed and mouthed back at him, but he didn't want to tangle with Stretch.

Stretch says, "It's fools like him that make kids so distrustful and hate the grown-ups around here. Makes it dangerous for anybody. It makes you worry about havin' your kids hit by a rock, you know, with a man like that. He don't even know what a kid is."

That man doesn't know how lucky he was that he missed Salt-Noody with the brick because Stretch would have done more than threaten him if he hadn't.

Stretch has two cats in his shop that Salt-Noody brought him to keep the rats away. But because the building is adjacent to the building the Hamites live in, the cats won't stay long. The rats are the same rats as in the Hamites' building, and they frighten cats away.

When Stretch covers up a rat hole, he does it in such a way that that rat's not going to come back. You know how rats are—they always find another hole or make one. Covering up rat holes is usually an exercise in futility. But when Stretch covers up a rat hole, what he'll do is take a long piece of galvanized tin and run it along the whole side of the wall where the rats would come in so there's no place where they can come in, and they're not going to go but so high in getting over anything. So people who live in that block pay him rather well because it seems to be one of the blocks in Harlem that's most infested with rats.

He doesn't have any helpers other than Salt-Noody and two other kids on the block who are not Hamites. Hebro helps him sometimes with heavy jobs. He likes to show the Hamites how to do things and make furniture, so in a way they've become apprentices of his. Most of them are pretty good electricians. They all know how to turn on the electricity after Con Edison comes and turns it off. If anything goes wrong with the electricity in their building, the Hamites know how to steal electricity from the buidling next to it, or even two buildings away. Their attitude is that Con Ed can afford it because they overcharge everybody in New York City anyway, especially blacks. "They charge more for electricity in black communities. It's like a black tax that they put on us."

So he's taught them a little bit about carpentry and electricity and fixing electrical appliances and a little bit about tarring roads. When it came to putting up the pigeon coops that Salt-Noody and a few of the other members of the Hamites built, Salt-Noody did most of the work, but his mentor was Stretch. It turned out to be one of the most impressive pigeon coops in the whole town, and at the time Salt-Noody did the work he was only thirteen.

Stretch is proud of the fact that he has been able to guide the Hamites and help them in many little ways. If they want some advice from an adult—they don't trust most adults—they turn to Stretch. They know that he's not going to tell them anything wrong and that he's going to try to guide them away from what he thinks may lead to trouble. They've come to regard him as a kind of father figure. They know that if anything "comes off" that they can't handle, Stretch is not going to let anyone take advantage of them.

Stretch has known most of the Hamites all their lives. He never asks them anything about their personal lives, why they don't go home or anything like that. He knows that most of their parents don't think too highly of them, and he knows that if home was that great they wouldn't be living at the spots.

He knows that they smoke pot and drink a little, although they don't smoke in front of him. But when he comes up to the spots he sometimes smells it.

Stretch is an old-timer. He's smoked, he's used drugs, he's sold drugs. He smoked a lot of pot before most people of his generation knew what pot really was—long before any of the Hamites were born. And he stopped smoking before any of them were born. So he knows what it is and sees it as just a phase that young people go through. In fact, most Harlemites see pot smoking as part of growing up.

Stretch never says anything to the Hamites about pot. He knows that none of them is a hard-drug user now, except Lee, and he knows that they're proud of what they're doing and that they need some encouragement. Every time he comes up to one of the spots he'll tell them how nice it looks and comment on anything new they've added.

Stretch immediately saw the value of Jill to the group, and he showered her with compliments and encouragement. He would tell her things like, "Yeah, you really turned this spot into a home with the curtains and the flowers." Sometimes he says, "Wow, this looks better than my apartment."

And when Salt-Noody made the partitions with the beer-can rings and the door curtain of the same material and the string spiderweb, he told him that they'd probably want him in Hollywood if they knew what he was doing here and that he had better be careful to finish school before one of those Hollywood people came looking for an interior decorator and stole him away. Salt-Noody went around with a smile on his face for about five days after that, and nobody could wipe it off.

Stretch comes up once or twice a week just to see if everyone and everything is all right. If he doesn't see one of the Hamites for more than a week, he'll ask about him because he has a constant fear that they'll get into trouble, not by their own doing, but because there are so many pitfalls in Harlem life that it's almost impossible for anyone to escape all of them.

He's not one of the run-of-the-mill idealists who expect great accomplishments from kids out of Harlem. He says it's a great achievement for them just to stay away from dope and out of jail, or just stay in school. He's sort of a "sideline bettor," filled with hope and betting on these kids. He says, "If they can make it, and so far they are—I mean, you know, like they went in hands down against the hard life, against the street life that keeps beckonin' to all the kids in Harlem—if they can make it, others can make it, too, and it's hard, bro."

He says it's even hard for an adult to walk the straight and narrow in Harlem, and if there's anything that he can do to help the Hamites he's going to go out of his way to do it "because what that means is that we might have a generation who's gonna change the trend, if only in this neighborhood."

Stretch has seen generations go down the drain on the block, kids who had everything basic going for them, kids who had brains, courage, talent, and vitality, but actually they didn't have a chance. "Maybe any other place but Harlem. Anyplace else they coulda made it, and they woulda gone to college, had a good life, got married, raised their kids, and made their parents proud."

But he's seen a couple of generations come up and go down the drain, just get swallowed up. Either gang fights or drugs or something equally ridiculous. But now for the first time in this block in more than two generations, there seems to be a relatively large group of kids who are going to make it, or who are trying to make it, and who've got a pretty good chance of succeeding because they're so determined. "If you get a large group who're makin' it, they can show the others who're comin' up behind them that it's possible to beat the odds—to beat the jail odds, beat the drugs odds, beat the losin' odds, and go on and win."

Stretch feels that's what's needed now more than anything else, "a good example to show the kids that they can win, and if they don't win they'll be doing as good as anyone else before them 'cause nobody else has won around here either. Losin' has been a way o' life here. What the neighborhood needs is a new tradition, a positive one, a winnin' one."

Stretch believes that the Hamites can do it, and he wants to help them do it. He has a real "mean on" for anybody who tries to prevent them. Stretch says, "If I see somebody wanna sell these kids some drugs, I'ma take him and wrap a crowbar 'round his head."

Stretch says, "These kids, they ain't got no parents, they ain't got nobody helpin' them. And everything seems to be against them, but yet they determined to come out winners on their own. And that's somethin' that everybody who's got any sense should wanta invest in, you know, take part in, because they gonna make it, and you can look back and say, 'Yeah, I had somethin' to do with it,' and feel good and know that you're changin' this whole scene. That thing in Harlem of losin' out is changin', and like you had a important part in changin' that."

Stretch is very contemptuous toward the Hamites' parents. He says somebody ought to take all of them and put them in jail for abandonment. And all the Hamites, he says, "All those kids oughta have medals of valor for what they already done." He hopes that his grandchildren can be as beautiful as they are, as independent as they are. "They're the kind of kids that would make anybody proud to be associated with them and proud of what they're doin'."

And it's because they are so beautiful that they attract beautiful friends like Stretch, a very good guy—like Dujo says, "very mellow people." Stretch says he wants to "teach them all how to make some money without throwin' rocks all their lives, without gamblin'. That's somethin' not enough kids in Harlem know."

ELEVEN

Snooky

Snooky, fourteen, is the youngest and the smallest of the Hamites. He's often the butt of family jokes. The others are continually teasing him, but he takes it in a good-natured way most of the time. He's more or less the mascot of the group. He's also the troublemaker—cars, guns. I guess Snooky really left home because his moms threw his pops out. He says, "You know what a wino is, don't you? Well, my father is a whiskey-o—a guy who walks the streets and stands on the corner with a bottle of whiskey in his hand. He says bars make him feel locked up, so he likes to drink out in the open. That's why my moms put him out. About two months later, I tipped, too."

Snooky's moms was constantly putting him and his older brother out of the apartment, at least once a month. No less than one weekend a month she would get drunk, and she would decide that Snooky and his brother Paul were no good and proceed to put them out. They would come back sometime during the night or at latest the next day. However, the last time she put Snooky out I don't think he wanted to come back, and he didn't. He'd probably been looking for an excuse to go shack up in one of the spots anyhow. So now he's a full-fledged member of the Hamites, and he does his share. He works in the numbers joint after school. He runs errands and does a variety of necessary chores. He also watches the spot.

Snooky has a car fetish. If he could only get a car, half of his dreams would be realized. Nobody knows how he acquired the great urge for a car, but he wants a car first out of life, and everything else is secondary. When Snooky talks about cars, he does it with reverence. He talks of cars the way a truly devoted minister might talk about God, or the way golf nuts can remember a hole-in-one they made twenty years ago and still taste it. This kid talks of cars with sheer ecstasy, especially a Cadillac. He once took a joyride in a Cadillac and smashed it up. Despite the aftermath, being arrested and receiving a hard time from his mother, he still considers that one of the greatest experiences of his life.

The Hamites are always teasing Snooky. It's their way of telling him they love him. For instance, there is a kid in the block that the Hamites try to persuade Snooky to fight. The kid's a bully. The Hamites regularly assure Snooky that he can beat this bully, whose name happens to be Jasper, if he really wants to or if he would just give it a shot. But Snooky is afraid of Jasper. Hebro is forever telling the Hamites to "leave him alone because he's just young, and everybody goes through that fear thing when they're young. All he needs to do is fight the dude one time to find out that he's not that bad and get rid of the fear thing. Even I was scared of some dudes when I was young. But when you fight a dude, it's like the fear leaves, you know."

Snooky says, in his own defense, that he's really not afraid of Jasper. "As a matter of fact," he says, "I got this big fat stick down in the basement, and it keeps tellin' me that Jasper ain't all that bad, and like if he keeps messin' with me, one o' these days I'ma listen to that big stick 'cause I think it's right." Snooky fights many other kids. The truth is that he gets into too many fights, and the other Hamites often have to come to his rescue. But he doesn't seem ready or willing to fight Jasper, and they continue to give him a hard time about it.

Almost everything Snooky does, somebody's teasing him about it. Dujo says that Snooky is a virgin. Then he says, "Tell me you not, Snooky." He's always telling Snooky to stand up for himself. But Snooky has never denied the accusation. They sometimes get him on center. Shaft says, "Go on, Snooky, tell the truth. You never had any, did you?" And Snooky doesn't answer. He slowly drops his head in a rather embarrassed fashion.

One night Snooky was raving about cars. He was telling the group about how he took a joyride in a Cadillac twice, but the second time he got caught. He'd probably heard somebody making a comparison of Cadillacs and women, so he said offhandedly, "You know, that's a dynamite ride, and it heats up real quick, just like a young girl."

After a brief silence, all the Hamites laughed, and Chips asked, "How would you know?"

Shaft, as usual the main prod, asked, "How would you know, Snooky? You never had any. You're still a virgin. And you'll stay that way as long as you keep hangin' out with Marva. Man, that broad is bent."

Next, Dujo began to inquire about Marva. He asked Snooky what does he do with her. Snooky didn't reply for a long moment. Marva is a couple of years older than Snooky, and she likes him, but it's a platonic thing, so everybody says. They're not really into a boy-friend-and-girl-friend-type relationship.

On this particular night while they were teasing Snooky, somebody decided to call for a serious discussion on the topic. I think it was Dujo. He spoke first and said Marva was a supervirgin and it didn't make sense "for Snooky to be hangin' out with her if he never had any because he should be goin' around with a broad or get tight with a broad who jams."

Nita, who also likes to tease Snooky, told him not to worry about it and assured him that she's going to give him some and if he is still a virgin on his sixteenth birthday, she'll give him the best piece he'll ever have. It seems that Snooky really looks forward to it because he tells Nita that when he gets to be sixteen she's going to be the first one to know about it. Sometimes he warns her jokingly, "Nita, I got a birthday comin' up tomorrow."

Anyhow, this night he got tired of everybody talking about Marva, and he asked Dujo what a supervirgin is. Dujo asked him if he knew what a virgin is, and Snooky replied, "Yeah, I know what a virgin is. A virgin is a girl who's still got her cherry."

"Yeah, that's right," Dujo said, "and Marva is a supervirgin because she's got two cherries."

When the Hamites see that Snooky's beginning to resent their jokes about his friend Marva and his virginity, they usually change the subject and stop teasing him. In this session they went too far, and Snooky spoke up. When Chips asked him why does he hang out with Marva," he said, "She's a good friend of mine. Y'all don't know the girl, she's really mellow people. I mean she's serious people. That means she's for real, not phony, got no airs, and she's not a jive sorta person. She'll tell you how she feels, and whatever she says, you can depend on it."

Dujo asked him, "But what do y'all do when you hang out, other than go up on the roof and watch pigeons fly and that kinda light stuff?"

"Well," says Snooky, "Marva's got long fingernails, and she likes to bust pimples, and I got a lotta pimples, and it feels good when she does it, and that's what the relationship with Marva is all about."

So Mumps says, "Yeah, then do it if that's how you get off," meaning if that's how he gets his kicks, why should it bother anybody else? And so they just let it drop there.

Snooky's fascination with cars is a menace that is likely to get him into serious trouble. In fact, about two months ago Snooky took a car and went joyriding again. He experienced a police confrontation as a result. I asked Snooky to tell me about it, but the Hamites said, "He won't tell it like it is," so I asked Dujo, "Okay, you were down with him, you run it to me. You helped Snooky steal the car, right? Okay, tell me."

Dujo told me how it happened. "One night a couple o' months ago, me and Snooky had just come downstairs from one o' the spots, and we saw Mr. Jimmy there cursin' out the raise, and we came up close to see what was goin' on because everybody was crowdin' around and laughin'. He was drunk, and he was cursin' the raise out. He had said somethin', and the raise just, you know, they had his—I guess he was drivin' or somethin' 'cause they had his wallet and they was double-parked next to him. The raise just threw his stuff out the window on the ground and drove away. And he said, 'I'm gonna get those sons a bitches for that.' Then he said, "I'm gonna report these sons a bitches,' and he got in his car and followed them.

"He was drivin' all crazy then, and he went down to the precinct, 135th Street, but nobody went in with him. They just stayed out and hung around for a while, and soon everybody started goin' back to the spot.

"Anyway, Snooky and me was the last ones to go back up to the spot because like we was on the stoop, rappin'. And Snooky said, 'I feel like drivin',' and I said, 'Yeah, I do, too.'

"He said, 'Let's go get Mr. Jimmy's car.'

"I said, 'Don't you know we takin' some big chances? Like it's in front o' the police station.'

"So we went down there, and it was in front o' the police station where he left it because he'd gone to follow the cops. We thought, well, they probably would arrest him anyway for drunk drivin' when he got into the police station and started talkin' all that nut-city rap about he wanted to press charges or have the raise arrested for throwin' his wallet on the ground. Anyway, it's like we knew where he kept his keys. He always kept a spare key under the ashtray.

"The ride was down a little ways from the station, like closer to the corner of Eighth Avenue. I said, 'Snooky, you lay on point for me.'

"So I got in and I drove the car away from the precinct and outta that block, and Snooky got in the ride with me, and we drove up Eighth Avenue, and the muffler went out. The muffler was draggin' on the ground and makin' noise. But I kept on drivin'. I stopped and got out and let Snooky start practicin' on parkin', and you know Snooky is a freak for rides. Yeah, that's his natural hang-up. We had two pints o' wine in there—it was Mr. Jimmy's wine—and we had drank one pint. Snooky fixed the muffler, tied some kinda rope around it to hold it up. Then we drove uptown to 160th Street where we went to pick up Michael Green and where Fat Roy lives at, but they was sleepin', everybody except Michael Green, he was awake watchin' television.

"I told him we like had a ride downstairs. He said, "Aw, man, why don't you dudes stop bullshittin'. Why'd you come up here this late?' 'Cause it was two o'clock in the mornin'.

"I said, 'Michael, we not jivin'. Why don't you come downstairs there and see it?'

"He saw this gray Cadillac parked out there, and he said, "Yeah, is that really yours?'

"And so I said, 'Yeah.'

"Then Michael said, 'I wanna drive.'

"I said, 'Man, I ain't never seen you drive. You sure you can drive?'

"He said, 'Yeah, I can drive. I wheel like the king o' the road.'

"I told him it was my uncle's ride and we had to be careful with it, and I told him that's why I couldn't let him drive it 'cause I didn't wanna have to answer to my uncle if he messed it up. The fact of the matter was I didn't believe that the dude could drive—like that was just somethin' comin' outta his mouth.

"I said, 'I can't do that, no offense, man, I don't know whether you know how to drive or not.'

"And he said, you know, like, 'Off that—take me back to the crib.'

"So I took him home.

"Me and Snooky was still ridin' around. But it got a certain time, like five o'clock in the mornin', and I said, 'This is when the raise is travelin' up and down Bradhurst.'

"Snooky said, 'It's no raise 'round here, why don't you let me drive 'round the block?'

"I said, 'No, man, 'cause I don't wanta get into no trouble.'

"He kept on insistin' that I'm tryin' to hog the ride and don't wanna let nobody drive. It's like he's tellin' me if the police came I'd get into just as much trouble as he would 'cause I don't look that much older than him. I said, 'If you drive I'm not gonna be in the car.'

"All of a sudden I gave him the key, and I got outta the car, and he was drivin' around by himself. I got out at 146th Street and Bradhurst, and I just stood there and watched him drive off. On 147th Street the raise was taggin' behind him. They latched on to him. They heard the muffler draggin' again, and like five o'clock in the mornin' that's a whole lotta noise 'cause it's so quiet out there. And they peeped the ride sorta swervin' a little, so they tried to pull up in front, and Snooky stepped on the accelerator and speeded up. I'm just standin' there on 146th Street, pinnin' all of this.

"They was tryin' to get in front of him, but he kept on speedin' up. They followed him and stayed on him, and when he speeded up they speeded up, too. They were drivin' right behind him. They blinked the lights a couple o' times, but he didn't stop or pay no attention to that. He just nutted. I guess he was tryin' to outrun 'em. They kept blinkin' the lights, but he kept nuttin' on 'em. The raise was determined to stay on him, and when they peeped him drivin' fast, they drove fast and pulled up in front of him, and Snooky kept on goin' and hit their ride."

"He ran into the police car?"

"Yeah, that's what he did. He crashed right into it. And I saw them grab Snooky and throw him in the police ride.

"They handcuffed Snooky. I guess they thought he was crazy or just criminal because everybody don't go around runnin' into the police. Snooky acted like he was scared when they snatched him outta the ride. Snooky musta panicked and just froze in the ride. They grabbed him and snatched him out, threw him against their ride, you know, put his hands behind his back after doin' that quick-feel number, and threw him in the back seat. And then one parked Mr. Jimmy's ride, got back in their own ride, and drove away.

"So I walked back around the block and sat down on the stoop. All of a sudden I saw the raise in Mr. Jimmy's ride comin' through the block. Like I jumped off the stoop, gettin' ready to split, 'cause I thought Snooky had probably dropped a dime on me. They had Snooky by the collar and stopped on the stoop. And they said, 'Do you know this kid? Do you'all know how old he is?'

"And it was me, Melvin Jackson, and Daddy-o on the stoop. And we said, 'He ain't no more than twelve years old.' And they got upstairs to the spot, and they asked Jill who she was. It seemed that Snooky had told 'em that Jill was his mother. Jill said she was his sister and guardian and what kinda trouble was he in 'cause he lived with her and he was in her custody. You know, like Jill's pretty swift, and she knew how to handle that. They told her that she should come down to the precinct 'cause it looked like he'd stolen a car and was in some trouble. They said the charges was drivin' a car without a license, you know, and possession of a stolen car.

"And so Jill said okay, she'd be down there as soon as she got dressed because she was in her nightgown. She said she would be along later because she had to get dressed and take a bath and all that. But what she wanted was a little bit o' time to go and get Miss Joann, Snooky's moms. She told 'em that they could go on down there and she'd meet 'em at the precinct.

"Snooky was laughin' because he thought he put somethin' over on 'em with Jill. They actually believed that he lived there with Jill, his sister, and that he was in her custody. But Jill figured that if anybody was gonna get him out and maybe had to sign somethin', she'd better go and get Miss Joann, which was what she did.

"Later on, Miss Joann went down to the precinct, and almost everybody in the block went down there. A lotta people went to see what was goin' down. When Miss Joann came out, she was mad. The first thing she said was, 'I'll bet you was down with 'em, too, you damn bum,' talkin' to me.

"And I said, 'No, I wasn't, Miss Joann, I wasn't down. If I was down, I woulda been flagged, too.'

"She said, 'You was down, nigger, 'cause he was there, and I know you was down with him.' And she was walkin' mad. I mean she was burnin', man. Then she got in a cab on the corner and headed back uptown. We waited 'cause we still wanted to know what came off with Snooky, and she showed back in about five minutes. She was steady cursin' me out. She said,'Yes you was, you was down, too, you little slick-ass nigger.'

"It seemed like she was mad at me because he got popped and I didn't get busted. You know how people's moms can be, man, when somethin' like that comes off. You know Fat Leon? Well, Fat Leon was there, too, and he said, you know, 'Miss Joann, if I was with your son, I woulda got caught, too.'

"And she started cursin' Fat Leon out, too, and he started laughin'. So I just strolled on away, and I said, 'Yeah, yeah, if I was there, that's all.'

"I came on back uptown. I went up to the spot and sat down, wonderin' whether Snooky had dropped a dime on me yet or not. And so, push came to shove. I guess it was Miss Joann puttin' the pressure on him. She kept sayin' like, 'Wasn't Dujo with you? Wasn't that damn Dujo with you? He's always gettin' you into trouble or leadin' you into somethin' that you ain't go no business in.'

"Anyway, it's like he had rapped on me, and I was mad. The first thing I thought about was like kickin' this dude's ass, and so I'm up at the spot, and like he was slick. He didn't come back to the spot. Now, what he did is that he went up to my aunt's house, and my aunt was mad 'cause she knew I was down with him, too. That's what made her so burned at me. I went up there, and she took me to Miss Joann's.

"My aunt was in the kitchen with Miss Joann, and she heard me 'cause I was arguin' loud with Snooky, and he was sittin' in the chair when I grabbed him. I said, 'I should stomp you, chump.'

"Then Snooky said somethin', you know, or did somethin', and his moms, Miss Joann, went into her act and threw everybody outta the house, you know, like not just Snooky and Paul. This time she threw all the boys out. She threw David and Abe out, too.

"Like she was really mad 'cause it was early in the mornin' and somebody got her outta bed, and then she said Snooky kept on lyin' and all that. But as far as I was concerned, he hadn't done enough lyin' 'cause he hadn't done enough lyin' to keep me out of it. It was about ten o'clock in the mornin', and I was comin' up for a final, you know, like I was pissed. I was mad about Snooky havin' dropped a dime on me.

"When we finally got together up at my aunt's house, I was tellin' him, I said, 'Man, like why did you rap on me?'

"I grabbed him around the collar, and I was gettin' ready to hit him, and my aunt came outta the bathroom, and she was screamin'. She cursed me out, but she didn't tell me to get out or nothin' like that, so I just walked out. If I was to lay there any longer, I probably woulda gotten sassy with her, you know, and it woulda been a mean scene. That, I didn't want.

"It's just that she used to get on my nerves sometimes. So I just tipped, and I told him that when he comes downstairs I'm gonna hurt him, and my aunt was shoutin' out the window, 'You ain't goin' do nothin'.' And she was hollerin' about what she was gonna to to me if I laid a hand on Snooky.

"And I told Mumps, 'That damn Snooky rapped on me.'

"And he said, 'Yeah, you oughta put somethin' on him 'cause he knows it's wrong to be rappin' on somebody,' and he asked if I wanted him to help me, and I said no, man, I could take care of that dude by myself.

"Anyhow, I went over to the spot and I started laughin', and we just sat there and ate some potato chips and drank our sodas. We just sat on the stoop, talkin' about somethin' that didn't even make sense, just sittin' there, runnin' off the mouth. I told Mumps, 'I'm gonna go and tell Snooky that I'm not gonna bother him so he'll come downstairs. Then I'm gonna catch him and whip his ass.'

"But Snooky didn't go for it, like Snooky can be a swift little dude sometimes, and he didn't fall for it. I didn't see him out on the street all that day. He stayed at my aunt's house for two days, and then it was all right for him to go home. Miss Joann wasn't mad at him no more. He just laid in the cut, stayed outta sight until everythin' blew over. And he hadn't dropped a dime on me to the police. He just told Miss Joann that I was with him. I didn't get into any trouble for it, and I didn't stay mad for a long time.

"After a while, it just straightened itself out. When I told Snooky I wasn't gonna bother him, he wasn't sure, and he thought I just mighta had somethin' foul or treacherous in mind. A few days later, he showed back on the set, and I was high. As a matter of fact, we was all high and sittin' on the stoop, runnin' off at the mouth. Fat Leon was sittin' in the doorway of 202, and I didn't even notice him. I saw

Snooky, and he peeped me. He probably figured I still had some violence on my mind and was still gonna do a job on him, you know, beat him up or somethin'. I wasn't gonna job him, I was gonna let somebody else do it for me.

"Leon had said somebody stole some money from him outta the numbers spot. He said they took this little penny job with five dollars' worth of pennies in it. I said, 'Yeah, I heard Snooky was up there at the spot this mornin', and he was rattlin' a whole lotta change.'

"So Leon came by the spot and snatched Snooky out and started punchin' on him, and I came down and started laughin.' But Leon got carried away, like I didn't really want to hurt Snooky as bad as he was beatin' on him, so I jumped in there and started swingin' for Snooky.

"Snooky's always had a way o' doin' it. You can't stay mad at him long. He's always startin' somethin' and gettin' everybody involved in some kinda static, and, you know, like nobody can stay mad at him. If there's one person who nobody's mad at, it ends up bein' him when everything is over and cool. That just the way Snooky is. He's a car freak, a gun freak, you know, and he's just like one o' them petty-trouble freaks."

Snooky doesn't do badly in school, but he says he doesn't believe they're teaching him the truth. He admires the Muslims and would like to attend the Muslim school. He wouldn't like to be a Muslim, the life is too strict, but he would like to go to their schools because he believes they teach the truth. If you ask him anything about whether or not a pig has veins, he says, "That's one little untruth that they might teach."

But he says he's never heard them say that, and he doesn't believe that the Muslims really say that anyhow, about pigs not having veins. And everything else he says that they teach at their schools or that he's heard them talk about is peace. So he says he wants to stop attending the regular city school and go to a Muslim school, a mosque school.

Snooky smokes pot and drinks wine and gin. Dujo frequently gives him smoke on credit, and he manages to pay his way. He doesn't drink too much, and he won't drink during the week. He goes to school regularly, and he's in the last year of junior high school. He wants to go to college, too, and become an engineer. He's hoping that one day, when he learns enough about engineering, he can "go someplace and find a whole lotta pieces of cars, like in some old used-car junk lot, and get all the parts and put it together and make me a car that's better than any car that's out there on the road. Like it drives so quiet, nobody will ever hear it start up. And a car that can get more miles. You put one gallon of gas in it for every fifty miles, or somethin' like that." It's Hebro's opinion that "if Snooky can accomplish that goal he'll be the only person ever to begin as a car thief and rise to the ranks of automotive geniuses, and he won't have to do nothin' else in life."

Snooky, being only fourteen years old, doesn't take life as seriously as most of the others do, just yet. He still likes to play around most of the time. He is one of the few Hamites who can go and see movies over and over again, especially the black movies, films such as *Shaft* and *Super Fly*. He saw *Black Gun* like three times. He can spend the whole day in the movies on Sundays when all the "mini-boppers" are in there, running up and down the aisles, making more noise than a herd of wild elephants. It doesn't seem to bother him. Maybe that's because he's not so far removed from them himself. Perhaps another reason why he spends so much time in the movies is that Hebro, who works there, lets him in free at the side door, or if he's at the front door taking tickets, he lets him go in without a ticket.

Snooky derives a special pleasure from going to the movies at night because it makes him feel older. This is the first year he's been able to go into the movies at night by himself, and he gets a kick out of it. He doesn't want to be the youngest one in the group, and he doesn't want to be treated any younger than anyone else. Sometimes when he's out on the streets, some of his friends from the block pass and hit him playfully or grab him, and he gets mad and insults them for "blowin' my cool around my fellows," the Hamites, the people whom he wants to be respected by as an equal member in their society.

He tries to do all the things that everybody else in the group does. He especially admires Chips, Mumps, and Dujo. He admires Shaft, too, but Shaft is always criticizing him, so he doesn't let on just how much he actually admires him.

Snooky misses his father. He said they used to have some mellow times together. He used to like his pops even better when he was drunk because that's when he gave him the most attention, him and his brothers David and Paul. That was when they'd be clowning together and he'd be telling them all kinds of crazy stories and dirty jokes. The only time his pops could relax with him and the other kids was "when he was drunk and wasn't too serious. But it seems like when he wasn't drunk he always had pressures on his mind that couldn't let him relax and be a real father instead of just a real strict father who's like other grown people and always playin' the father part."

Apparently, when his pops got a little bit drunk on the weekends, instead of every day, he would take some time out and be friends to his children.

Somehow Snooky got the impression that his mother didn't care for his father as much when he was drunk and being friends with his kids as she did when he was sober and being "real strict" with them. Snooky would never have left home if his pops had still been there. But, he said, as far as he was concerned, everything worth staying home for had gone when his father left because he thought his mother was a little bit crazy and "Pops understood me."

His father beat him sometimes, "But he wasn't one o' those crazy fathers who's always beatin' somebody for nothin'."

And when his father beat him, he could accept it because he knew he had done something wrong, and he also knew that his father would do something to soften the blows later. He might give him some money, or he might take him out someplace, like to the movie with him. He said his mother never took him to the flick. But long before his mother put his father out, and this was also before his father started drinking every day and keeping a bottle in his pocket or in his hands all the time, he used to have more time for him. "Now he just don't seem interested no more and ain't got no time for us."

Miss Joann never took the children out. "The only time she took us out was when she took us shoppin' or someplace to see about school, or to the doctor or the dentist, somethin' like that, you know. Most o' the time she just didn't bother with us, and if we asked somethin' or if any of us asked her somethin', she was always grouchy, like somebody was botherin' her. You know, sometimes she would even tell us, 'Why don't y'all get away from me and don't bother me or stop botherin' me?' "

Snooky felt that when he left home he wasn't "botherin' her" anymore.

He sees his father once in a while out on the street, and his father never fails to ask him if he's got any money. His father will offer him a dollar or two. Snooky usually refuses it because he doesn't think his father can afford it, but sometimes he accepts it rather than offend his "movie buddy."

Every time he goes around to see his mother, "She's always talkin' some weird stuff about she's gonna send the police around here and have 'em clean out the whole place, all of us, and put everybody in jail ' 'cause y'all ain't doin' nothin' 'round there but usin' dope and carryin' on, stealin' stuff, and bein' juvenile delinquents.' "

He stopped denying it long ago, once he realized that all she wanted to do was get that sermon off her chest and she never listened to anything he said in rebuttal. So it didn't make sense for him to go through the hassle of defending himself. He would just say, "Yeah, yeah, Ma," and maybe he'd ask her for some money or food stamps. If he asked her for five dollars, she might give him three dollars, or maybe two dollars, and tell him he'd better come on home and stop acting so crazy. He thinks that she acts pretty crazy, too, crazier than he does or most people he knows. When he tells her, "I saw Daddy today," just to get her reaction, he says all she ever says is, "Oh, yeah, was he drunk?" and begins preaching about how no good he was and how he left her for the bottle. She says she thought he was married to her, and he was really married to the bottle, and she wished she had known it long before because he put her through "so much misery." She should have saved herself "a whole lotta misery and hardship by makin' him get out years before I did." She doesn't know "how she suffered so long with that man. God musta gave me strength. Any other woman that man woulda drove crazy."

Snooky gets tired of listening to that worn-out tale of woe, and he doesn't go around to see her often. He might visit his mother maybe once every two weeks. He sometimes has supper with her, but he won't stay long enough to "hear all that noise" about his father. As far as he's concerned, "Pops is still a pretty mellow dude. He's just out there doin' his thing. His thing happens to be drinkin' whiskey. It's not like he was out there drinkin' wine, right? It's like Mumps said about the junkies, they just out there doin' they thing. That's all anybody can do is his thing, whatever it is in life that he was meant to do. It's like Dee Dee sayin' that everybody's gotta follow the course of his star—that star that leads him through life—and you know he can't get off that track even if he wanted to.

"All my pops is doin' is followin' his star, and his star happens to take him to the liquor store a few more times than it takes other people. I guess junkies are followin' they stars, too, but it's not like that, it's not the same thing. He don't bother nobody. I mean he don't go around hittin' nobody in the head or muggin' somebody one way or another and breakin' into people's cribs and rippin' off they things, you know, or takin' people off, pullin' stickups and things for, you know, to follow his star. It's like his star just sorta leads him to wherever it is he's supposed to go without him botherin' anybody else too much."

Snooky says that once when he was "visiting" and his mother was asking him when was he going to stop acting so crazy and come on home, he told her, "When Daddy stops actin' crazy and come home, too!"

He said his mother's retort was, "Well, I guess you gone for good 'cause he can't come back here no more."

"I didn't say nothin' because I felt that it's okay for me not to come back anymore, and I didn't wanna come back, you know, now and live with her."

She is his mother and he loves her, he guesses, or at least he tries, but he can't see "livin' with the woman. She just took me through too many changes."

He tried to talk to her once, and he said, "Ma, why don't you and Daddy make up and try and like go back together or somethin'?"

She told him that his father was Aquarius, and he didn't understand that. He knew it was some kind of sign in the horoscope " 'cause Dee Dee was always rappin' about that," but he didn't believe in that stuff, and he said, "Well, Ma, what's that got to do with anything, his sign and his bein' Aquarius? It's like he treated you all right. He didn't beat you up all the time, right?"

He new his father had hit her a couple of times, but he figured she knew as well as he that she had it coming to her, and he knew that wasn't what she had against him.

"He's been Aquarius all the time, I mean all his life, and it didn't matter before, right? Before you put him out?"

His mother told him, "Aquarians are messed-up people, and it's nothin' you can do to change 'em. The trouble with Aquarians is that they're too loyal, they get downright devoted. They become real devoted to whatever vices they take up in life, be it drinkin', gamblin', religion, no-good women, dope, or whatever. And nobody can come in and interfere with that devotion. Anybody else is just gonna be in the way and just be ignored or get walked on. There's nothin' nobody can do about it. He's just a poor lost soul. Boy, your daddy will be forever loyal to that bottle. It's like he's married to it, and he'll be one of the most faithful husbands the bottle ever had."

Snooky wasn't really satisfied with that explanation, so he asked Dee Dee and Jill about it, and they both said, "Yeah, Aquarians are like that."

When Snooky had it confirmed by two respected authorities whom he had so much faith in, then he bought it. He said he was happy that he was not an Aquarian. He's Aries, and he's happy about that.

Jill's constantly warning Snooky about drinking too much of that "pluck" because he likes wine. "He likes that old funny-tastin' wine that they drink a lot of out there now. A lotta people say it goes good with smoke. I keep tellin' him that he better stop messin' with all that before he gets a jones for it because it might be some of it in his blood."

He becomes a little concerned. The junkie is perhaps one-half of a social stratum above the wino, and the idea of becoming a wino is a little more frightening to young people than the thought of becoming a junkie. So for a while Snooky switched from drinking wine with his smoke to drinking gin. One week he buys a bottle of gin, and the next week he'll buy a pint of wine. If he has a hangover from the pluck (wine), he might just stay off it for three or four weeks. He goes on the wagon for one or two weeks at a time, and when he says to somebody, "Let's get some wine because I haven't had a drink of wine in two weeks," he feels as though he's sort of entitled to one.

Jill tends to worry about Snooky a lot as though he were her younger blood brother. And she's always mothering him, one way or another, and constantly worrying about him as an expression of her maternal instincts, especially when Snooky is talking about guns. He's fascinated by guns, and for his age he's knowledgeable. He knows more than any of the other Hamites about guns and artillery. He's almost as fascinated by guns as he is by cars. He tells everybody about this great gun he saw in some magazine or someplace, and how he's going to get a gun. When he starts talking about guns, Jill asks, "What's the matter with you?"

Maybe she senses something in his constant chatter about guns that the other Hamites are insensitive to. Sometimes she jumps up and says, "Why don't you stop rappin' about guns all the time? Are you gun-crazy or somethin'? Maybe you seen too many movies. You better stop goin' to the movies. Maybe you don't understand that guns really kill people."

And he'll stop for a while, won't say anything about it for days. Sometimes he'll be talking about guns and Jill will enter the room, and he'll stop talking or change the subject because he likes Jill and he doesn't want to put her through changes.

Snooky can explain the difference between a .357 Magnum and a .44 Magnum. He knows that a .44 Magnum is the largest handgun in the world. He says people usually carry it as a sidearm "when they're huntin' in the jungle for big game 'cause a magnum bullet can kill a lion if it hits him in the head, and it'll stop an elephant, so you know what it'll do for people. But they make too much noise, and they're too powerful for people to carry 'em in the city 'cause they'll go through too many walls and kill people like two or three miles away—all kindsa dangerous stuff like that." He really finds it fascinating.

Snooky also knows which guns the various police forces use in fifteen major cities and how long policemen in New York City and most other cities have been using .38s as their official revolver. He knows that there's a difference between a two-inch .38 and a three-inch .38 barrel and that the amount of accuracy of the weapon depends on the length of the barrel.

He can also tell some interesting and truly fascinating gun stories. He said he read about how these five sailors went hunting huge Alaskan bear up in Alaska, and they had .50-caliber rifles. He says, "You gotta get a special permit to get a fifty-caliber rifle in this country 'cause they don't allow private citizens to own 'em. They only issue 'em out to the police force as riot guns—and fifty-calibers that's enough to stop anybody.

"Well, anyway, that's the largest-caliber rifle there is. These sailors on shore leave one day, went huntin' up in Alaska for a Alaskan bear. That's supposed to be the biggest bear in the world, you know, larger than the Kodiac bear and the brown bear. And if they stand up, they about eight feet tall, seven or eight feet tall. Well, anyway, you know, like these sailors didn't know that much about huntin' and guns. They got steel bullets to put in they guns. Then, when they shot the bear, they all emptied they guns into this bear. But the bear had enough life left in him to get to all five of 'em and kill 'em. And that's what happened.

"The reason this came off was because, because they put those steel bullets in it, and the steel balls went through the bear so fast that the hole would almost close up right away, or the bear wouldn't hardly feel it or wouldn't have time to bleed. So it was really a nut-city number for them to put the steel bullets in the guns 'cause that'll go right through somebody that's comin' at you—even with a thirty-eight—so fast that they still get to you. Even though you've snuffed 'em, it's gonna take like a little while longer to die, so much later that they'll be able to off you a couple of times, and a few other people, too, before they die."

Snooky will tell anyone who will listen why the New York City policemen use .38s instead of .45s: "Because a forty-five don't have as much accuracy as a thirty-eight, and a bigger gun'll do too much damage. And the most accurate handgun around is the P-thirty-nine, a German-made gun."

He likes the Luger, too, and he would love to have one. He seems to have a special thing for foreign guns.

The youngest of the Hamites likes to go look at guns. He can see the dummy guns in Forty-second Street store windows, but he says he wouldn't want any dummy guns. He's been to places like Coney Island where he's shot rifles, and he says he'd like to have one to go on the roof or the top floor and shoot rats. He wants a real gun. He wants any kind of real gun.

Dujo said maybe he ought to be a gunsmith. He says no, he doesn't really want to make guns. He'd like to know how to take a gun apart, but he thinks he could do that anyway. He's seen pictures of guns dismantled. He says, "You know, like they all built pretty much the same, at least on the same principle," and he believes that if he learns to take one gun apart and put it back together, he can do the same thing with any other gun.

Snooky claims he can "make a piece, but it just wouldn't be as good as a piece that's made in the factory. Really all a dude needs is a rubber band, a strong pipe, and a nail to shoot somebody. If I wanted to shoot somebody, I could do that, but that's not what I want. I just want to have a piece because it would feel good. It's like I would like to have a car."

Jill says, "The last thing Snooky needs is a gun 'cause Snooky's always gettin' in fights with people, and if he had one, somebody would get iced. Besides, the whole place would be stinkin' up more than it is now with dead rats all over. And not only that, if Snooky got on the roof, he'd probably be tempted to shoot some of those pigeons, and I'm not so sure that that's all he would shoot at, the rats and the pigeons. Snooky ain't wrapped too tight, you know, because o' those flicks he sees, with all the bad guys and the good guys shootin' each other up and one guy comes in and kills everybody else. Those're the flicks he sees three and four times."

And Jill's not sure that Snooky realizes what a big difference there is between movies and what comes off in real life. "He knows he's gonna have guns one day—it's not a urgent thing right now—just like he's gonna have a car. It would be nice to have it now, but he can live without it. Because the desire is so strong, I know he's gotta get it. It's just a matter of a little time. But a gun, NO."

When Dujo hears Jill getting on Snooky's case about guns, he always come to his defense and says that Snooky is a lot cooler than Jill thinks he is. "He gets in a lotta fights 'cause people're always messin' with him, but he don't go around startin' all those fights that he gets into."

Of course, Dujo is being a bit partial to Snooky. Now and then, Dujo tells Snooky that he should try to have some other goals in between getting the car and getting the gun, something he can do right now. "Somethin' that won't take as much time and you won't have to go through changes to get 'em."

Dujo tells everybody they should have some long-range goals, and some short-range goals to make the long-range goals seem easier. So he suggested Snooky shouldn't stop wanting guns, but he should set some short-range goals for himself before the car goal and before getting the gun. He told Snooky that one of the short-range goals he might set up for himself could be to get a piece from some girl. "You know, as a goal before you get the guns and the car, 'cause you might get a car and run into somebody or have a accident and get killed, and it would be a shame to get killed and never find out what a broad was really like. And the gun thing, you can cop that anytime if you have the bucks and really want one. You could go out and cop one now, but who needs a gun unless you really gonna off somebody?"

Dujo feels hopeful about Nita teasing Snooky, and "She might do it if he could really convince her that it was important to him."

Dujo tells Snooky, "Since you so tight with supervirgin Marva, maybe if you was to sit down and talk to her one time and tell her, when she bustin' those pimples, how much you dig her and how important it is for you to get some before you reach fifteen, she might just give it up. As a matter of fact, one of the reasons she might be a virgin is because she could be just ashamed that she don't know how to do it and might feel that some older dude would embarrass her. But if you was to be for real with her and tell her like you never had a piece either in life, maybe then she would say, 'Yeah, okay,' and she'd feel, well, y'all both new at this jammin' thing and nobody can embarrass nobody else. She might just come on. She might just be ready and waitin' for you to make your move. And maybe that's why she's so tight with you, 'cause she feels safe with you, like you don't know that much about it either. Maybe she's waitin' for you to make a move."

Snooky went for it. He said, "Yeah, that's what I'm gonna do."

He was going to set up a short-range goal before he becomes fifteen, which is in about five months, to get a piece from a broad. And after he's done that, "like I'm just gonna keep on concentratin' on gettin' my car. Yeah, the gun thing can wait, it's not so important as a car."

When he'd thought about it for a while, he said, "Maybe nothin' is as important as the girl goal." His virginity doesn't seem to bother him as much as it disturbs the others, but he told Dujo that he was going to make that a goal. He's going to let him know when he's had some, and he wants him to give him some free smoke. Dujo said, "Yeah, all right." He would give him some free smoke as a celebration or congratulatory gift when he got some. That was enough to cool him out for a while and stop Snooky from worrying about the gun.

TWELVE

Hebro

Hebro is sixteen years old, he's six feet, three inches tall, and weighs 217 pounds. He wants to be a football player. He's the strongarm for the Hamites, or the unofficial peace officer. He goes around knocking people out, and he's the big brother and protector for the family. Many in the block, I'm certain, allow the Hamites to get away with numerous offenses that they wouldn't ordinarily tolerate because they don't want to deal with Hebro. They know if they "come down" on any members of the family, they will have to answer to Hebro.

Hebro smokes pot and drinks wine, but he does it in moderation. He does practically everything in moderation. He keeps himself in good physical shape. He's undoubtedly the "straightest" member of the Hamites. Hebro doesn't actually live at one of the spots. He still lives with his folks across the street, and he takes some of the Hamites up to his house from time to time. He says his pops is all right. He says he digs his parents. He once told me, "When I was a little kid, my pops used to tell me, 'Boy, I'll kick you ass.' And when I got as big as he was, he said, 'Boy, I'll cut your throat.' And he meant both threats."

I suppose the respect that he has for his father is still based on fear because whenever his pops tells him to do something he hurries up and does it. And Hebro hurries for no one else. Hebro stays at the spot on the weekends, and in the evenings he's there after he finishes his job. He works after school and on the weekends as an usher in the local movie theater. Most of his spare time is spent at the spot with the Hamites.

Stretch asked Hebro, "Why don't you think you ever used scag, or did you? What do you think stopped you from probin' the scag scene like so many of the young dudes around here?"

"There are two things that I'm allergic to that I know of, and that's coffee and scag. I don't mess wit' 'em 'cause they make me sick. I mean deathly sick."

Whenever a stranger or anybody else is foolish enough to come around and start some trouble with the Hamites, it doesn't take him long to discover his folly. Hebro usually educates him quickly. Nobody has to tell Hebro what to do. He just goes up to the stranger and knocks him out. That's Hebro's position in the group. He knows what's expected of him, and he does it. And he likes being feared by people.

The junkies, too, stay away from the building where the spots are located, mainly because of Hebro. Hebro once hung a junkie off the roof by his ankles and had him dangling and hollering. Lee asked Hebro why was he so hard on junkies, and he said that they were foul, real foul.

"For example, I saw some junkies do some really foul stuff about three o'clock one mornin' out on Eighth Avenue. This man had come outta a hallway, and somebody had slit his throat from ear to ear, and he was bleedin' like a pig. So it's like the dude staggered against a storefront and started to sink down to the ground. He was fallin' and tryin' to stay on his feet, and he didn't know where he was. Maybe he was drunk, too. But he was halfway clean.

"He had on a suit, and he looked like he mighta had some money. When he first like came outta the hallway, outta the buildin', there was nobody in sight. But as he started like fallin', the junkies swarmed all over him from outta nowhere. I mean, a second before, you didn't even see 'em. They came down on this dude like buzzards, man. Nobody saw 'em comin', nobody saw where they came from. They tore the dude's pockets off his pants. I mean they didn't bother to take what was in 'em out. They just tore 'em off. Tore his jacket off him and everything.

"The dude is hurt, and this is serious stuff, and you would think anybody would call a ambulance or do somethin'. You know, ask the man, 'Mister, what's wrong? Can I do somethin' for you?' Or try to get the police so they could take him to the hospital. But the junkies was just takin' him off. They took his watch, they took his shoes, they took his coat. They just took everything. All this was done in about maybe twenty seconds. They left him there like in his shirt. I don't know why they didn't take that. Maybe it had too much blood on it. They left the dude layin' there in his shirt and socks and in a pool of blood, and they just disappeared. They had picked him clean.

"I'm layin' back, just pinnin' it, and I'm sayin' to myself, Them dirty, rotten mothas. I went over there and peeped at the dude, he was in a pool of blood, and I guess the man didn't need the stuff they took 'cause he bled to death on the spot right where he fell. I called the police and told 'em that there was a man here with his throat cut, and it looked like he was dyin'. They came, and they took him away.

"I've seen junkies do all kindsa foul stuff. Junkies are like wolves or buzzards. Man, they ain't people. Everybody got a little bit o' feelin' or sympathy for anybody, I mean it don't have to be nobody you know or anybody related to you, but junkies ain't got no sympathy for nobody. That's why I ain't got no feelin's for them. It's hard for me to look at junkies like they people 'cause they don't act like people. I've heard that rats will eat their young—or wolves, if one gets hurt, the pack eats him. Dopeys are the same way, you know. They ain't even got no sympathy for each other.

"They could be at a shootin' gallery, gettin' off, and if, let's say, one junkie should go into a coma or somethin', like he's OD'in', instead of tryin' to bring him out or save the dude's life, the first thing the other dopeys goin' think about, it's gettin' what he's got. They be hopin' he's got some scag, or maybe they saw him puttin' some money in his pocket. Everybody's just goin' be on him in the spot and pickin' him clean. Ain't nobody thinkin' about savin' the dopey's life.

"That's the kinda stuff sharks do, you know, or to me it's like vultures. They be out there, layin'. The buzzards don't be sympathizin' if there's somebody dyin' on the desert. They be out there thinkin' about, yum, yum, they waitin' for the dude to die. It's the same wit' 'em. They all seem to be waitin' for each other to die. It's like that's all they live for, to do somethin' foul to somebody or even to each other. You know, it's like if one of the junkies sees another dopey cop, and he puts it in his pocket, and they don't see him no more till late at night, well, they still got it in they mind that they saw this dude put some money in his left back pocket early this mornin'. I think they the foulest people on the face o' the earth.

"Now, if I had my way like, I'd solve the dopey problem. I'll tell you what I'd do. You know, in China they had a dope-fiend problem when Mao Tse-tung came to power, and he told the dopeys they gotta come on and clean up. He gave 'em like more than a year to do it, and he set up all these clinics and everything for the junkies to come and kick their joneses and clean up. But not enough dope fiends showed. They didn't pay that much attention to it 'cause they dug bein' junkies. It's like that was their thing. That's what they wanted to do, and they said, 'Hell with Mao Tse-tung.' But after a while he went around and just started wipin' out the dopeys. Everybody he saw in a nod, I guess.

"It's kinda different over there 'cause it was a opium jones. Not like scag. And, you know, like the dude wanted to build a new nation, and he just didn't have time for dopeys, and besides, he's gave 'em a chance to clean up and they didn't wanta take it. After a while he told 'em—I guess they thought he was jivin' or somethin'—but he told 'em, 'Please, this is the last time I'm askin' y'all, you clean up or die.'

"And they still didn't pay any attention to him, so what the dude did is that he sent trucks and planes around and started scoopin' 'em up, and they say that he just iced thirty million junkies in cold blood. Everybody thinks Hitler was a serious dude, but Mao was much more deadly. Like this dude went and iced thirty million dope fiends. Later on, he iced all the cats and dogs in the country 'cause it was cheaper than feedin' em. Now, ain't that somethin' cold?

"But Mao was right. If the country was doin' bad and he was tryin' to get 'em out from under the white man's foot, he can't have some ol' simpleminded dude who don't wanna do nothin' but nod or dream or just shoot dope holdin' him back. So he got rid of 'em.

"That's just what I would do. I would tell all these dopeys I'll give 'em about three months to clean up and square up and get off all the street corners, get outta all the shootin' galleries—and everybody sellin' dope, you know, you gotta ice the dope dealers, too. I wouldn't have any kinda prison system goin' for 'em. That cost money, too, like keepin' them dudes in food and clothes in prison. Just tell 'em, 'Hey, man, ain't nobody got time for that 'cause we got a new program here and you're either down wit' it or you dead.'

"And I'd give the dudes in jail an opportunity to get outta jail. Now, the deal would be this. Say you doin' life, usually for murder or somethin'. I'd go around the country and get the coldest dudes I can find and give 'em a quota like for every junkie they ice. They would get like a half a week off their sentence.

"We goin' clean up the dope dealers, too, 'cause we goin' ice them first, and then like the dope fiends who don't wanna clean up, they goin' get iced. You get all these killers, truckloads of 'em, and put 'em all over the city where you know the dope fiends hang out, like all up and down Eighth Avenue, all up and down Lenox Avenue, but the Eighth Avenues and the Lenox Avenues in all of the cities all over the country. And you have signs up all over the place like, 'It's Judgment Day comin',' and like, 'That's gonna be the day o' cleanin' up.'

"You have countdown signs every day, just like the newspapers show for Christmas that you got twenty-one more shoppin' days to Christmas. You have these signs bein' put up, put ads in the newspapers. You put it on television and on radio that junkie doomsday is comin', you got twenty-one more days to clean up or it's over for you. And you just do that every day, and you emphasize it stronger and stronger, and as you start gettin' down to the wire and you tell 'em, you know, every day on the radio you have a minute of silent prayer for all the dopeys who didn't clean up 'cause this is gonna be doomsday. You have a national advance funeral service the day before for all of 'em who didn't clean up.

"The next day you just turn loose the killer squad on the places where they hang out. You have a doomsday prison come-out. They gotta kill. Everybody's got a quota. They goin' get a half a week off their time for every junkie they kill, and they don't have nothin' but baseball bats to bust heads open with. And not ordinary baseball bats, but you get baseball bats with lead tips on 'em so that when they hit a dude they bust his head open and you have blood flowin' down streets like a bloodbath.

"I mean this is stuff that history won't even wanna talk about. I mean historians ain't goin' say nothin' about this 'cause this would be a infamous act—'cause, you know, it's goin' sound kinda cold and foul, and it might be if somebody didn't know what the situation was and was just lookin' back on it. But, you know, Americans can take it 'cause this country's done a lotta foul stuff. And it wouldn't be really that foul 'cause you gave everybody a chance to come on and clean up. It wouldn't be like you just snuck up on 'em and nobody knew what was comin'. Not like you just turned a goon squad loose on some poor defenseless and suspectin' nice people.

"After you do this, if you miss any dopeys who still alive, man, they goin' clean up so fast, I mean go someplace and cold-turkey it out and swear they ain't never used no dope and they wouldn't wanna know each other. You wouldn't see 'em hangin' around noplace. And it would be a whole new scene. I'm sure that'd be the solution for it.

"If I was to go to the City and say, 'Hey y'all give me a million dollars, and I'll clean up the dopeys for you, I'll solve the problem of junkies once and for all,' they would probably say, 'No, we can't do that 'cause that's too cruel.'

"It's cruel to have 'em out there goin' through all the miseries that they goin' through and at the same time puttin' other people through all kindsa changes behind that old foul stuff that they be doin', hittin' a old woman in the head with an iron pipe for her Social Security check. That's pretty foul, too, man. And I know they do it. That's why I don't have any sympathy for no junkies. Now, I could see throwin' a dopey off the roof or hittin' 'em in the head with a baseball bat 'cause I know what they'll do. I ain't got no sympathy for those creatures out there who ain't got no sympathy for nobody or even themselves.

"If you was to tell the City somethin' like this, behind white folks bein' such hypocrites anyway, they would say no, we can't do that 'cause that's too foul. But they'd be BS'in' 'cause dope is a big-time industry out there, and the people in power, they are not interested in gettin' rid of the dopeys 'cause they makin' the bucks. You don't have that many white dopeys. White folks don't care 'cause they lose more than that in the war and don't even think about it. It's mainly a problem wit' black folks.

"Junkies usually hang out and crib in black neighborhoods, and they rip off black folks, and the white folks just lay back and make the money. They make the bucks in the courts and through the rehabilitation programs that never rehabilitate nobody. They make the bucks through the import-export, the smugglin' thing, you know. They make the bucks through sellin' needles and syringes and through sellin' milk sugar to cut it wit'. They make the bucks through sellin' the wine to go along with the methadone that people seem to have to have now with their scag. They make the bucks through sellin' the little cellophane bags that everybody puts the dope in, or sellin' the tinfoil that people but blow in, you know, and they make the bucks by sellin' the Cadillacs that the big dope dealers use to flash and let everybody know that they dealin' dope. They make money through the police. It's a big-time industry. One way or another, officially or unofficially, the dope industry in this country employs at least as many people as General Motors.

"Now, everybody be talkin' that talk about inflation. It's like, you know, it would really be a big inflation if the dope industry had some real money problems, but 'cause this is somethin' that has to be done, it's just like dope fiends have to use their dope just like people gotta eat, you know, you gotta have food. So nobody even worries about that. Let's say suddenly there was no more dope in the world and the people who was employed in that industry became unemployed, you'd have to have a whole different kind of unemployment system 'cause nobody could afford to deal with all these people. You know, if you got money, and you white, in America you don't have to worry about no dope fiends. You know, they ain't comin' in your neighborhood and mess wit' you. You got police protection. The only people that ain't got no police protection is poor black folks. But the police and the law says, 'Yeah, well, that's too bad. Y'all got a bad problem, but y'all better not take any sho'nuff steps to solve it. Y'all better come on and stay within the law, which means that you better keep on sufferin'.'

"The junkies out there, they be takin' people off, maybe robbin' places, but we leave the spots open here and they don't come in. They know that we got a television, but if they come in here and I catch 'em they ain't comin' out. They know they goin' end up in the morgue. All they need, and they know this, is for me to catch 'em wrong. If I catch the dudes in here, I'm goin' break they backs before they go out the window. If I come down the street, the junkies out there, they walk on the other side of the street 'cause they know I don't care for 'em. I ain't got nothin', you know, in my heart for 'em but some violence. I'll commit mayhem on them mothas in a minute, and they know it. They get in flight when they see me comin'. I got more feelin' and sympathy, you know, for that roach on the floor over there than I got for a junkie.

"I remember when we first took over the spots, they was comin' in here. Three of 'em was sleepin' in the spot upstairs. They just came in here and bogarted us outta the spot. We was younger then. Well, some of the fellows wanted to go up there and throw some hot water on 'em and that silly sorta thing. But I thought that was light stuff. I said, 'Well, let me throw 'em out the window.'

"But them guys didn't wanta do that, they too softhearted and all. So I said, 'All right, y'all wanta throw somethin' on 'em. Why don't we just throw some lighter fluid on 'em or gasoline, you know, and fire 'em up. And when the word gets around about that number, ain't none of 'em goin' come back here no more 'cause they goin' start lookin' at the place like the inferno, and it'll give the buildin' a choice name. You'll just have real people comin' here.'

"But, you know, the dudes didn't wanta do that. They said that's too cold. They wouldn't go for it, so we poured some hot water on 'em and burned their asses up—I mean somethin' good. They ain't come back no more. If like any of the family have some static with the dopeys, they usually try and keep it from me that some dopey out there did somethin' to one of my people. We'll just have that as his epitaph: Here lies So-and-so, Dopey So-and-so, Junkie So-and-so, who did somethin' to one of the Hamites, as you call us, and Hebro found him.

"So a lotta times I hear about stuff that came off a week or two weeks after it went down 'cause nobody would tell me before. Very often the dopey done got in flight before that 'cause somebody probably ran it to him that that's one of Hebro's people and he know that he can't stay around here. They more afraid of me than they are the police 'cause they know if I'm lookin' for a dopey the other dopeys don't want him around 'cause I'm some heavy pressure and they don't want it on 'em. So ain't nobody gonna be around him, even the dope dealers out there. We usually don't have no static.

"A dope dealer is harder on black folks than whitey is. In the Ku Klux Klan they go around doin' foul stuff to black folks, but at least we know that they the enemy and they ain't comin' in the neighborhood. But you find dope dealers out there doin' foul stuff to your own people. You know all they doin' is sabotagin' it from the inside. They sabotagin' the whole black program. It's like people out there tryin' to make bucks figure if the people stupid enough to buy dope and pay that expensive price for their own self-destruction, somebody's goin' ice 'em one way or another. They so anxious to die, they payin' a heavy price for it. I guess they figure if they don't do it, somebody else is goin' do it."

"Hebro, you have a job, don't you? Don't you work in the flick around there on the block after school?"

"Yeah, I'm a usher there. I work there on Saturdays and Sundays and after school. That's kinda mellow. I get to see all the flicks, and I meet a lotta broads from all over the neighborhood."

"Yeah, are you in a position to let the Hamites in for free?"

"Yeah, you know, I'm not supposed to. But when my people come around, sometimes I get some tickets, and I get passes, and I give 'em to Jill and Connie and Dee Dee. But you know what happens. Snooky and Salt-Noody, Mumps and Dujo come around, and sometimes everybody comes, you know, the whole family, and I open the door, the side door, for 'em. The other two dudes let their people in, and I don't say nothin' on 'em, and I know they ain't goin' say nothin' on me. It's like a understandin'. And that's cool, too. It's like havin' a position in the community. It's like in a way, you got some power. You can do somthin' for somebody.

"And I get a lotta respect. If I tell people they smokin' in the wrong, nonsmokin' section, ain't too many people goin' give me no mouth about it. I only had to knock out about three or four dudes who got simpleminded on me, you know, mouthy. I told 'em they not supposed to be drinkin' in there. As a rule, I don't get no static. I don't go around gorillain' nobody. Once everybody gets to know you, you don't get no more static. Like they've tried you, you been tested, and you proved your point, what you all about, and like that's where it is now. You know, it's peaceful there, and it's quiet. It's dark.

"But the kids on Saturday, on the weekends, can sho'nuff be a hassle. It's really more like a nursery on Saturday and Sunday. Moms and pops throw 'em out the house 'cause, I guess, they want to jam. They just give 'em some money, let 'em go to the flick, and they be in there all day. I'll put 'em out, so they act halfway cool, but how cool can kids act? They got too much energy, and they gotta make noise. I think kids would go crazy if they didn't make noise.

"But other than that, it's sorta a cool gig. And more than that, it keeps me off the street. If I'm out there, I'm liable to get into some trouble. Sometimes I get out here, and I'm just as human as anybody else, I get bored, and I want somethin' to happen to me, want to go dopey-huntin'.

"This way I got some money, and I don't have to ask my pops for nothin'. My pops gives me some money when he gets paid, but most of my clothes I buy wit' my own money. Havin' the gig at the flick gives me a feelin' of independence. I don't have to play the real kid role and go and say, 'Hey, Daddy, can I have this or that? Daddy, I need a new pair of shoes, or jacket.' It's like I got my money, and I just go and cop, you know. It takes away some of that beggin' thing.

"It ain't no great gig, but it is a gig. You have some strange experiences in there. Sometimes a dude'll be in the john, and he be sittin' there all day, and you have to check it out. You come back two hours later, and you see the same pair o' shoes is still under there. You lookin' under the door of the john, and he ain't moved yet. You can go in there, and you find that the dude is dead. Junkies be comin' in the flick, and they be sittin' on the toilet like takin' off, and they just OD there and keep on takin' off. Yeah, I seen a couple o' cases of people OD'in' on the toilet in the flick. That's just part of the game.

"In a couple o' years I'm goin' get away from all o' this, you know, all this madness out here. I'm goin' go to college, play some football, and forget I ever saw Harlem. Like this ain't it. I mean this ain't the place to do no kinda serious business. And I know I'm not goin' be here too long. When I leave Harlem and get in college, I'm never even goin' look back. I'm goin' act like this scene never happened to me. The one thing I've got that's halfway decent here is the fellas and the family. If I didn't see a way out, I think I'd just hang it up 'cause this ain't nothin' to live with. I just couldn't take it. I think I've had my fill of it. I can think of stuff that goes on out in the street and get sick. Maybe that's a third thing that I'm allergic to, Harlem life. Yeah, that makes me sick, too, when I think about it. I'm allergic to coffee, scag, and Harlem life. Now ain't that some serious shit?"

Dee Dee says that all one has to do is look at Hebro, and he can tell right away that he's a Taurus. "It's like Hebro has always just wanted to be what he is naturally. Big and strong. He doesn't care to bully people 'cause he believes that that's askin' for trouble, and if you ask for trouble long enough, somebody's gonna give it to you."

Hebro used to admire Karate Bob, Nita's father. Hebro talked about Karate Bob with reverence. "Like this dude was always movin'." He'd like to be as bad a dude as somebody like Karate Bob, but he wouldn't want to go around gorillaing people because to Hebro's way of thinking, that's suicide. So he can settle for being strong like Big Lester, Mae the drug dealer's old man. He says he saw

Lester "hit a dude, a big dude, and knock him all the way across the street. The dude didn't stop stumblin' and fallin' until he hit the other side of the street."

Hebro admires this kind of thing. He said he'd never seen anybody hit that hard in his whole life. He used to take a little karate, but there was too much practicing involved. Somebody told him he would have to break his hands eventually, to do the "real karate thing." He knows he doesn't need that much karate because he's a pretty big dude. "I'm a big dude, and people ain't goin' be messin' wit' me anyhow."

He wants to be an athlete. He yearns to play professional football someday. He says he was made to play football, "you know, a rough game." Hebro raved about the movie *The Longest Yard* because it was about some "sho'nuff rough football." He says he knows that as an athlete he's going to be abused economically. "They still don't like to give black athletes no real money. But that's where the money is, and that's where big, strong dudes can really put their natural abilities and strengths to a good cause."

Hebro says he believes "all the big dudes and the strong dudes and the fast dudes are paid a lotta bucks to keep 'em off the streets from robbin' people and pullin' stickups. They take care of athletes, and it's gettin' better because they got a black baseball manager now. They even pay ball players like Wilt Chamberlain more money than they pay white dudes."

He knows that there's still a lot of prejudice in sports, but he thinks it's getting better. By the time he finishes college and goes out to play professional football, he feels that things are going to be changed so much that they are liable to have a black football team manager "or somethin'." He believes that things are changing. He cites the case of John Carlos. "You remember, one of the brothers who put the hand up with the black glove at the 1968 Olympics in Mexico? They was doin' their protest thing for their people and what they believe in. Juan Carlos was like six foot, three inches, weighed two hundred pounds, and he was built. They used to call him the fastest man alive. But he ain't been able to get a job since 1968. One time he got with the Toronto Argonauts, but they peeped him. Every time a team finds out who he is, that he's a black dude who raised a black glove in protest for black people in America.

"The white folks in America could go along wit' King and his marches and everything, but here's a brother like John Carlos, they wouldn't even let him make a livin'. It's like he didn't make up any lies on America. All he was doin' was sayin', 'Hey, I don't dig this prejudice.'

"And he wasn't a professional athlete then, but they not goin' let him make any bucks 'cause he was man enough to show how he felt about it.

"That whole sports scene is kinda hard and rough 'cause, you know, you goin' have to walk with a whole lotta stuff. I bet they give white athletes more money on the side, they give 'em property, some shares in stock that nobody knows about. Yeah, but you know they gotta have somethin' for us black dudes to do. Can you imagine the kinda problem they'd have if all the black dudes, let's say Wilt Chamberlain, people like Jim Brown, was out there committin' crimes, you know, and Bubba Smith. That would be like some hard law-enforcement problems all around.

"It's not as easy as it was to fool blacks 'cause like today blacks know more than they knew a few years ago. The white people wouldn't publish it in *Sports Illustrated* about John Carlos, but they could get him a job in a minute, and the man could be gettin' a salary that he deserves 'cause he was a believer. He was young, you know, and in school at the time, and all the college students was doin' the same thing. Everybody was protestin'. They graduated from school, you mean they ain't goin' let 'em get a job? They better! But in the sports world they got away wit' it by what they doin' to John Carlos. If blacks had the strength or a strong organization, we could do somethin' about it, I mean do somethin' and make ourselves heard, and say we goin' see to it that the man gets a job or we goin' strike, like all the blacks on every football team, baseball team, 'cause here's one o' the greatest livin' athletes this country's ever seen, and they won't give him a job just because he was young once."

Hebro, because he is serious about wanting to become an athlete, leads a pretty righteous life. He doesn't drink much. He likes to drink orange juice. And he smokes some herbs, but he won't dabble with anything else. He doesn't like gin, but it doesn't bother him to see the other Hamites getting high on smoke and drinking wine and vodka or gin because that's "their thing." He wants to keep his body in good condition.

"You know, there's a natural instinct, maybe it's a part of that, you know, survival instinct, where you don't wanna do nothin' that's goin' hurt you. Liquor's goin' hurt you. I mean not just what it does to the system and makes you weak and somebody could come and do a job on you, start takin' you through changes, but, you know, it messes up the mind, and it messes up your stomach. It's like the natural thing is to survive and do somethin' that's not goin' hurt yourself. Liquor is legal, but it's not healthy. When the law goes against nature, ain't nothin' nobody can do but ignore the law. Now, if the folks that made the law had any sense, those dudes would be changin' the law because they know it's a stupid law.

"The real religion in this country is the dollar, and they'll kill everybody to get it. Now, people who don't admit this either is ignorant or they just stupid or they lyin', you know. When they have all those food scandals and they know that some drugs are harmful, they won't take 'em off the market—you know, certain legal drugs, and the foods when they get bad, people don't wanna take 'em off the market. They still wanta sell 'em. I guess they send it up to Harlem, say, 'Sell it to black folks.' The real thing is the dollar, you know. Same thing with the whiskey. As long as whiskey is makin' all that money, they go on, and you see ads in every magazine, every newspaper, Buy whiskey, buy whiskey.

"Now, a whole lotta people walkin' around here thinkin' like the god sign in this country is a cross. No, that ain't the god sign. The god sign is really the dollar sign. That's what people worship, that's what they pray to, and, you know, if you goin' really get down to it, I guess that's what keeps the country goin' 'round. Everybody else says, 'God protects, God provides, and God saves, and God does this, and God will make a way.' My moms is always sayin', 'God will make a way.' If the dollar is doin' everything that God was supposed to do, or people say only God can do, then the dollar must be God, right? That makes sense to me.

"The Muslims know about the dollar. They real serious about bucks, you know, they some serious moneymakers. They have that thing up there, the star and the crescent, over their temple. But their real god is money, just like it is for all the other religions in this country. When they first started out wit' those Steak 'n' Take places, the sandwiches was pretty good. But then they started makin' these sandwiches that didn't have any steak in it. It became really a bread sandwich with some onions thrown on it. It was just a come-on like all the white businesses and all the other money worshipers in America.

"I think the most for-real dude out there in the religion game is Reverend Ike. He gives sermons on makin' money, you know. He ain't jivin'. He goes around talkin' a little stuff about God for old people who like to hear that, like the old sisters in the church, 'cause if you don't mention God two or three times, they forget that they in church and they start not believin' it. But he makes it plainly understood that he is for money and that God is money. He's the closest thing to a sho'nuff religious man in America."

To Hebro the group he protects is his congregation, and their candid and open relationship with each other is what he believes in. "I believe in frankness myself. It's like that's how you get your point over. That's how people know what's on your mind and don't go around messin' wit' you all the time, you know. It's like we can—take Dujo, for instance, he's not that frank. It takes him a long time to get his point over. I mean he goes in a sorta roundabout way. I'm frank. Like Chips is frank. Chips is all right. He's really mellow, a swift brother. He's down, and his head is on right. You know, it's like all the Hamites are together. We know who we are, what we are, and we're not afraid to say it. It don't make sense to be afraid anyhow 'cause if you don't say it other people will. Now, when Chips had this thing where he says like, you know, he thinks Nita's cute. I mean he digs her, but it's just that she's a black broad—she's a little too black for him. It's like that's just a personal preference thing. Everybody's got his preference in broads. Like some dudes dig fat broads, some dudes like skinny broads, some dudes dig short broads, and some dudes like tall broads.

"You know, it's the same way wit' other things. Everybody don't like the same kinda car, and everybody likes a different kinda high. And I think when people dig somethin', they oughta be man enough to stand up and say it. I think Nita is the most beautiful broad here, but that's just my preference. Now, nobody can tell me not to dig her, and I can't tell nobody else to dig her, you know, 'cause if they like somebody else, solid, but it's just the way the light falls on that sister, man.

"You know, like the light could be comin' through the window there on a day like last Sunday. She comes outta that room and stopped at the window, and when she turned I thought I was seein' a dream, that broad looked so beautiful. I wish I could write some poetry. I just told her, 'Don't move.' And she stood there, man, and I looked at her, and you know what it's like, my peter got harder than it had ever been in my life before. I had to put my hand in my pocket to hold it down so that she wouldn't peep me goin' through this thing about her. And I told her I just wanted to see somethin' afterward, you know. I told her I wanted to look at her. But it's like she was sorta shinin', and she looked so good. I really just wanted to eat her alive. But it's like that's a personal thing. With just me and what I see, and everybody's got their own like personal thing.

"You know, I've never been attracted to light-skinned broads. Maybe it's got somethin' to do with what I think would go good with me, or maybe in the back of my mind I'm thinkin' about the kinda kids we would have, but I don't think in terms of color or complexion. When I get into it wit' a broad, it's like it's just somethin' that happened.

"Anyway, I'm goin' come right out and tell you that I don't dig somethin' if I don't like it, and I'm goin' come right to the point. I'm not goin' call a meetin' like in Dujo's style. I'm just gonna tell it to whoever the person is, and just what's on my mind. Like that's the only way we make it here. I guess that's one o' the main reasons why we been tight for so long, because everybody knows that everybody else wants them to say what's on their minds. I mean you come on and speak your piece, like somebody say somethin' wrong or you feel that it's not right, you go on and you speak on it. Don't hold no secrets on it 'cause all that's goin' do is, you know, like keep the problem goin' and it's gonna happen again. Sooner or later you goin' have to come on out and speak on it. So you do that from the jump.

"I mean if you get it out front from the jump, then everything is where you can start like hashin' it out, and if it gets that tough, you go on and you do battle about it. But if people never speak on it they just won't know what it is, they won't know what's happenin'. Frankness, I think, is good for any relationship, if it's like sho'nuff frankness, and not somebody just tryin' to hurt somebody's feelin's. I mean, let's say, a broad is stinkin', you can't go up to her and say, 'Hey, baby, you sure smell bad.'

"I mean that's goin' to hurt her, but if she ask you somethin' like, let's say, a broad was to ask, 'Hey, how does this look?' and it looks funny on her, and you up and say, 'That's outta sight, that's really swift, you are hooked up, mama, and together.' Then she goes outside and she lookin' funny, you ain't doin' her no favor, and she's goin' be mad at you, you know. The next time she ain't goin' even bother askin' you. She's gonna say, 'Like this dude, he's goin' come out wit' stuff, tellin' me some noise.' Now, the frank thing, she's gonna appreciate that 'cause she'll put it together and really get hooked up right before she goes out and lets some strangers peep her.

"So I believe in frankness, I think it's one o' the most valuable things that people got goin' for 'em. Like if you ain't got nothin' else and you got some frankness, that leaves you unpoor. You can not have a penny, not a cent to your name, but if you frank, you worth somethin' to somebody 'cause everybody can use some frankness, even those who don't know it. It's just a matter of time before they find out where it's at. You know, I dig it when people tell me that I'm wrong, and I'm not goin' go and ask nobody who I feel not goin' run it to me, like be scared or somethin', or goin' try to hurt my feelin's. And I think I made some good connections with my people here, you know, the Hamites. We all tell it to each other like it is. You know, we don't hold back nothin' on nobody."

THIRTEEN

Chips

Chips is seventeen, and the smoothie of the Hamites, the swiftest one there. He takes numbers on the night track, and he always has enough money to lend to the other Hamites. He's also the lover of the group. It was Chips who attracted Connie into the family. Once Connie was a challenge to Chips, but after the conquest he lost interest. Chips enjoys himself. He smokes pot and drinks wine and plays a lot of basketball, but he leaves scag alone. He's been close to it for most of his life, but he never touches it.

He's got ambition of a kind. He's a serious student in school, and he says he'd like to get a scholarship to play basketball at some college and finish college and go into pro ball. It is possible. He's an exceptionally skillful ball player. Everybody admits that.

He likes to dress in the latest fashions. He wants to be like Walt Frazier and play a mean game of basketball, dress "real suave," wear custom-made white mink coats, and drive a custom-made Rolls-Royce. That's his idea of success, and he strives diligently toward his goal. He is a very determined young man when it comes to doing what he wants to do. He's had an amazing amount of success at doing this sort of thing, for his age.

Chips has two chipped teeth, whence cometh his name. His parents used to live in the same building where the spots are located. When they moved out almost two years ago, Chips stayed. He's always been "out there," making money somehow on the streets, one way or another.

Chips grew up in the middle of the drug thing. Both parents were into it. When he was thirteen years old he met Sheryl, who tried to turn him on to drugs and couldn't succeed, but they got tight nevertheless, and he was always around the drug scene. When Sheryl's mother Mae was in the dope business, he dealt a lot of drugs for her.

Just about every one of the Hamites has a favorite saying, like Salt-Noody's always saying, "Ain't nobody nothin' anyway." Well, Chips has a favorite saying, too. He'll say something is "fast, real fast," and he isn't necessarily referring to speed. He says things like, "faster than a shit fly in panic." Once I asked him, "How fast is a shit fly in panic?" And he answered, "A shit fly in panic is faster than a hummin'bird, and a hummin'bird can fly faster than the eye can follow." He plays basketball, so he appreciates speed. He'd like to have a sports car when he has made it, or something that's fast, to go with his custom-made Rolls-Royce.

If anything should happen when he's in college to keep him from becoming a professional basketball player, he says, "If something should happen so I couldn't play, if I was to hurt a knee or something, then I would go on to medical school." Because he thinks "the doctor is like the best legitimate hustle they got going."

Biology is his favorite subject now, and he would major in that, or chemistry, or zoology. He's assuming he'll have enough money because he has a knack for making money on the streets. And he's certain that if he becomes a doctor instead of a basketball player, he'd still be able to pull down enough "long money" so that he could have his white mink coat and his custom-made Rolls-Royce and his fast sports cars, a Maserati or Ferrari or something like that. He would still be able to live in the style he wants to. He would simply obtain his goal by a different route. He anxiously wants to do it, he wants to do it as soon as possible because he believes that life is supposed to be lived fast. He likes fast women, too. That's why he and Sheryl were tight for so long.

I asked him why he leaves scag alone when he's been so close to it all his life, and he answered, "I feel as good as I wanta feel behind some smoke and wine, so why bother with anything else? Especially somethin' that would make you look bad and put you down. I've seen dope change people and turn them into something mean. I mean from Dr. Jekyll to a permanent Mr. Hyde in only a few months. Man, that's not for me. I can't use it. I could see what drugs do to other people, and I was certain it would have the same effect on me, you know, a psychocriminal effect. Like my old runnin' partner Glen, now, he's sho'nuff, sho'nuff strung out. We smoke all the reefer we want, drink all the wine we want, but that don't make us winos or potheads. It's like you could smoke all the herb you want, and you know it don't bother you physically. You can run around and play as much ball as you want, and you still feel good. But you know if you were goin' around jonesin' and you tried runnin' out on a basketball court and playin' some ball, the strain of it would probably kill you. It would take everything outta you. And me, I appreciate bein' in good physical condition, and I never messed with anything that's gonna jeopardize my physical health."

Chips worked for Mae from about 1971 until the apartment was burned out in 1973. Chips says, "Mae would have a gate on the outside of the apartment door, and two heavy iron gates on the inside of the door, and the door had five locks on it so if the narcs or raise ever busted the joint it would take 'em so long to get in past those gates, you could get rid of a whole factory in that time. Out of the windows, in the toilet, and everyplace. I guess she never thought about gettin' outta there if a fire broke out in the joint. Anyway, I worked for her until the fire. I sold it, and I carried it, too. I saw a lotta people "comin' out," and I knew a whole lotta stuff that was goin' down, so I used to keep my eyes open, peepin' a whole lotta things, and then I'd shoot it to her, and she'd thank me or give me some money or somethin', and then I used to always ask her if she wanted me to do somethin', if I could do somethin' for her. And after a while, because I was tight with her daughter Sheryl anyway, I used to just stay up there. First of all, she let me sit on the garbage can."

"Wait a minute, back up there. What does 'sit on the garbage can' mean?" I inquired of Chips.

"You know how the junkies are always buyin' wine to mix with their meth and their scag? They like to have the wine near the spots where they go and cop. So Mae realized it was a good business to have the wine, but not in the same spot where they got the scag 'cause it'd be too much traffic, people comin' up there for one bottle of wine. This is bootleg wine. You get it for seventy-five cents in the store, but it runs from a dollar twenty-five to a dollar fifty in the bootleg spot. Now, that was my thing. I used to be sittin' about a quarter of a block down from where the dope spot was, sittin' on the garbage can, foolin' wit' a bottle of wine. I would sell wine like hotcakes at a dollar fifty a bottle. They'd go in and get their scag and their meth, and they would pass me sittin' there on the wine box or on the garbage can, and I'd just be dealin' it out. I used to sell sometimes five or six hundred bottles a day. She came and picked up the bucks every time she brought another case, she was kinda swift. The broad was really no dummy. And she kept check on everything. She kept everything goin' around in good workin' order.

"Nobody was just usin' scag because scag out there wasn't that tough. They was mixin' scag with meth, and the wine came in behind that, especially when all the methadone junkies got on the scene outnumberin' even the scag junkies. Then the wine really became a main thing.

"The liquor stores usually don't like the junkies around there 'cause the junkies take over and chase away all the regular wino and whiskey customers. The owners just weren't strong or forceful enough to keep them away. The regular winos wouldn't be goin' to the garbage can and buyin' the bootleg wine. They wouldn't go to the places where the junkies cop 'cause the junkies would take them off—beat 'em up and take their money, and all that kind of old foul stuff. So the junkies went to one spot, they went to the garbage can or the liquor store, and the winos went to the one that the junkies left alone. The winos wanted to have some peace, they didn't want any violence. And the junkies, they'd get violent over somebody's dollar fifty in a minute.

"I never had the slightest desire to try any scag. I had seen too much. You know, both o' my parents was junkies, man, and I've seen scag mess a whole lotta people up, and I always said to myself, No, it ain't goin' get me. It might get the whole world, everybody I know and everybody I'm related to, but if there's one thing that I can say without any doubt in this world, scag is not gonna get me. You know, it's like I'd had all that good fortune to see what it did to so many other people. So many other unfortunate people.

"Mae started feelin' she could really trust me, so she started movin' me upstairs and had me in the crib, like layin' on the door. She'd have two people up there on eight-hour shifts, and she'd always have somebody downstairs peepin' on the two people upstairs to make sure that nobody threw anything out the window to somebody else. And she'd have somebody across the street peepin' on the peeper. Across the street was the shotgun, too, in case anybody tried to take the place off. They had to come down through there unless they off the dudes upstairs. They could always holler out the window and say, 'Hey, here they come,' and the shotgun across the street would be layin' for 'em, you know, to take 'em off or just pop 'em off.

"She had a system that was really together. You didn't open the two gates. All you did was open the door by reachin' through one gate when the customer rang the bell, and you peeped out the peephole and you pinned him. He still couldn't get in at you. If he was silly enough to stick a pistol in and say, 'Hey, open that gate,' that was gonna take some time, and there was a light on the window you could flash to the shotgun across the street. There was a shotgun upstairs, too. If everything wasn't right, he was gonna hear it. The place's security was so solid, you know, it's like a fly couldn't slip through unnoticed.

"The big suppliers always wanted to put some dope in Mae's hands because they knew she was a operator and she knew how to make the bucks. She used to have so much money around that we'd be stealin' three and four hundred dollars a day and she wouldn't miss it. She had shoppin' bags full o' money all around the house. Her grandson Tommy, if we knew that little dude was gonna burn the whole crib down, we coulda taken the money and Mae woulda thought the fire got it. That little dude burned up about six shoppin' bags full o' paper money and fifteen five-gallon paint cans o' change. But somehow the baby got outta there. I think it was a cop that got him out, and I think the cop got some of the money, but nobody saw him come out with any o' the shoppin' bags. They say that the police and firemen was fightin' over the change. They say the paper money all went up in smoke, but the raise and the firemen was fightin' over who was gonna get the change in the paint cans. Now it musta been at least five thousand and ten thousand dollars in those cans. Mae was mad.

"She had other shoppin' bags o' money in other cribs that she didn't take care o' business at. She'd just run right out and get sixty thousand, you know, just like that. She'd just take a shoppin' bag full o' bucks, give it to the heavyweight man, and say, 'Here, you count it, and if anything is short let me know, and you could come by and get it, or we'll just make it up the next time.'

"When I first started workin' for Mae in 1971, when I was sellin' the wine out o' the garbage can and shoppin' bags, she was givin' me a quarter on the bottle. Later on, when I got up in the crib, I was stealin' so much money that it didn't matter whether she paid me or not 'cause the hustle was bein' able to steal some bucks. That's how you got most o' the money. That's when I really started dressin', man, I mean I was dressin' to death when I was up in the crib. When the house burned down, Mae decided to lay dead for a while.

"She had all kinds o' long funny money, like shoppin' bags full o' money, to cop. When she went to cop, she just went and took the dude the shoppin' bag. Her system was so well organized, so well schemed out, that she could down probably more scag and blow than anybody else around. There wasn't that many heavyweights who could supply her need.

"Benny used to sit out there in his Lincoln Continental with a couple of kilos of coke, and I used to take it down in the basement. That's where the factory was. And everybody was stealin' some of it. People was stealin' from her and stealin' her blind, but she was still makin' all kinds of shit pots full o' money, and she just never missed it. If we didn't steal so much, she woulda had more money than she knew what to do wit'.

"I guess the broad was kinda glad people was stealin' some of it. She couldn't put it in the bank because like she didn't have any visible means of income. So she had it here and there and all over town in shoppin' bags. Everybody who knew about the shoppin' bags was always tryin' to get up to the cribs and get next to the shoppin' bags.

"That was her daughters' main attraction. Every dude who knew about it always wanted to stay tight wit' em, and that's why, you know, like they always had a fistful o' bucks. They could dip into the shoppin' bags anytime they wanted to. Sheryl used to always be on Mae about the bucks when I first got tight with her, like, 'Mama, give me some money,' and she'd say, 'Don't bother me about no money. You know where the money is. Damn, you been takin' as much as you want till now.'

"She would like sneak in there and come out with two fistfuls of money, and she'd say like, 'Hold this for me.' Most of the time she would never ask for it back, which made that a very sweet scene, I mean, a mellow thing. I sure was in love wit' her. How could you not be in love with the broad who's always comin' on and givin' you fistfuls of money to hold for her and forgettin' to ask for it back?

"Mae was hooked up with Lester, you know, Big Lester from Seventh Avenue. He was her man then, and 'cause he had his number spot and all that up on the avenue and the after-hour joint, I used to take money up there for him to pay off the raise upstairs who would be collectin' from his spots. I even paid sergeants and lieutenants who would be in the car. Somebody'd drive them around, I'd just go down to the car. Mae'd give me a paper bag or a fat envelope and say, 'Here, you take this down to the car. Make sure you give this to the sergeant, make sure you give this to the lieutenant.'

"I was only fifteen or fourteen years old at the time, but I looked older. I used to come down the block with a kilo of coke under my arm, and the police would look at me and know what I had, but they wouldn't mess wit' me 'cause they knew I was the bagman. I was the man who was gonna be bringin' them money. It's like I almost had a armed police escort. The raise would keep an eye on me. They'd be peepin' because the raise on the beat, they was taken care of, too, and if they wasn't they couldn't say nothin' 'cause they saw the sergeant and the lieutenant comin' around there to collect.

"They were cool. They just fell in line with everybody else and stuck their hands out and started gettin' their share like somebody with some sense. I mean what else could they do? Go around and squawk, get bounced out for blowin' somebody else's thing? No, they were cool, everybody was cool. This is the solid truth. They would peep me comin', and they would see to it that nobody else would hassle me or try to take me off while I was makin' my rounds.

"Some dudes in the block knew what I was doin', that I was carryin' stuff like a high-priced courier. I used to see some of the takeoff artists like just pinnin' me, but they knew that the raise was pinnin' me and the raise would be pinnin' them, too. So they just laid back, and nobody ever tried it. And besides that, the shotgun would be walkin' on the other side of the street behind me. And between the shotgun and the police, I was probably the safest dude in New York city, walkin' around wit' pounds o' dope on him.

"Mae was tight with Lester, but she was goin' with these two cops, too, who used to patrol the block. She was really a swift broad. The broad was really together. She would juggle and handle a whole lot of stuff at the same time. And anybody who looked like they might be able to give her some trouble, Mae would just neutralize them. The problem was solved before it ever got started.

"There was these two cops who used to patrol the block, and they knew that a whole lotta stuff was goin' down and that the real bucks led to Mae's door. So she just hooked up with both of 'em. She started screwin' both of 'em. So, you know, that was extra protection. She was goin' wit' that other raise, too. You know that raise who became a narco? Yeah, Greedy Joe was his name, Greedy Joe. He was the smartest of all those dudes out there. You know, when Greedy Joe got on that special narcotics squad, he used to bust everybody right and left who wasn't comin' on wit' some bucks.

"People who tried to get in on Mae's territory or give her some competition in the block or in the whole community, he would pop 'em. Mae would finger them for him, and he would take half of their stuff, or just turn in enough to make it a decent bust, and he'd take the other stuff and give it to Mae and Mae would down it for him, or he would just give it to her and Mae would give him a nice piece of money outright and she'd just go on and down it. They had a real sweet thing goin' for a while. Until the fire.

"That fire did a whole lotta people outta money. There were a whole lotta people on the take. She might just about had a drug industry goin' in that spot. Yeah, well, it's like the whole industry died. The block ain't never been the same. There ain't been that much money in this block since the fire. The police still got like three or four number joints here, but they ain't got no kinda industry like that one woman had put together in this block all by herself through her own efforts, energies, and ingenuity. Yeah, that broad was sho'-nuff swift.

"Mae was a fence, too, she had some of everything in her crib, hot stuff piled up all along the wall. When the dope fiends used to come to buy stuff from her, they used to be tryin' to play her. Let's say they brought a hi-fi or stereo, they'd bring it in parts. They'd bring one part, and then they'd bring another part when they needed some more dope. But she knew this, and she would stay ahead of them by givin' them the dope with a extra whack on it.

"She had all these hot goods piled up in her crib. When the fire came she had a hard time explainin' it to the police or to anybody who asked.

"Two dudes took her spot off, once, and she knew who they was, and she put a contract out on 'em. She gave the contract to the police 'cause she wanted 'em iced as a lesson to anybody else who might try and put her in the cross, but after she put out the contract, she had a change of heart. She felt sorry for 'em, so then she had to go and buy the contract back from the police. Yeah, ain't that somethin'? The truth of the matter is that, you know, the broad was a genius. That's all there was to it. I learned a whole lot from her, some real devious shit."

Chips likes fast women, but he can't stand "Y" women. When asked what the Y women are, he said, "Those are superwomen who think they're men. They wanna control men, they wanna be the boss on the scene."

He calls them Y women because he read an article in one of the girlie magazines about men being hyperaggressive if they possess two Y chromosomes. He's had biology, and he's hip to chromosomes, and, besides, reproduction fascinates him. So does all of biology, but especially reproduction. He says that the article was contending that women can have Y chromosomes, too, and they become aggressive and domineering.

"We know some broads wanna be men, not especially butches, but probably some o' them, too. On the inside in their genes they got Y chromosomes. It's healthy for a male, but it's gonna freak a woman out. That Y chromosome is gonna make itself known in the broad's personality, in many ways she goin' act like a dude, and that's what a Y broad is. This thing is too powerful to cool out, and some of them may not wanna be as passive as women are supposed to be anyway, and they be goin' through a masculine thing.

"Like they might wake up one mornin', when they hit puberty, and discover they don't really desire men sexually. This Y chromosome, you see, is conttrollin' 'em, and they end up wantin' broads. Of course, there's some frustration in it, but what they goin' do? That Y chromosome won't let 'em be like a passive or nice, sweet woman. They goin' run out and start wars. Gonna wanna knock a man down. Wanna yell at him and scream and tell him what to be, and tell him what to do and how to do it.

"I don't care what anybody says, all that liberation BS is somethin' they could throw out the window. Women can be liberated and still be women. But the women who wanna be the bosses, who wanna take on the man's role, probably wanna be on top of the man, too, when they gettin' off sexually. And when it comes to certain things that men do, like buildin' bridges, puttin' a army together, desirin' to conquer some foreign country, to take over somethin' from somebody else by force, you know, all that's male stuff, man. That's the Y chromosome.

"You know, it would probably be a strange dude who's born from a woman with a Y chromosome, too. That's like havin' your mother and your father in one package. That kinda broad could say 'my child,' and, Jack, she'd sho'nuff be tellin' the truth. It's like, man, I sure wouldn't wanna get hooked up wit' a broad like that. Besides, what do she need a dude for? Some thrill, or what? I mean like she can do the whole thing all by herself, right?

"Well, the dude with the X chromosome probably be in the same scene.

"It's like I think that's what Sheryl is all about, and her mamma, too. You know, they Y broads. That's why they go out there tryin' to be gangsters and takin' care, you know, they wanna take care o' all the business. They really can't help it. It's not like they wanna be men, like those are the broads who'd probably like to be straight-up broads, but they can't. There's this thing inside that's controllin' 'em. It's like it's somethin' deeper than bein' possessed by a demon 'cause it's like nobody can exorcise it. It's too deep."

"Well, tell me something, Chips," I asked. "Why are you always picking on Nita? You dig her? I mean why do you always tease her about being so dark and shiny?"

"She just won't face the facts of life, and she's gonna try to change 'em," Chips said. "You know all that stuff about black is beautiful. It's a nice rap for the younger kids who don't know no better, people runnin' that down, but nobody really buys it. Now, I know where that black-is-beautiful thing is, and I know it's a lotta BS. If somebody was to practice it a little bit, then maybe us folks could really go for it, but all I'm tryin' to do with Nita is open her eyes and show her that she shouldn't be goin' for that jive rap those loudmouthed clowns out there preachin' when none o' them are practicin' it 'cause she's gonna end up, you know, like goin' for the flam. Like they gonna take her off behind it 'cause she'll be one o' those people who's buyin' it.

"Nita's got a whole lotta things goin' for her. She ain't gotta buy no fairy tales. She don't have to grab hold of no smoke ring just 'cause it may be fashionable. All I'm tellin' her is to open her eyes and look around her and see all the hypocrisy that, you know, that black noise is supported by. They all marryin' light-skinned broads with straight hair, and a sister like Nita, well, she's got about as much chance wit' 'em as she's got of turnin' white. Nita got about as much chance wit' the into-somethin' brothers as she's got of turnin' white overnight.

"But Nita is right about her gator thing. I'm not talkin' about whether it's right or wrong or whether the brothers shouldn't be doin' that for peace and unity and everything, that ain't my thing anyway. I'm not into that. I think all those people full o' noise out there, runnin' that down all the time. I go on and do my thing, and I know if they got a opportunity to do better, they would jump at it, too. All those same dudes was out there a few years ago, when all it took to be a militant was a dashiki and a afro, and they had the big 'fro up on their heads, and they had their dashikis, and they be runnin' 'round shakin' hands like five or six different ways, wearin' you out wit' a handshake. Man, by the time a dude finished shakin' your hand you didn't wanna see him no more. The dudes who was for real about it, they all restin' in peace. I never got into that bag.

"Yeah, I got a afro, but that's 'cause I dug it, and it looked good on me. I don't wanna be mistaken for anything other than bein' me. I'm suspicious of everybody who makes a whole lotta noise about how black they are. These dudes was always gettin' on television, talkin' about how much they love their people and how much they love black people. You say, 'Hey, man, what've you done for black people lately?' Well, that's the question that stops the show. I mean it's like I've heard and seen all that. Everybody's seen it. And you see these dudes and what they into, all of 'em out there just gamin'.

"For some it's just sellin' some dope or takin' some digits [numbers], but they goin' around hustlin' bein' black. The other people who didn't care nothin' about it to begin wit' saw that this was the fad that was payin' off, so they went for it, too. They started cashin' in on the hustle just like everybody else. What it amounted to was that as long as it paid to be black everybody started bein' black.

"There was a time when they was actually sellin' more afro wigs to white broads than they was to the sisters because bein' black had become so fashionable. And once it did, it's like everybody jumped on the bandwagon like dudes who hadn't been black in twenty-five years, wouldn't know what it meant to be black. But, you know, half of 'em didn't know what a ham hock was, man. Couldn't tell collard greens from wild cabbage. Most of 'em, if you mentioned chitterlin's to 'em they wouldn't know if it came from a cow or a goat. It's like everybody got on the kick because they made it so easy for 'em.

"I saw this dude, I don't wanna call his name, but a brother who was a disc jockey. About four years ago he came into a joint and had this white broad wit' him, and the broad had on a afro wig. Some white broads are tryin' to pass for black, and they look strange. Maybe they use some kinda skin darkener, or put on some sister liquid makeup or somethin'. And some of 'em look almost black. Well, anyway, this dude comes in the joint, and it just hurt people's feelin's, man, because he was gonna try and chump everybody off. Here comes this clown into the joint with his white broad, tryin' to pass her off as black. Nobody said nothin', you know, but he coulda just come on in if he had any heart. People woulda had more respect for him if he had just come in wit' a white broad and acted like it was his woman. I mean if you a man that's what you do if she's yours. Hell wit' what people say. If you gonna be worried about what people say, you ain't goin' never be able to do nothin' that you want to do. People always got some kinda complaints or squawks about somethin' if it's really you 'cause if it's really you it's not gonna be anything that's gonna completely satisfy somebody. Those fools out there talkin' all o' that noise oughta know better.

"Any fool can look around and say, 'Yeah, I'll go along with this program of a group of militant blacks, as long as it don't cost me nothin'.' That's what people been doin'. But when it starts to cost, ain't nobody goin' for it. It's human nature for people to be concerned about Number One. Do you think that you can go out there and get a whole lotta dudes, say, 'Hey, you know, we wanna pull a strike on the federal government 'cause somethin's gotta be done about the economy. We goin' stop workin', and we ain't gonna pay taxes. We gonna go on welfare, demand that we be put on welfare, and not gonna pay no taxes.'

"People not gonna go for it because they concerned about themselves. They believe in blackness and civil rights and equality and all that stuff up to a point, but not to a point where they have to sacrifice their own goals and their own comfort and their own pleasures in life.

"If all those people out there who run around hollerin' about the blackness thing was down for makin' a big personal sacrifice, there wouldn't be no problem. Let's say all the blacks in the country decided not to pay taxes until we get sho'nuff equal representation in the Senate, in the Congress, and on all levels of government, and let's say we go and we get everything that was promised to us, ever since the forty acres and the mule, and then we want that with interest on it, but say all the blacks would have to agree to be down together when the weight comes down. If we got twenty-two million blacks, let's say we got six million blacks—that's a quick guess—in the national work force. Like supposin' that six million blacks go on a taxpayin' strike against the federal government, what could they do? I mean what could they do? Everybody knows they couldn't put six million people, even blacks, in jail. It would cost so much just to feed 'em bread and water that it wouldn't make sense.

"We'd have to get all those dudes out there who hollerin' about all that blackness to be the main leaders. 'You gonna be on the front lines because we know how much you love black people. We know how much you love blackness because you been tellin' us so loud for so many years. Now here comes put-up time. We want you to come on, put up.'

"They gotta be the main ones. I bet they be the first ones, like them loudmouthed dudes in jail who're always talkin' riot, and when the riot thing comes off, they get all sick, go to the hospital. That's what happened at Attica, you know. I bet those other players, those superblacks, would be doin' the same thing.

"When black folks are in need of somethin' strong, like a strong spiritual basis or somethin' strong to believe in, you got everybody runnin' off BS, man. Runnin' down this noise and that noise. Rah, rah, rah, and yeah, yeah, yeah, this is just some more rap takin' us back to the churches with those amens and the hallelujahs. This is another era of the same old thing.

"I want everybody to stop BS'in' themselves and jivin' each other. It's like I'm not down on blackness. The last thing I'm against is any kinda blackness, but I don't wanna see anybody, especially somebody who is as mellow as Nita is, go for a flam. You see, to my way of thinkin', all of that hollerin' about black is like bringin' the black emotion thing outta the Baptist church and those sanctified churches and bringin' it out into the street and in the public and on television, and it's not gonna git over anymore here than it did in the church, so we might as well go back to church and holler about how much we love God, it'll do just as much good as tellin' ourselves how much we love each other when the junkies and muggers and everybody goin' around here doin' numbers on each other. It ain't no love, Jack. You got everybody runnin' that love game and showin' that hate much stronger than the words they express it in. The younger kids who comin' up now, they see what we doin' to each other. They know this ain't no love. What I'm sayin' is that you can save the noise, let's see somethin'. If anybody would show me some real acts of it, I'd be the first one to get down.

"Listen, I was at the Hilton Hotel year before last, when the black doctors had their convention there, you know. And it's like every one of those dudes had light-skinned squeezes, Jack. All their old ladies was about as light as they could find 'em, especially those dudes over forty years old, and like a lotta the young ones, too. Maybe they all gators and need some flash or somethin', you know. Or maybe they still in that old bag, and they scared the kids might come out too dark and have a hard way to go in this life, and they tryin' to give 'em every advantage, even a light complexion. But it seemed to me, they just don't believe that black is all that beautiful.

"I guess you know what's important to those kinda black folks is they can't have their pictures in newspapers and magazines with broads who are too dark-skinned, right? So they probably take that into consideration when they get hooked up. They figure they gonna be some kinda socialite, and they gotta have somebody as their squeeze who's gonna be kind of presentable in a flick, somebody whose picture won't come out too dark in the *Amsterdam News* and in *Jet* and *Ebony*. They all tryin' to get as unblack as they can from generation to generation.

"I'm suspicious of all people who go around hollerin' all that stuff about what they are and stand for instead of doin' it. If you really down wit' somethin', like people gonna know it. They gonna know it behind what you do more than what you say. You don't have to run around and say black is beautiful. They goin' know it because you got that beautiful black woman wit' you as your main squeeze.

"Think of how many brothers who have made it, even the real black-on-black brothers with that extrahigh visibility. Think about how many of 'em are married to black-on-black broads. You can count 'em on one hand, those that I could think of anyway—entertainers, athletes, doctors, lawyers, gangsters, and everybody else. They might mouth that black rap, but they ain't hookin' up wit' nothin' too black. And all those broads you hear swearin' about holy blackness, I'll bet they buy more skin lighteners than anybody else, and they'd panic like junkies in the street if Nadinola ever takes its product off the market. That's all I'm sayin' to Nita.

"I ain't never been in no kinda movement, and I ain't never been too attracted to broads who are too dark. Everybody's got his thing, and I know what mine is. It's like some dudes want dark-skinned broads, some dudes want light-skinned broads. Some dudes wanna drive economy cars, I'd rather walk, myself. But to each his own. You know, if you can go around here and, say, somebody tell you what you supposed to like, man, you didn't know what you dug anyhow. It really don't matter if you so weak-minded that you goin' let somebody tell you, I mean you supposed to be really be goin' for a broad 'cause she's dark-skinned or she's light-skinned. It's like the broad's really goin' be in big trouble 'cause you might hook up with her, but it's gonna be plain that you don't dig her. I mean you really don't dig her. It's like all you doin' is goin' along wit' the program, that's like always bein' a sad creature, like a obedient child, even when it comes to your feelin's, and that's a very personal thing just between you and the person you got the feelin's for.

"It's just like if you gonna grow up in life, you can't go on bein' a obedient child and doin' what your mamma and your daddy told you you supposed to do or be—it's your mamma and your daddy, you know, your black leader or your minister or priest or whoever it might really be. That's like listenin' to the President and him tellin' you like you not hungry because we in a recession, or somethin' like that, and you don't get hungry because he said it ain't cool to be hungry now.

"I mean you can get involved in some real flam stuff if you really start thinkin' about it or carryin' it to its final conclusion. Everybody today who goes along wit' 'em and tries to be the obedient child, once you get out from under their roof and their control, it's like it's goin' to be your loss. You goin' blow everything that you want. You goin' miss out on all the shots that you want to make in life, and you just might end up bein' a obedient child who went along with your parents' game right to the best, the grave. That would mean you never even lived, which is kinda foolish because you know they can't live for you and what they might want is not gonna make you happy. It's like you s'posed to go on and do your whole thing.

"You only got one life. You only got one to blow. You got only one to live, and it may be a disappointment to your parents and anybody else, but they livin' theirs unless they stupid. And even if they are, you don't have to be stupid, too. It's not goin' gain you nothin', and it's not goin' really like profit them nothin'.

"Now, it's like a whole lotta folks are tryin' to be the parents for blacks. I mean people be gettin' out there and talkin' all that noise. Some of 'em, they really need it. Some of 'em, they really lookin' out for their own pockets. It's like if you a black broad, it makes sense for you to be runnin' all that noise because you know you stand to gain by it, but the average person out there who is not a sister know that they don't go for it. But like if they gamin' and they know what they doin', that's cool. But if they not runnin' down that song on a flam, it's like they gotta be crazy or confused because they not livin' their own lives.

"And aside from that, if you listen to what people run to you, you know, the other parents after you leave home, who tell you what you supposed to do if you goin' be livin' right or if you goin' be a righteous brother, you in big trouble in Harlem because everybody'll be tellin' you that you supposed to be usin' dope. Like they goin' say that's the swift thing to do. If you goin' be a sho'nuff fast dude out here, it's like you gotta go and start destroyin' yourself with a needle and that white boy. It's like you gotta start committin' twenty-year suicide unless you luck out and you end it wit' a OD or dirty needle, you know somethin', you'll end it in two or three years or maybe one year if you real lucky. If not, you'll go out there and join the army of twenty-year suicides.

"You can't be weak-minded and survive in Harlem. Anybody who's weak and listenin' to everything he hears out here ain't got a tiny chance. It's like he's lost from the jump, the dude that wants to be a good and obedient son, not only to his parents or maybe not to his parents but to his society and those people who control him. You know, parents are always talkin' that noise about they love you, too, and that's for your own good. You gotta find out what you all about. You know, you go on out there and go along with the game, too, but only for what you want—Número Uno.

There is an epilogue to this book, but only time can write it.